Hebrew Poetry
in the Bible

Helps for Translators

Hebrew Poetry in the Bible

A Guide for Understanding and for Translating

by Lynell Zogbo
and Ernst R. Wendland

UBS Technical Helps Series

UNITED
BIBLE
SOCIETIES

New York

Books in the series of **UBS Helps for Translators** may be ordered from a national Bible Society or from either of the following centers:

UBS Europe Distribution Centre   United Bible Societies
Danish Bible Society   1865 Broadway
Frederiksborggade 50   New York, NY 10023
DK 1360 Copenhagen K   U. S. A.
Denmark

ABS-5/05-100-500-QWD 3 106535

Contents

CONTENTS

Preface

One of our colleagues has written a book in French with a captivating title: *Traduire sans trahir* ("Translating without betraying"). The title is challenging. Many people do indeed wonder whether faithful translation is possible. How often do we hear the phrase "Something is lost in the translation"?

Probably the ultimate challenge for the Bible translator is translating poetry. The task is not small, since nearly one third of the Old Testament is in some kind of poetic form. To complicate matters, many translators cannot read this poetry in Hebrew, the language in which it was written. If they can read Hebrew, they may lack the skills necessary to adapt these poems into real poems in their own language.

Indeed, in many parts of the world, much of Old Testament poetry has been translated like any other portion of Scripture. Some translators have arranged their translation into lines to give the impression of poetry, but this does not ensure that the beauty of the Hebrew forms is expressed.

This book is meant as a practical guide for the translator with limited or no background in Hebrew. Its main purpose is to convince translators that, in certain contexts, rendering biblical poetry as poetry in their own language is a worthy goal. It suggests ways translators can compare the stylistic techniques of the Hebrew text with those in their own language. In this way they can try to create the same poetic effect in their translations. It points out typical problems that Old Testament translators face and suggests ways to set out the text that will help the reader.

We are grateful to many colleagues who have shown interest in this book, especially Randy Buth, who provided an initial outline and several examples for chapter 3, and Jan Sterk, whose writings on the subject provided an important impetus. Special thanks go to Loren Bliese, Louis Dorn, Ted Hope, and Giles Williams for providing case studies of poetic transfer in various languages (see Appendix). We also wish to thank Bob Bascom, Loren Bliese, Margaret Bohoussou, Reinier De Blois, Eric Hermanson, Phil Noss, Don Slager, and Timothy Wilt for their helpful comments on various drafts. We thank Edesio Sánchez-Cetina for providing examples in Spanish, and Elisabeth Gbongue for help with typing. We want to express our deep gratitude to all our poet-translator friends on the African continent who have taught us so much.

When not otherwise cited, all Scriptural references in English are from the Revised Standard Version. Any translations from French were done by L. Zogbo. Where quoted material contains words in bold type or in italics, these words have been highlighted by the authors of this book and are not bold type or italics in the original passage quoted.

We hope translators of the Old Testament will be encouraged by the discussions and suggestions offered here and will consider rendering Biblical poetry as poetry in their own languages.

Abbreviations

Bible Versions

CEV	Contemporary English Version	NJPSV	TANAKH (or New Jewish Publication Society Version)
FRCL	French common language translation, *français courant*	NRSV	New Revised Standard Version
KJV	King James Version	REB	Revised English Bible
NAB	New American Bible	RSV	Revised Standard Version
NIV	New International Version	TEV	Today's English Version (or Good News Bible)
NJB	New Jerusalem Bible		

Books of the Bible

Gen	Genesis	Hos	Hosea
Exo	Exodus	Hab	Habakkuk
Deut	Deuteronomy	Matt	Matthew
1,2 Sam	1,2 Samuel	Rom	Romans
Psa	Psalms	1 Cor	1 Corinthians
Pro	Proverbs	Gal	Galatians
Eccl	Ecclesiastes	1 Thess	1 Thessalonians
Isa	Isaiah	Heb	Hebrews
Jer	Jeremiah	Rev	Revelation
Lam	Lamentations		

Hebrew Transliteration Table

The following system of transliteration has been adopted in order to keep all references as simple as possible for those readers who are not trained in Hebrew.

The English vowels, *a, e, i, o,* and *u,* represent the nearest equivalent sounds of the corresponding Hebrew vowels. Gemination of consonants caused by *dagesh forte* will be represented by a single consonant unless the information being discussed requires the distinction. The presence of *dagesh lene* will not be reflected in the representation of *gimel, daleth,* and *kaf,* since the resulting difference in English pronunciation is negligible or nonexistent. Consonants are represented as follows:

א	'	ט	t	פ, ף	f
ב	b	י	y	צ	ts
ב	v	כ, ך	k	ק	q
ג	g	ל	l	ר	r
ד	d	מ, ם	m	שׂ	s
ה	h	נ, ן	n	שׁ	sh
ו	w	ס	s	ת	t
ז	z	ע	'	ת	th
ח	ch	פ	p		

Those who work with the Hebrew text will, of course, wish to consult their copies of the text directly.

Chapter 1:

Translating Poetry in the Old Testament

1.1 Introduction

In most translation projects translators begin by translating the New Testament. When this job is done they move on to translate the Old Testament. By this time translators may be quite experienced, having spent three or four years working with biblical texts and actively applying translation principles. So it is usually mature, confident translators who begin an Old Testament project and who assume that they will be simply continuing on in the same kind of work. But such translators may be in for a surprise, because translation problems in the Old Testament are different from and oftentimes more difficult than those found in the New Testament.

Some of these problems have to do with the time gap between the time the Old Testament was written and our modern times. The New Testament was written less than two thousand years ago, but parts of the Old Testament were probably written over three thousand years ago. The New Testament text was written by a limited number of authors over a relatively short period of time, amounting to less than one hundred years. The Old Testament texts, on the other hand, were written by many more authors over a much longer time period covering nearly one thousand years. While we know quite a bit about the social, political, and cultural context of the New Testament, we know much less about the world of the Old Testament. Because the manuscripts of the New Testament are not nearly as old, scholars are more sure of the texts. In contrast, in the Old Testament there are over five thousand places where we are unsure what the original text said. Though most of these textual problems concern minor issues, they complicate the task of translation.

Added to these problems, the Old Testament has a greater variety of subject matter and many more different types of literature, or "genres," than found in the New Testament. The translation of the literary form we call "poetry" presents one of the greatest challenges to Old Testament translators.

1.2 What is poetry?

Scholars today cannot agree on a standard definition of poetry. They cannot find a definition that would apply to all languages, or even one that would apply in every respect to an individual language like English or Hebrew. The first question we might ask is this: Is poetry universal? In other words, does poetry exist in every culture and in every language of the world?

It appears that some form of poetry does occur in every language. Western civilization has a long history of poetic works, such as the early epic poetry of

1

the Greeks (for example, the Iliad and the Odyssey), through Shakespearean sonnets of the Renaissance period, right up to modern songs heard on radio and TV. The Orient and the Middle East have an even longer history of written poetic works. But poetry has also existed and still exists in nonliterate societies around the world—in Australia, Micronesia, Africa, and South America. Though they may not have been preserved in writing, songs and poems from these cultures have been passed in oral form from generation to generation and can still be heard today.

1.2.1 Features of Poetry

Though poetry is not easy to define, it is easy to recognize. Though the exact form poetry takes may differ from language to language, in every culture there is a special kind of language that is recognized as being artistic, beautiful to listen to, full of feeling, and different from ordinary speech. Scholars have attempted to define some universal features of poetry and to determine how poetry differs from prose. **Prose** is a written form of language that resembles the style used in ordinary speech. Though many defining features of **poetry** have been proposed, here we will mention only a few of the most important ones.

One important feature that distinguishes poetry from everyday speech is the difference in the **goal of speaking**. In ordinary speech style or in plain written prose, a person simply attempts to communicate a message to another person or group of persons. The form of language may be important but it is not essential to the message. In poetry, on the other hand, the **form** of the message is prominent. The words and the way they are used are highlighted. Poetry is "language chosen and arranged to create a specific emotional response through meaning, sound, and rhythm" (Webster's Dictionary: 1981). As the great African-American poet, Langston Hughes, commented, poetry lets us know "how people feel" more than "what they think" (1968:11).

Poetry is difficult to define and to translate because it goes beyond the usual interaction of everyday speech and experience. It can move us to tears, make us laugh, or encourage our faith. Poetry plays a special role in each society. It is often considered precious and is therefore carefully preserved. In literate societies it is written, read, and reread. In oral cultures poetry is usually committed to memory and communicated by word of mouth from generation to generation. In many cultures poetry preserves the most important traditions of the society—its origins, its history, and its sacred beliefs. It expresses the deepest feelings of the individual or the group.

Another defining feature of poetry is **repetition**. This is one of the ways we recognize that the speech form before us is different from the ordinary. It lets us know we are dealing with what some call "elevated style." Repetition may involve many different elements of language: a line or set of lines, a word or group of words, a sound, a syllable, or even meaning. Each one of these types of repetition is found in English poetry, and at least some of them occur in the poetry of every language.

For example, we find repetition of theme, line, and word in the beautiful lines of Psa 130.5-6:

> I wait for the LORD, my soul waits,
> and in his word I hope;
> my soul waits for the LORD
> more than watchmen for the morning,
> more than watchmen for the morning.

Besides the repetition of words and lines, there are many repetitive consonants and vowels in the original text. This makes this poem even more beautiful to hear in Hebrew than in any translated version.

Another feature of poetry is the prominence of **figurative language**. In the above lines the author speaks of his soul waiting for God, when in common language he could have simply said "I." He compares himself to a night watchman who must stand watch, waiting for the end of his guard duty. He is sure that God will come to his aid, even as the night watchman is sure the sun will rise. Through figurative language the poet has created a memorable picture of his faith.

Finally, poetry is most often **organized in lines** or measured utterances. This applies not only to written forms of poetry but to oral forms as well. When poets or scholars first write down oral forms of poetry, the words usually appear in the form of balanced lines. Often these lines have a certain beat, or rhythm, due to a pattern of stress or accent.

It is important to note that what is considered poetic in one language may not be so in another. In some languages such as Greek or Latin, there are complicated systems of accent patterns within the lines (called "meter") which are combined to form long epics. Among the Godies, a small ethnic group living in the rain forest of Côte d'Ivoire, poetry consists of very short lines repeated over and over in song. In Japan a poem may be made up of just five words arranged in a particular order. What makes words sound poetic or beautiful is language-specific. That is to say, each language has its own forms of arrangement and its own standards of beauty.

The difference between poetry and prose will also be language-specific. Indeed some scholars think that the boundary between the two is not always clear. Rather, there may be a kind of continuum or progression of forms, with casual prose on one end, and classical poetry on the other. In some languages there seem to be gray areas where we speak of "free verse" (poetry that is like prose) or poetic prose (prose which resembles poetry in some ways). However, in most instances speakers will be able to recognize the difference between a poem and a prose statement in their own language, even if they cannot define it.

1.2.2 Differences between prose and poetry in Hebrew

A good example of the difference between poetry and prose comes from the Old Testament itself. In the book of Exodus we have two texts that recount the same event. Exodus 14 tells in prose what happened when the King of Egypt finally decided to let the Israelites leave his country. It is a well-ordered and stirring tale with lively dialogue (14.1-5) and geographic detail (14.2). The story begins with background material, has a slow build-up, suspense (14.10), and a climax statement that highlights the Lord's great work of deliverance (14.30). Then the

3

outcome of the experience is presented: the people have complete trust in the Lord (14.31). Below is an excerpt of the final part of the story taken from the Revised Standard Version (RSV):

> When Pharaoh drew near, the people of Israel lifted up their eyes, and behold, the Egyptians were marching after them; and they were in great fear. . . .
>
> Then Moses stretched out his hand over the sea; and the LORD drove the sea back by the strong east wind all night, and made the sea dry land, and the waters were divided. And the people of Israel went into the midst of the sea on dry ground, the waters being a wall to them on their right hand and on their left. (14.10, 21-22)
>
> The Egyptians pursued, and went in after them into the midst of the sea, all Pharaoh's horses, his chariots, and his horsemen. And in the morning watch the LORD in the pillar of fire and of cloud looked down upon the host of the Egyptians, and discomfited the host of the Egyptians, clogging their chariot wheels so that they drove heavily; and the Egyptians said, "Let us flee from before Israel; for the LORD fights for them against the Egyptians." (23-25)
>
> Then the LORD said to Moses, "Stretch out your hand over the sea, that the water may come back upon the Egyptians, upon their chariots, and upon their horsemen." So Moses stretched forth his hand over the sea, and the sea returned to its wonted flow when the morning appeared; and the Egyptians fled into it, and the LORD routed the Egyptians in the midst of the sea. The waters returned and covered the chariots and the horsemen and all the host of Pharaoh that had followed them into the sea; not so much as one of them remained. But the people of Israel walked on dry ground through the sea, the waters being a wall to them on their right hand and on their left. (26-29)
>
> Thus the LORD saved Israel that day from the hand of the Egyptians; and Israel saw the Egyptians dead upon the seashore. And Israel saw the great work which the LORD did against the Egyptians, and the people feared the LORD; and they believed in the LORD and in his servant Moses. (30-31)

In the following chapter, on the other hand, we have a poetic account of the same event, known as the "Song of Deliverance" (Exodus 15). This passage is strikingly different from the prose account. Below are a few stanzas of this great poem:

> 1 "I will sing to the LORD, for he has triumphed gloriously;
>   the horse and his rider he has thrown into the sea.
> 2 The LORD is my strength and my song,
>   and he has become my salvation;
>   this is my God, and I will praise him,
>   my father's God, and I will exalt him.

3   The LORD is a man of war;
        the LORD is his name.

4   "Pharaoh's chariots and his host he cast into the sea;
        and his picked officers are sunk in the Red Sea.
5   The floods cover them;
        they went down into the depths like a stone.
6   Thy right hand, O LORD, glorious in power,
        thy right hand, O LORD, shatters the enemy.
7   In the greatness of thy majesty thou overthrowest thy adversaries;
        thou sendest forth thy fury, it consumes them like stubble.
8   At the blast of thy nostrils the waters piled up,
        the floods stood up in a heap;
        the deep congealed in the heart of the sea.
9   The enemy said, 'I will pursue, I will overtake,
        I will divide the spoil, my desire shall have its fill of them,
        I will draw my sword, my hand shall destroy them.'
10 Thou didst blow with thy wind, the sea covered them;
        they sank as lead in the mighty waters.

11 "Who is like thee, O LORD, among the gods?
        Who is like thee, majestic in holiness,
        terrible in glorious deeds, doing wonders?
12 Thou didst stretch out thy right hand,
        the earth swallowed them. . . .

It does not take a literary expert or even someone who knows Hebrew to
recognize the distinguishing characteristics of each text. First, we note that the
poem is easily set out in short lines, often parallel to each other, while the prose
description is not. Second, the goal of speaking is different in each text. The
words of the poem are personal and intense (note the use of the first person "I").
Their purpose is not to recount a story or simply to convey historical
information. They are a deeply emotional call to praise a saving God (verses
11-12). They are a verbal celebration directed to him.

Many of the paired lines of the poem are rhythmic, even in the English
translation from the Hebrew. Some lines pick up the theme of the preceding line
and intensify its message (verse 2b):

> This is **my God**, and *I will praise him,*
> **my father's God**, and *I will exalt him.*

Some lines are repetitive and very moving (11):

> **Who is like thee**, O LORD, among the gods?
> **Who is like thee** . . . .

5

The passage is full of images and figures of speech: the enemies are "thrown into the sea" (1); "the floods stood up in a heap" (8); the enemies "went down into the depths like a stone" (5); they "sank as lead" (10) and "the earth swallowed them" (12). God is not presented as the quiet, composed actor seen in the prose rendering, but as a "man of war" (3), a mighty and furious ruler. He is both human and superhuman: "At the blast of thy nostrils" (8) . . . "Thou didst blow" (10). The expression in the poem is more condensed than in the narrative account, but it is also more powerful and stirring.

In the poem participants are not introduced in any systematic way. No scene is set; no background information is given. We hear first of "the horse and his rider" (verse 1), and only later are these more specifically identified as "Pharaoh's chariots and his host . . . and his picked officers" (verse 4).

Further, within the poem there is no strict progression along a time line. The poet assumes the hearer or reader knows the story. Events occur out of order and repeat themselves. In the first stanza the enemies are cast into the sea. In the second stanza a flood covers the enemies. But then the poet turns back and starts up his description all over again: God intervenes, sends his destructive force, and the water stands up. Next the poet flashes back to the time when the enemies were plotting the destruction of the Israelites. Their rhythmic, repetitive threats draw out the suspense (though even these too seem out of order!): "I will pursue, I will overtake, I will divide the spoil . . . I will draw my sword. . . ." Then once again the enemies are covered by the sea, and they sink into the waters.

The prose rendition of the flight from Egypt gives all the narrative detail with the logical and temporal progression of events. We can easily learn the story and retell it. The poem, on the other hand, seems to be a jumble of rhythm, repetition, imagery, and emotion. Of course this apparent jumble is, in fact, a finely crafted work of art! It is not a story. It is a celebration, a remembrance, and a powerful song of praise to God.

It is important to remember, however, that there are not two sets of differing features, one which characterizes poetry and the other prose. We cannot say, for example, that repetition is only a feature of poetry and not of prose. In the prose portion above there is also effective use of repetition. The repetition of "the Egyptians, their chariots, their horsemen" (Exo 14.23,26) lets us know that the defeat of the enemy is complete. The repetition of the expression "on dry ground, the waters being a wall to them on their right hand and their left" (Exo 14.22, 29) underlines the miracle of Israel's deliverance.

Features such as repetition, word play, figurative language, rhetorical questions, and irony occur in both poetry and prose. But there is a difference of intensity in the use of these features. In poetry these features are piled up, one on top of the other, and are thus made to stand out. They appeal to our senses and our emotions. They catch the eye or ear of the audience and make this speech form very distinct from everyday language.

1.3 Can poetry be translated from one language to another?

Many translators may ask if it is possible to translate poetry from one language to another. Another question is, Should we attempt to do this in our language?

Apart from the domain of Bible translation, we note that great poems have been translated the world over. Shakespeare has been translated into Japanese, French, and Swahili. The work of French poets such as Rimbaud and Baudelaire have been translated into English and Japanese. English literature has been enriched by the translation of American Indian, Spanish, Chinese, Nigerian, and Philippine poetry, to name only a few. Granted, some translators of poetry may feel the need to resort to notes to do justice to a translated text. But despite the obvious problems, people the world over find great pleasure in reading poetry in translation. No one doubts that the translation of poetry is a worthy goal.

In this manual we assume that biblical poetry is often best rendered in translation by its own equivalent, poetry itself. We have already mentioned that poetry is a special speech type whereby the form of the message is highlighted. The message of the poem is important. It is the heart of what the poet wants to say. But also important is the way the message is presented. As is evident in the rather literal rending of Moses' "Song of Deliverance" in English, the rhythm, repetition, and figures of speech all combine to produce a powerful message of divine deliverance and human rejoicing. As we have seen, it is possible to tell the same story in prose, but prose cannot communicate the same emotion or create the same effect.

In the Hebrew Bible some of the most powerful and important passages are in poetic form. We think of the deeply emotional Book of Psalms and the stirring messages of the prophets—Isaiah, Joel, Jeremiah, and others. We think of the rhythmic wisdom in Proverbs and the lyric beauty of the Song of Songs. These poems deserve careful treatment so that the real beauty and power of the original can be felt and the complete message can be experienced, rather than simply understood. If we reduce poetry to prose, the biblical message may lose its effect and, in a very real way, be robbed of some of its truth. Consistently translating poetic lines into flat prose is not being faithful to the text. It is not dynamically or functionally equivalent translation.

In the past, scholars and translators have been slow to understand the important role poetry plays in the Old Testament. In the documents found at Qumran (known as the Dead Sea Scrolls), only rarely are poetic passages written in poetic lines. The early versions in Greek, Latin, Syriac, and Aramaic did not line up poetic material into poetic lines. However, later translators did present poetry in a poetic format. RSV (1952) was the first translation in English to do this throughout the biblical text. Many versions written in the twentieth century have followed this pattern. Poetic formats have helped readers identify which parts of the text are poetic in the original. A more literal rendering of repetitive passages has captured some of the poetic flavor of the original.

More recently, however, some modern versions have purposely avoided poetry in certain contexts as being unnatural or inappropriate. Indeed, in English-speaking countries of the Western world, both the role and style of poetry has shifted. Formal, rhyming, or meter-based poetry is no longer common, and the context where poetry is read today has perhaps changed from what it was before. Poetry is read in intellectual circles, studied by students, enjoyed by children, and sung in songs. But it is not considered common reading material. It is therefore assumed that ordinary people wanting to understand the message of the Bible may be confused or put off by poetic forms. Adapting to this new situation and this new need, many common language versions sometimes render poetry as prose (Today's English Version [TEV]), or they attempt to substitute poetic or rhythmic prose for formal poetry (Contemporary English Version [CEV]; Newman 1993).

Thus, while it is in principle a very good thing for poetry to be translated as poetry, there may be some exceptions. As we will see later, this depends on the function of poetry in the language of the translation. A translation team confronted with the task of translating the Old Testament needs to come to grips with this problem early on. A policy needs to be adopted as to how to handle poetic passages. Knowing how and when to translate poetry as poetry is a key concern. This will require research and hard work involving both the source text (the Bible) and the language of translation.

The goal of this manual, therefore, is to help translators evaluate the need for translating poetry as poetry in their own language and to help them successfully carry out this task. We hope to assist translators to:

- consider the life setting and the role of poetry in the Old Testament and to be aware of the various literary types or genres that occur (chapter 2)

- understand and identify important features of Hebrew poetry (chapter 3)

- decide when it is appropriate to render biblical poetry by poetry in their own language and to identify stylistic features in the target language which can be used in translation (chapter 4)

- gain insight into some special problems involved in translating biblical poetry (chapter 5)

- learn how laying out poetry in a special printed format can help the reader better understand a poem (chapter 6)

- understand how poetic principles can help determine the meaning or structure of some difficult texts (chapter 7)

- gain insight into how to handle quotes of Old Testament poetry in the New Testament (chapter 8)

In the Appendix we have included three case studies of how biblical poetry can be rendered as poetry in the language of translation, as well as one translation team's efforts at establishing principles for translating poetry in their language.

We hope that translators will be encouraged to try their hand at rendering at least some Hebrew poetry in poetic form in their own language.

Questions for Reflection

1. What Bible translations are available to you or to people speaking your language? Do these versions make a distinction between prose and poetry? How can you identify which passages are prose and which are poetry? (You may want to look at Gen 2.23-25; 3.14-19; 4.23-24; and Ecclesiastes, chapters 1 and 3.)

2. Look at Exodus, chapters 14 and 15, in several different versions. Are there any differences in the way these texts are presented? Do all the versions print these passages in the same way?

3. If a translation is already available in your language, study Psalms 1, 23, and 103. Are these poems rendered as poetry in your language? What features in your language help you to identify these passages as poetic? Which passages are well translated? Which passages are unnatural or difficult to understand? Give reasons for your opinions. (If there is no translation in your own language, refer to translations done in other languages.)

4. Compare Judges 4 and 5 in a version that you are familiar with. Notice that these two chapters tell the same story. What event is being described? What are some of the differences between the two accounts? How can you recognize that chapter 5 is written poetry? Which version of the story do you prefer and why?

5. Do you think that it is important to translate the poetry of the Bible as poetry in your own language? Why or why not?

6. What are some main features of poetry in your language? Give some examples. Can these same features be used to translate biblical poetry? Explain your answer.

Chapter 2:

Life Setting and Genres in Hebrew Poetry

2.1 Introduction

No poems—not even today's modern forms—are created in a void. They are created within a cultural context or "life setting." There are social, geographical, religious, and even political circumstances that give rise to a poem. In many preliterate societies today, poetry is found only in song. These poetic forms focus on various life experiences: birth, initiation, marriage, death, and war (songs of victory, taunting chants, calls for revenge). Songs and recitations celebrate past events and are used to teach younger generations important truths about the clan or the larger social unit.

2.2 Life setting of Hebrew poetry

We know little about how poetry and song arose in the ancient Hebrew culture. Most scholars think the first songs were sung in commemoration of historical events; for example, Moses' Song of Deliverance (Exo 15.1-18), Miriam's response (15.21), and the Song of Deborah (Judges 5.2-31). It is possible that parts of the Old Testament narrative preserve bits of these very old songs. Some scholars think, for example, that the very short poetic lines in Genesis are remnants of a very old oral tradition. Thus, Adam's stirring response to Eve's appearance, "This at last is bone of my bones and flesh of my flesh . . ." (Gen 2.23), and Lamech's promise of vengeance spoken to his wives, "If Cain is avenged sevenfold, truly Lamech seventy-sevenfold" (Gen 4.24), may be older in origin than the narratives in which they occur.

Some scholars suggest that, in its earliest form, Hebrew poetry was more communal in nature than individual, and more centered on cultic or religious matters than on private ones. They think that the first songs were probably hymns of celebration and prayers of confession or thanksgiving and that the role of poetry expanded to other activities such as teaching and prophesying. Certainly by the time that David, the most well-known songwriter in the Bible, was composing, poetry had taken on a more individual flavor. Many of the psalms attributed to him are personal, referring to specific circumstances in his life.

However, other scholars are quick to point out that in Hebrew culture there was no sharp distinction between everyday concerns and cultic ones. Activities were not defined as "secular" or "sacred." Were the first poems really communal and cultic? If, indeed, the short poetic lines attributed to Adam and Lamech in Genesis are quite old, then poetry was used to express individual emotions from a very early date.

11

It is also difficult to know just how much creativity was allowed in early times. If current situations in preliterate societies are any indication, the themes and literary styles of the songs were probably relatively fixed. The poet was free to add his or her individual touches in word choice and line combination, but not allowed to change the content or form in any significant way. However, by the time the book of Amos and the later chapters in Isaiah were composed, there was quite of bit of creative freedom, as mixing literary styles became common.

The historical books of the Old Testament give us some clue as to the use of songs in their original setting. In 1 Chronicles 16 we learn that psalms were part of the worship ceremonies taking place in the temple in Jerusalem. We know that psalms were sung and not just read, since many are marked by notes at the beginning of the poem (commonly called **superscriptions**). These indicated the melody to be used and sometimes the type of musical instrument that should accompany the song (see Psalms 45, 55, for example). It is likely that priests sang Psalms 24, 48, 81–82, and 92–94 during the ceremonies associated with certain sacrifices. According to tradition Psalms 120 through 134 were sung by travelers as they made their way to Jerusalem for the various religious festivals such as Passover, the Feast of Weeks, and the Feast of Tabernacles. Texts from the New Testament (Mark 14.26) confirm that selected psalms were sung at festival times.

Much of the Old Testament went through a long editorial process, so that, as noted above, parts of poems or parts of books could be very old, while other parts may be relatively recent. The Book of Psalms, for example, is a collection of songs that differ considerably in age. There are older psalms that refer to the ancient theme of order over chaos (Psalm 29). There are much later poems, such as Psalm 137, a lament following the exile. Most scholars feel the Song of Songs has a rather late date, but it may contain portions of very old love poems. The unusual passage in 3.6-11 may have been handed down through the ages and inserted into a much more modern love poem. It is also possible that the writer of Ecclesiastes took ancient poems and proverbs and incorporated them into his text as part of his argumentation.

2.3 Types of Hebrew poetry

Up to now we have been speaking of poetry as a single category. But in most cultures there are many different types of poetry. The term **genre** is used to refer to a literary type characterized by a distinct style, structure, or content. Thus, in describing literature in English, we may speak of novels, autobiographical material, folktales, riddles, "how-to" manuals, and poetry, to name only a few. Within each category we can further subdivide according to type. For example, in the category of "novels" we may distinguish historical, spy, and detective novels. Within the category of poetry in English, there are several types, depending on the form of the poem (free verse, sonnet, and others) or its content and function (lyrical, religious, satirical).

2.3.1 Genres in Hebrew

What genres exist in Hebrew poetry? Unfortunately there is no general agreement on a fixed number of literary types. The number of categories depends on the analyst. Indeed, it appears that, in the Hebrew language itself, there were no neat categories to define every genre. The Hebrew word *shir* is a general term meaning "song" or "poem." The victory song in Judges 5 is called a *shir*. This term is used to describe the Song of Songs as well as various psalms (30, 46, 48, 65–68, 108). This term combines with others to refer to more specific types of songs or poems: *shir yedidoth* "a love song" (Psalm 45), *shir hamma'aloth*, "a pilgrim song" or song of ascents (Psalms 120–134), or even *shir leyom hashebbath*, "a song for the day of the Sabbath" (Psalm 92). In its feminine form *shirah* it refers to the song of Moses (Deut 32), Psalm 18, and other texts as well, with no apparent difference in meaning.

Another term *mizmor* applies to fifty-seven psalms, most of which are marked as having musical accompaniment. Many of these are songs attributed to David (*mizmor ledawid*), Asaph, or the sons of Korah, and are individual laments (47, 64–65, 76–77, 87–88). Many of these same psalms include two titles. They are both "song" (*shir*) and "psalm" (*mizmor*). Sometimes the *mizmor* is further qualified. Psalm 100 is a *mizmor lethodah*, "a psalm of thanksgiving."

The term *maskil* describes 13 psalms (32; 42; 44–45; 52–55; 78; 88; 89), some of which can be qualified as didactic, or teaching psalms (see Psalm 78). When this term occurs within a text, RSV has translated it "psalm" (Psa 47.7), but other versions translate "instruction." Here again, however, there is an overlap between categories. Psalm 45 is a *maskil* and a "wedding song" at the same time. Psalm 88 is qualified in its title as a *mizmor*, a *shir*, and a *maskil*!

Qinah is the word used to describe a lament, as when David mourns the death of Saul and Jonathan (2 Sam 1.19-27). Many psalms also fall into this category. The word *mashal* most often refers to proverbs or wise sayings of all types, while *chiydah* is a riddle or enigma of the type Samson used to confound his opponents (Judges 14.14). *Ne'um* and *massa'* both refer to oracles against threatening nations, while *ne'um Yahweh*, "oracle of Yahweh," becomes a more specific name for the message of Yahweh as it is transmitted by the prophets. Other categories recognized within the biblical text itself are *berakah* "blessing" (Psalm 67) and *qelalah* "curse" (Psa 7.3-5) (Alonso Schökel, 1988:8-13).

2.3.2 Genres according to Gunkel

Perhaps because there is a certain degree of overlap in the definitions of the genres in Hebrew itself, scholars have been trying for centuries to organize Hebrew poetry into types. One of the most famous of these scholars, Hermann Gunkel, divided Psalms into major and minor genres on the basis of life setting or traditional use, subject matter, and style of the poem:

Major	Minor
hymns	blessings and cursings
thanksgiving songs	pilgrimage songs
royal songs	collective/communal songs of thanksgiving
communal lamentations	wisdom or didactic psalms

13

| individual lamentations | liturgical songs |
| songs of trust | mixed songs |

Below are brief descriptions of some of these genres.

A **hymn** is a song or poem which praises God. It often includes a reference to the great acts of God or gives other reasons for praising him. Examples of such poems are Psalm 8; 18; 19.1-6; 34; 104; 108; 116; 118; 124; 129; 148. Some of these hymns are individual, that is, sung by a single person (Psalm 118), while others are communal, or sung by a group (Psalm 118 and 124). In Israel the setting of such hymns may have been the Passover celebration or the Festival of Weeks and of Tabernacles. The category of hymns has often been subdivided. For example, Psalms 8, 19, 104, 108, and 148 are sometimes called **creation psalms** because of their particular content.

A **thanksgiving song** gives praise for deliverance from a particular menace or for forgiveness of sin. These songs may have been sung in the sanctuary, perhaps at the time of a sacrifice. Some thanksgiving songs include Psalms 9-10; 30; 32; 34; 40.1-12; 92; 107; 116; 118. Note that this type may be very close to a hymn, though its focus is narrowed to thanksgiving for victory, forgiveness, or other specific blessings. Psalm 100, for example, is marked as "A Psalm for the thank offering," but it could certainly also qualify as a hymn or creation psalm.

Many scholars recognize a distinct category, **royal psalms**, which make some reference to the king. Psalms 2 and 110, for example, are thought to be composed for a king's coronation. Psalm 45 seems to be composed for a king's marriage. Royal psalms may include prayers or thanksgiving for the king's success or victory. They may include a declaration of God's support of the king, or a reminder of God's promises to the family line of David. Psalms 18, 20, 21, 45, 72, 101, 110 all include such references. Today many of these psalms, or certain passages from them, are called **messianic**, because New Testament writers used them to refer to Christ, the Messiah, who was to come from the descendants of King David.

A **lament** or "dirge" is a sad song or poem which expresses distress over some unhappy situation: sickness, death, defeat, persecution, or other catastrophes. The lament may be a cry for help expressed by the entire community, as when the people of Jerusalem lamented the fall of that city (Lamentations). Laments may also be individual, as when David mourned over the deaths of Saul and Jonathan (2 Sam 1). This genre is the most common literary type in the book of Psalms.

In some laments (Psalm 51) the poet expresses sorrow over his own sin. This type of lament is sometimes called a confessional or **penitential psalm** (see also Psalms 32; 143). However, many individual laments go beyond the distressing situation at hand. As the lament unfolds, the distraught person often finds new hope or has his faith renewed, and concludes by praising God (see Psalm 32).

Some scholars distinguish another category, **imprecatory psalms**, which call down curses or God's judgment on enemies. Such psalms include 35, 69, 83, and 109.

Dividing poems into genres, as Gunkel has done, is certainly a useful exercise if it helps us to identify poetic features of individual poems or to indicate something of their religious function. However, we must realize that all attempts at categorizing psalms or any other biblical poetry are subjective. Some poems seem to fit into several categories at the same time. Some categories can be subdivided into even smaller ones. It must be remembered that, though poems share certain common features, each poem has its own unique characteristics. As one scholar correctly points out, "many works resist tidy classification" (Alonso Schökel, 1988:19).

2.3.3 Categorizing by the goal of speaking

Another approach to categorizing poetry is to concentrate on the particular **function** or **goal** of speaking. Thus we can identify poems that are meant to praise, to teach, to celebrate great historic events, to speak of love, or to proclaim "the Word of the LORD." This gives a new and sometimes overlapping set of categories that do not appear in Gunkel's list of major genres. Among these some of the most important are:

Didactic poetry: its primary goal is to teach. This type of poem concentrates on themes of the so-called "wisdom school"—the perfection of the law, for example, or the importance of "fearing Yahweh" (Psa 19.7-14; 119). There is often a contrast drawn between the wicked and the righteous, or the wise and the foolish (Psalm 1; Eccl 7; Proverbs 14). It may give practical advice on how to live one's life. Pro 23.29-35 speaks against drinking too much. Pro 7.1-27 advises young people to avoid immoral relationships. Proverbs 31 sets out characteristics of a good spouse. Didactic poetry may consist of a single pair of parallel lines (Pro 13.20) or may be composed of much longer literary units (Psalm 119).

Liturgical poetry, termed a minor category by Gunkel, is characterized by its probable use in Temple worship or at specific religious festivals. Liturgical poems often have refrains which may have been repeated in unison by the entire congregation (Psalm 118, 136). They often contain references to the place of worship: God's holy hill, his tent, the altar (Psalms 25, 43), or to particular religious vows or offerings (Psalms 56, 81).

Love poetry is typified by the Song of Songs. According to many scholars the poems of this book share several features with Egyptian love songs. They describe the deep, loving relationship between a young woman and man. Some other biblical passages make explicit reference to love and marriage (Psalm 45; Isaiah 62), while in at least one passage, a love genre is used in an ironic way (Isa 5.1-5).

Prophetic poetry's aim is to communicate a special message from God to his people. Poetry was a common means of criticizing social inequality and injustice. Through poetry the prophets questioned political decisions and uncovered misdeeds in the religious or cultic community. There is no doubt that some of the harshest and some of the most comforting poetry of the Bible is found in the mouths of prophets.

Prophetic poetry is the richest of all types of poetry because different kinds of genres are often combined to communicate the prophet's message. In the book of Isaiah, for example, we find examples of a praise song (Isa 63.7-14), a creation poem (Isa 51.12-16), a love song (Isa 5.1-7), a judicial case (Isa 45.20-21; see also Micah 1.1-7), and a taunt song (Isa 24.1-23). Within the prophetic context the use of a particular genre may express irony. For example, the "love song" in Isaiah really serves to condemn Israel for their unfaithfulness to God. The prophet's message may be interspersed with curses (the five woes in Habakkuk 2) or satire (Isa 14; 37.22-29). Mixing genres tends to heighten the emotional impact of the message.

2.4 Conclusion

To conclude, we note that trying to understand the original setting of a poem and determining its goal of speaking and its genre can be very helpful exercises. But we must always remember the limitations with which we are working. Since we lack documentation, we cannot be absolutely sure about the life settings of many poems in the Bible. Further, the classification into genres is very subjective. We cannot take every poem of the Hebrew Bible and automatically place it in a single category such as "hymn," "love song," or "didactic poem." There is much overlapping and mixing. What is helpful is to think about the form of the poem, how it is like or different from other poems, and what its unique message or purpose is.

Questions for Reflection

1. Read the following psalms and match each one up to a specific genre mentioned below:

Psalm 1	thanksgiving
Psalm 20	wisdom
Psalm 12	lament
Psalm 30	hymn (praise)
Psalm 104	royal

Now try to find your own examples of psalms that fit into each of the above categories. Give reasons for your choices.

2. Read carefully through Psalm 44. Try to identify sections that have different functions or goals of speaking.

3. Study chapter 1 of the book of Ecclesiastes. Identify as many different genres as you can. Think about how you would classify this chapter. Should the entire chapter be classified as a single type? Why or why not?

4. Quickly read through the book of Joel and identify three different goals of speaking. List the passages concerned. Could these texts be translated as poetry in your language? Explain your answer.

5. Study the third chapter of Habakkuk. Do you have any type of poetry in your language that sounds like this? If so, does it describe God or some ancestor or chief? Could you render this chapter as poetry in your language? Give reasons for your answer.

6. How many different types or genres of poetry are common in your society? Mention some of the more important ones and think about how and when they are used. Can you associate certain genres with specific ceremonies, rites, or feasts? Are certain genres associated with specific subjects (love, war, deities)?

Chapter 3:

Features of Hebrew Poetry

3.1 Introduction

In order to translate a poem, we must first be able to understand its meaning. In chapter 1 we have seen that the form of a poem and all the poetic devices that the author uses to compose it are an important part of its meaning and contribute to its overall message. To translate a poem from the Old Testament successfully, one of the first steps is to identify the poetic devices that occur in the original. By analyzing these features the translator gets a feel for the structure and style of the poem and begins to understand its intricacy and its beauty, in addition to its message.

Unfortunately not every Old Testament translator can read the original text. But any translator who has a good grasp of the poetic devices that exist in Hebrew will be able to identify many of these features in a translated version. When searching for such poetic features, it is best to use versions that are more literal, rather than common-language or dynamic ones. More conservative translations such as RSV, New International Version (NIV), New Jerusalem Bible (NJB), or TANAKH (New Jewish Publication Society Version, or NJPSV) retain many poetic features of the original Hebrew.

In this chapter we present an overview of the major poetic devices in biblical Hebrew. We begin with those features that are easily identified in translation. These include structural features such as parallelism, word pairs, chiastic structures, inclusio, and refrain. Next we will treat some sound-related devices of Hebrew poetry which are nearly impossible to appreciate in any version but the original. These include wordplays, and sound patterns such as alliteration, assonance, and rhyme. Even though these are not accessible to every translator, it is important to be familiar with these stylistic devices in order to follow discussions on the Hebrew text in commentaries and translation manuals. Following this we will give a brief presentation of some features which occur generally in Hebrew literature, but which are especially frequent in poetic forms. These include figures of speech, rhetorical questions, and keywords. We will then discuss the difficult subject of shifting persons in Hebrew poetry. We will conclude with some remarks on how to determine breaks in poetic units, and how the rather strict structures in Hebrew poetry still leave room for individual creativity.

3.2 Poetic devices that help define structure

There are many devices used by Hebrew poets which in some way help to define the structure of a text. These include parallelism, chiastic structures, inclusios, and refrains. By far the most common organizing pattern in Hebrew poetry is parallelism.

3.2.1 Parallelism

In geometry, parallel lines are lines that are equidistant from each other. They run alongside one another at exactly the same distance apart. In poetry, parallelism refers to two lines of poetry which are in some way similar. The similarity may be **grammatical** (with lines having the same structure) or **semantic** (with lines having very similar meanings). For example, in Psa 9.8 below, both lines have the same internal structure: a subject, verb, and object, followed by a prepositional phrase. These two lines also have approximately the same meaning:

> he judges the world   with righteousness,
> he judges the peoples with equity.

Parallelism may also be based on a similarity in sound, as seen in the following example from Isa 44.8b (Berlin, 1985: 105):

> Is there a god **except me** [bal'aday]?
> And there is no rock, **I know none** [bal-yada'ty].

When speaking about parallelism in poetry, Bible scholars use a variety of terms. A single line is called a **colon**, and two paired lines are called a **bicolon**. (The plural of "colon" is "cola.") These lines are often labeled **A** and **B**, as in the following example from Isa 1.3b:

> But Israel does not know,   (A colon)
> my people does not understand.   (B colon)

Some scholars consider a bicolon, or two cola together, to be one "line" or a "verse." According to this method each colon is called a "half-line." However, in this manual we will call a colon a "line" rather than a "half-line," because this is the terminology used in discussing other traditions of poetry throughout the world.

When three cola form a poetic unit, we speak of a **tricolon**, and when there are four, **a tetracolon**:

> Smoke went up from his nostrils,   A
> and devouring fire from his mouth;   B
> glowing coals flamed forth from him. (2 Sam 22.9)   C

> They have all fallen away;   A
> they are all alike depraved;   B
> there is none that does good,   C
> no, not one. (Psa 53.3)   D

3.2.1.1 Types of parallelism

For centuries biblical scholars have been aware of the existence of parallelism in Hebrew poetry. In the eighteenth century Bishop Robert Lowth identified three different types of parallelism and categorized them as **synonymous**, **antithetical**, and **synthetic** parallelism.

According to Lowth's definition, **synonymous parallelism** occurs when the parallel lines are similar in meaning. In the example from Isa 1.3 seen above, we can say that A = B:

But Israel does not know,	(A colon)
my people does not understand.	(B colon)

There are times, however, when synonymous lines have gaps. That is, some element in the second line is missing. This phenomenon is known formally as **ellipsis**. These gaps are intentionally left by the poet, often to make room within the line for another thought or expression. Because of the context, these gaps are easily filled in by the hearer or reader. In Isa 1.3a, for example, the second line has no verb, but the hearer or reader automatically assumes that the verb of the first line ("know") applies to the second line as well. The asterisks (*) seen below show that an element is missing at this point in the text:

The ox	**knows**	its owner,
and the ass	******	its master's crib.

In Lam 5.2 the verb is again missing, but it is easily identified:

Our inheritance	**has been turned over**	to strangers,
our homes	*******************	to aliens.

Antithetical parallelism occurs when a contrast or opposition is expressed between two cola or lines (A contrasts with B). Pairs of opposites are a frequent feature in this type of parallelism. For example, in the following set of parallelisms from Psa 30.5, contrast is shown by a set of paired opposites: anger/favor, moment/lifetime, weeping/joy, night/morning:

> For his **anger** is but for a *moment*,
> and his **favor** is for a *lifetime*.

> **Weeping** may tarry for the *night*,
> but **joy** comes with the *morning*.

Antithetical parallelism is extremely common in the book of Proverbs:

> A fool gives full vent to his anger,
> but a wise man quietly holds it back. (Pro 29.11)

> A wise son makes a glad father,
> but a foolish son is a sorrow to his mother. (Pro 10.1)

In **synthetic parallelism** the second line adds to or completes the thought of the first, modifying it in some way. Looking at the first line we cannot predict what the second will say. But when the two are put together, we recognize that they make up a meaningful unit (A + B = a complete thought):

> The fool says in his heart,   A
> "There is no God." (Psa 14.1)   B
>
> The Lord knows the thoughts of man,   A
> that they are but a breath. (Psa 94.11)   B

Note that the meaning of each of the two lines is not the same, but the balance of the two lines taken together is similar to that of other parallel lines.

Ellipsis can occur in this type of parallelism as well. Psa 9.9, for example, reads:

> The LORD is a stronghold for the oppressed,
> a stronghold in times of trouble.

Two elements of the first line are assumed in the second line. This leaves room for an added element, "in times of trouble" in line B:

> The LORD is   a stronghold for the oppressed   A
> **********   a stronghold *************** **in times of trouble**. B

This parallelism is sometimes called **stairstep parallelism**, because the second line builds on the first. Often a word or phrase from line A is repeated in line B:

> The LORD is near   **to all who call upon him,**
>   **to all who call upon him**   in truth. (Psa 145.18)

3.2.1.2 Word pairs in parallel lines

Another common feature of Hebrew poetry which has been recognized and studied for centuries is **word pairs**. In Hebrew and related Middle Eastern languages, pairs of words are commonly associated in poetry. Many of these are naturally related pairs such as "heaven" and "earth," "sun" and "moon," "day" and "night":

> Let the **heavens** be glad,
> and let the **earth** rejoice. (Psa 96.11)
>
> The **sun** shall not smite you by day,
> nor the **moon** by night. (Psa 121.6)

Others words are paired together because of cultural, historical, or geographical reasons:

Hear the word of the Lord, you rulers of **Sodom**!
Give ear to the teaching of our God, you people of **Gomorrah**. (Isa 1.10)

The LORD roars from **Zion**,
and utters his voice from **Jerusalem**. (Amos 1.2)

In **Judah** God is known,
his name is great in **Israel**. (Psa 76.1)

There may be over one thousand known word pairs in Hebrew poetry. Their occurrence serves to define and reinforce parallel lines, and they also help to create a sense of balance:

If I ascend to **heaven**, thou art there!
If I make my bed in **Sheol**, thou art there! (Psa 139.8)

3.2.1.3 Beyond Lowth's classification

In recent years scholars have come to question some of the basic assumptions concerning parallelism. Lowth's three categories have been criticized as being too simple. In most so-called synonymous parallel lines, for example, there are still differences in meaning, even though they may be very difficult to recognize or describe. We see an example of this in Psa 34.1:

I will bless the LORD at all times;
his praise shall continually be in my mouth.

If the author had wanted to repeat himself more exactly, he could have done so. Instead he purposely expressed the second line differently from the first.

Scholars today readily acknowledge that parallel lines can express many more relationships than the three types described above. The link between two lines may be **logical**, exhibiting relationships such as action-consequence, reason-result, condition-consequence, generic-specific, grounds-conclusion, concession-counterexpectation, or means-purpose. Often imperatives or commands are combined with a logical support: command-reason, means-command, or others. Sometimes the link between the two lines can be **temporal** (sequential or circumstantial). These are very common in the historical psalms. Some links are based on **formal** distinctions. These may be grammatical, such as positive-negative, question-answer, singular-plural, masculine-feminine. Still other parallel lines express various types of comparison. Below are some of the many relationships that can characterize the A and B cola in Hebrew poetry:

Parallelisms Based on Logical Relationships

1. A gives an action; B gives its consequence:

> In all your ways acknowledge him,
> and he will make straight your paths. (Pro 3.6)

2. A gives a concession; B gives a counter-expectation:

> though your sins are like scarlet,
> they shall be as white as snow. (Isa 1.18)

3. A presents a condition; B the consequence:

> If the clouds are full of rain,
> they empty themselves on the earth. (Eccl 11.3)

4. A presents a reason; B the result:

> Because he inclined his ear to me,
> therefore I will call on him as long as I live. (Psa 116.2)

5. A presents a request or command; B gives the reason:

> Arise O God, judge the earth;
> for to thee belong all the nations! (Psa 82.8)

6. A presents the means of carrying out an action; B the request:

> By the strength of your arm
> preserve those condemned to die! (Psa 79.11; NIV)

7. A is generic; B is specific:

> Your **country** lies desolate,
> your **cities** are burned with fire. (Isa 1.7)

> Even there thy **hand** shall lead me,
> and thy **right hand** shall hold me. (Psa 139.10)

Parallelisms Based on Temporal Relationships

8. A presents one event, B the next event in the sequence:

> Then they cried to the LORD in their trouble,
> and he delivered them from their distress. (Psa 107.6)

9. A presents an event, B the time setting of that event:

> But thou didst hear my supplications,
> when I cried to thee for help. (Psa 31.22)

Parallelisms Based on Form

10. A asks a question; B answers:

> Is there a God besides me?
> There is no Rock; I know not any. (Isa 44.8)

11. A makes a statement; B asks a question:

> A man's spirit will endure sickness;
> but a broken spirit who can bear? (Pro 18.14)

12. A is positive; B is negative (in this example, despite the positive–negative forms, note that the lines are similar in meaning):

> **Hear**, my son, your father's instruction,
> and **reject not** your mother's teaching. (Prov. 1.8)

13. A has one gender (masculine or feminine); B has another:

> May our **sons** in their youth be like plants full grown,
> our **daughters** like corner pillars cut for the structure of a palace.
>   (Psa 144.12)

14. A is singular; B is plural:

> O **offspring** of Abraham, his servant,
> **sons** of Jacob, his chosen ones! (Psa 105.6)

15. A presents a number; B adds one:

> There are **six** things which the LORD hates,
> **seven** which are an abomination to him. (Pro 6.16)

16. A presents a number; B exaggerates it:

> Saul has slain his **thousands**,
> and David his **ten thousands**. (1 Sam 18.7)

Parallelism Expressing Comparison

17. A gives a comparison; B the application of the comparison:

As a hart longs for flowing streams,
so longs my soul for thee, O God. (Psa 42.1)

As far as the east is from the west,
so far does he remove our transgressions from us. (Psa 103.12)

Other Parallel Statements

18. A may make a statement; B describes or comments on an element of A:

Oh, how I love thy **law**!
It is my meditation all the day. (Psa 119.97)

My help comes from the **LORD**,
who made heaven and earth. (Psa 121.2)

19. A presents one item; B its exact opposite (note in the following case, there are two sets of contrast):

The heart of the **wise** is in the house of **mourning**,
but the heart of **fools** is in the house of **mirth**. (Eccl 7.4)

Even this short list shows that describing the link between parallel lines can be quite subjective, since many features work together to make up a parallelism. Note that, besides the logical relationships defined above, word pairs play a crucial role in the composition of several parallel sets; for example, "ways" and "paths" in example (1), "father" and "mother" in example (12), or "east" and "west" in example (17).

Two actions may be related in time and have a logical link as well. Thus, in "they cried to the LORD/and he delivered them," there is a temporal link and also a logical one: action–consequence or possibly reason–result. In the proverb "keep your father's commandment, and forsake not your mother's teaching," there is the negative–positive link, a masculine–feminine link, and the word pair "father"–"mother." The generic–specific example, "your country"/"your cities" (7) can also fall under the singular–plural category, as can "wise"/"fools" (19). Thus it is very difficult to identify one single factor that ties two lines together. In most cases there are several features that link the first and second lines of a parallel set.

It is difficult, then, to make a definitive list of all possible relationships that can occur between parallel lines. However, it is important for translators to try to define the relationship of each set as specifically as possible in order to communicate these in their translation.

James Kugel was one of the first modern scholars to seriously question Lowth's three categories and to suggest that there are many ways of interpreting the relationship between two parallel lines. He notes that the relationship is never so simple as "A = B," "A does not equal B" or "A + B." He writes "B must inevitably be understood as A's completion" (1981: 13). He characterizes the most common relationships as:

26

A, and what's more, B;
not only A, but B;
not A, not even B;
not A, and certainly not B;
just as A, so B

Taking one of our examples from Isa 1.7, we note that Kugel's suggested analysis fits well:

Your country lies desolate,   (A)
[what's more] your cities are burned with fire.   (B)

We sense that there is a development or progression from one line to another. The second intensifies the first and brings its message home. It expresses the point of the passage in more specific terms. As Robert Alter notes on parallelism (1985: 615-616):

> The dominant pattern is a focusing, heightening, or specification of ideas, images, actions, themes, from one verse to the next. If something is broken in the first verset, it is smashed or shattered in the second verset; if a city is destroyed in the first verset, it is turned into a heap of rubble in the second. A general term in the first half of a line is typically followed by a specific instance of the general category in the second half; or again, a literal statement in the first verset becomes a metaphor or hyperbole in the second. . . .What this means to us as readers of biblical poetry is that, instead of listening to an imagined drumbeat of repetitions, *we need constantly to look for something new happening from one part of the line to the next.* [Italics added.]

Indeed, we notice that often the psalmist states something in ordinary language in the first line, but then he emphasizes his point with painful detail or forceful imagery in the second:

For you will put them to flight;
you will aim at their faces with your bows. (Psa 21.12)

Thou hast made thy people suffer hard things;
thou hast given us wine to drink that made us reel. (Psa 60.3)

If the first line is figurative, the second may be even more graphic:

For thou dost smite all my enemies on the cheek,
thou dost break the teeth of the wicked. (Psa 3.7)

The second line may be more personalized. In Psa 60.3 above, for example, the first reference to the Israelites is "thy people," while in the second line there is

27

a very direct reference to "us." Similarly in the verse below, the second line is more personal:

> For who is God, but the LORD?
> And who is a rock, except **our God**? (Psa 18.31)

This last example shows an important feature of Hebrew poetry: the varying and repeated names of God. In the Psalms and in other praise or petition poetry, it is very common for the poet to call out the name of God and to describe his attributes in different forms. In this way parallel lines show in detail who God is and what he does:

> Yet I will rejoice in the **LORD**,
> I will joy in the **God of my salvation**. (Hab 3.18)

These names draw us into an intimate interaction with God:

> Do not forsake me, **O LORD**!
> **O my God**, be not far from me! (Psa 38.21)

Such insistence on God's name invites the reader or hearer to have confidence in him even in times of trouble:

> Yea, **thou** dost light my lamp;
> **the LORD my God** lightens my darkness. (Psa 18.28)

3.2.1.4 More complicated patterns
Patterns of parallelism may extend further than just two lines. There may be alternating parallelism, when synonymous lines occur every other line. In the following example from Isa 1.10, the lower case letters **a** and **b** represent this pattern:

> Hear the word of the LORD,   a
>   you rulers of Sodom!   b
> Give ear to the teaching of our God, a′
>   you people of Gomorrah!   b′

The same logical, temporal, or semantic relationships that hold two lines together may also tie different sections of a poem together. In Isa 1.3, for example, the first two lines would traditionally be called synonymous (a-a'), as would the second set (b-b'). However, the two sets of parallel lines are tied together by a logical relationship that may be described as concession-counterexpectation:

The ox knows its owner,	a	Concession
and the ass its master's crib;	a'	
but Israel does not know,	b	Counterexpectation
my people does not understand.	b'	

In Psa 121.1-2 the relationship between the lines is quite complex. A statement in the first line gives way to a question in the second line. This question is answered in the third and fourth lines. In this set the second line expands on an element in the first:

I lift up my eyes to the hills.	Statement
From whence does my help come?	Question
My help comes from the LORD,	Statement
who made heaven and earth.	Expansion }Answer

Parallel sets, based on a similar pattern, may occur one after another. These sets often create a rhythm, which builds to a high point, followed by a concluding statement. In the following example from Psa 103.11-14, there are four sets of parallel lines:

> For as the heavens are high above the earth,
> so great is his steadfast love toward those who fear him;
>
> as far as the east is from the west,
> so far does he remove our transgressions from us.
>
> As a father pities his children,
> so the LORD pities those who fear him.
>
> For he knows our frame;
> he remembers that we are dust. (Psa 103.11-14)

Through the repetition of expressions and similar parallel structures, the greatness of God's love and mercy is emphasized. The sweeping rhythm and word-pair opposites of the first two sets ("heavens"–"earth," "east"–"west") lead us to a more intimate comparison: "As a father pities his children." At this high point the name of Yahweh (LORD) triumphantly appears. The comparison-assertion pattern of the first three lines ("as . . . so" in the English translation) is then changed into a final statement of reason. In what would seem to be a quiet tone, we are finally reminded of our human weakness and the willingness of God to strengthen and support us: "For he knows our frame; he remembers we are dust"!

To summarize our discussion of Hebrew parallelism, we note that it is the association of two poetic lines linked by one or more features. While the second line may be seen as completing, complementing, or intensifying the first, the two lines combine together to express one unified thought. Translators must take care not only to analyze the relationship between two parallel lines, but the relationship between nearby sets of parallel lines as well. As we will see in a later section (section 3.3), parallelism also has to do with sound, stresses and rhythm. Parallel lines resonate in our ears and are, at times, so strikingly beautiful (even in translation) that they are almost impossible to forget.

3.2.2 Chiastic structures

A variant of parallel lines is the **chiastic** or **X-structure** (also called **chiasmus** or **chiasm**). In this pattern two lines have corresponding elements, but their order is reversed. For example, the lines from the English poet, Goldsmith, "to stop, too fearful, too faint to go," can be diagramed as follows:

In the following lines from Psa 84.8, the vocative phrase "O LORD God of hosts" matches another vocative "O God of Jacob." The imperative verb phrase "hear my prayer" matches the phrase "give ear":

| O LORD God of hosts, | (a) | | hear my prayer; | (b) |
| give ear, | (b′) | | O God of Jacob! | (a′) |

Sometimes scholars abbreviate this structure as **abb′a′**. More complicated patterns also exist, involving three elements **abc-c′b′a′** (Isa 6.10):

Make the **heart** of this people fat,	a
and their **ears** heavy,	b
and shut their **eyes**;	c
lest they see with their **eyes**,	c′
and hear with their **ears**,	b′
and understand with their **hearts**.	a′

Chiastic structures do not always contain perfect matches in form or meaning, as Psa 1.6 demonstrates:

| for the LORD knows | (a) | the way of the righteous, | (b) |
| but the way of the wicked | (b′) | will perish. | (c) |

This imperfect X-pattern (**abb′c**) is built on contrast: "the way of righteous" is contrasted with "the way of the wicked," and the way of life ("the LORD knows") is contrasted with the way of death ("perdition"). Note also that there is a kind of grammatical chiastic structure, since **b** and **b′** are nominal, while **a** and **c** are verbal.

Chiastic structures are not as frequent as simple parallel lines, and they often stand out in the text. Thus they may signal the climax of a poem or some other important point (Bliese, 1988). In Psa 26.4, for example, an X-pattern seems to emphasize David's total refusal of all wrongdoing (Berlin 1985: 137):

I have never consorted   with scoundrels
And with hypocrites   I will never associate

Chiastic patterns also play a role in defining structures within poems. In Ecclesiastes a chiastic structure signals the beginning of the so-called "Time Poem" (3.1):

For everything   there is a season,
and a time   for every matter under heaven.

A chiastic pattern of positive (+) and negative (-) marks the end of this poem as well (3.8):

a time to love, (+)   and a time to hate; (-)
a time for war, (-)   and a time for peace. (+)

In contrast, the lines in the middle of the poem follow simple parallel structures:

a time to weep, (-)   and a time to laugh; (+)
a time to mourn, (-)   and a time to dance. (+)

Another chiastic pattern based on positive–negative meanings is super-imposed on the entire time poem (Loader, 1986: 34):

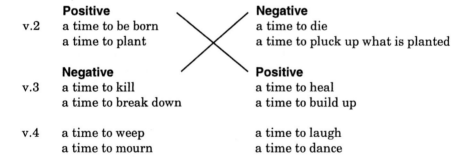

	Positive		**Negative**
v.2	a time to be born		a time to die
	a time to plant		a time to pluck up what is planted
	Negative		**Positive**
v.3	a time to kill		a time to heal
	a time to break down		a time to build up
v.4	a time to weep		a time to laugh
	a time to mourn		a time to dance

	Positive		**Negative**
v.5	a time to throw		a time to gather stones
	a time to embrace		a time to refrain from embracing
v.6	a time to seek		a time to lose
	a time to keep		a time to cast away
	Negative		**Positive**
v.7	a time to rend		a time to sew
	a time to keep silence		a time to speak

Note that the verb "throw" in verse 5, which might be interpreted as negative, is in fact positive. The Good News Bible translates this idiomatic expression as "the time for making love" (+), and the following line as "the time for not making love" (–). Following this analysis, this poem has a very tight symmetrical structure which can be summarized as follows:

v. 1	internal chiastic structure	a
v. 2	2 pairs of positive-negative	b
v. 3-4	4 pairs of negative-positive	c
v. 5-6	4 pairs of positive-negative	c′
v. 7	2 pairs of negative-positive	b′
v. 8	internal chiastic structure	a′

This is an example of the fine craftsmanship which characterizes much of Hebrew poetry—craftsmanship which is often difficult to appreciate in a translated version. Translators should be familiar with such patterns in the original text, so that the impact and significance may be maintained in the translation (see chapter 6 for format).

3.2.3 Refrains

Hebrew poetry is rich with lines that are repeated within a given text. A **refrain** can occur after only one line, or following a long stretch of material, where it may signal the end of a unit. In Psa 136, the line "for his steadfast love endures for ever" occurs every other line throughout the poem. This psalm was certainly used during public worship. It is very likely that one person chanted the narrative part of the poem, while the audience joined in with the refrain:

> to him who smote the first-born of Egypt,
> **for his steadfast love endures for ever;**
> and brought Israel out from among them,
> **for his steadfast love endures for ever. . . .** (10-11)

This device is also found in Psalm 118, where two different refrains occur:

> Let Israel say,
> **"His steadfast love endures for ever."**

32

Let the house of Aaron say,
"His steadfast love endures for ever."
Let those who fear the LORD say,
"His steadfast love endures for ever." (2-4)

All nations surrounded me;
in the name of the LORD I cut them off!
They surrounded me, surrounded me on every side;
in the name of the LORD I cut them off!
They surrounded me like bees,
they blazed like a fire of thorns;
in the name of the LORD I cut them off! (10-12)

In the Song of Songs, on the other hand, the refrain "I adjure you, O daughters of Jerusalem" occurs only a few times throughout the book. Yet it serves the important function of closing off a poetic unit (2.7; 3.5; 5.8; 8.4).

3.2.4 Envelope or Inclusio
This device is used in both narrative and poetic material. A word or phrase is repeated both at the beginning and at the end of a unit. In Ecclesiastes, for example, the saying "Vanity of vanities, says the Preacher; all is vanity" surrounds the entire book (1.2;12.8). On the other hand there may be an envelope around just a single verse, as seen in Psa 27.14 (NIV):

Wait for the LORD;
be strong and take heart
and **wait for the LORD.**

Similarly, in some psalms a line or set of lines may surround an entire poem. In Psalm 8, for example, an envelope made up of two lines surrounds the entire poem:

O LORD, our Lord,
how majestic is thy name in all the earth!

Thou whose glory above the heavens is chanted
by the mouth of babes and infants,
thou hast founded a bulwark because of thy foes,
to still the enemy and the avenger.

When I look at thy heavens, the work of thy fingers,
the moon and the stars which thou hast established;
what is man that thou art mindful of him,
and the son of man that thou dost care for him?

Yet thou hast made him little less than God,
and dost crown him with glory and honor.

Thou hast given him dominion over the works of thy hands;
    thou hast put all things under his feet,
all sheep and oxen,
    and also the beasts of the field,
the birds of the air, and the fish of the sea,
    whatever passes along the paths of the sea.

O LORD, our Lord,
    how majestic is thy name in all the earth!

Similarly in Psa 103, the phrase "Bless the LORD, O my soul!" occurs at the beginning and end of the poem.

Usually inclusios repeat the exact words at the beginning and end of a poem. Sometimes, however, there may be variants which mean the same thing, and these may not occur strictly at the beginning or end, but rather as a part of the introduction or closing sections. In Psalm 26, for example, we note that, though the introductory and concluding words in Hebrew (and the English translation) are somewhat different, there is an inclusio based on meaning:

Opening lines (verse 1):

    Vindicate me, O LORD,
    for **I have walked in my integrity**,
    and I have trusted in the LORD without wavering.

Closing lines (verses 11 and 12):

    But as for me, **I walk in my integrity**;
    redeem me, and be gracious to me.
    My foot stands on level ground;
    in the great congregation I will bless the LORD.

Thus "vindicate me" is matched by "redeem me." "Walk in my integrity" occurs in both passages. "Trust in the LORD" seems to be matched by "bless the LORD," and "without wavering" corresponds to the idea in the statement: "my foot stands on level ground."

A similar phenomenon occurs in Song of Songs. In this case several elements of the introduction of the Song ("companions," "apple tree," "desert," "Solomon," "vineyard") reappear at the end of the book.

In long stretches of poetry, inclusios based on single words or short expressions can help determine where strophes or breaks occur in the poem (see section 3.4 below).

3.3 Sound effects in Hebrew poetry

Sound is the building block of any poem, and in Hebrew there are several devices that can be used by the poet. Unfortunately nearly all of them, with the possible exception of rhythm, are not often kept in translation. Consequently they are lost to the person who cannot read the text in the original language.

3.3.1 Stress, meter, and rhythm

In our discussion of parallelism, we barely touched on one very important fact: parallel structures are built not only on similarity of meaning and grammatical form, but on sound patterns as well. Parallel lines have similar or regular stress patterns, which add to the overall feeling of rhythm and balance.

In Hebrew poetic lines, patterns are formed on the basis of word stresses, which usually fall on the last syllable of the word. The most commonly found pattern is 3 + 3, that is, three stresses in each colon. This pattern is seen in the opening lines of Psalm 92 (Alonso Schökel 1988; 35):

tóv	le-hodóth	la-Yahwéh	//	ule-zammér	le-shimká	'elyón
good	to-praise	to-LORD	//	and-to-play	to-name-your	Elyon
	3 accents		+		3 accents	

> It is good to give thanks to the LORD,
> to sing praises to thy name, O Most High.

Note that, while normally Hebrew words have one stress per word, sometimes words are pronounced together, in which case the group carries only one stress. This happens especially when there are grammatical particles such as prepositions or negative markers, which are pronounced with the following word in one beat. In the example above, the preposition "to" (*le* or *la*), which occurs four times, does not have its own stress; it is attached to the following word.

Though 3+3 is the most common pattern in Hebrew poetry, other patterns do exist: 2+2, 4+4, as well as 3+2, 4+3, 3+4, and others. Some patterns are associated with certain moods. For example the 3+2 pattern is often associated with a lament (see chapter 2), as in the following passage from Lamentations (3.19-21):

zekar	'ani	umerudi	//	la'anah	waro'sh
zakor	tizkor	wethashoch	//	'alay	naphshi
zoth	'ashiv	'el-libi	//	'al-ken	'ochil
	3				2

> Remember my affliction and my bitterness,
> the wormwood and the gall!
> My soul continually thinks of it
> and is bowed down within me.
> But this I call to mind,
> and therefore I have hope. . . .

It is, in fact, stress patterns which provide evidence that in Hebrew many proverbs belong in the same category as other poetic lines (Alonso Schökel, page 37):

dalyú	*shoqáyim*	*mippiséach*	*//*	*umashál*	*bephí*	*kesilím*
3			+		3	

> Like a lame man's legs, which hang useless,
> is a proverb in the mouth of fools. (Pro 26.7)

Many commentaries and books about Hebrew poetry talk about **meter**, which Webster defines as "a systematically arranged and measured rhythm in verse." Accepting this definition we can say Hebrew poetry has meter, but we must emphasize the fact that it is not strict meter as in Greek poetry, English sonnets, or other Western European forms. Hebrew poetry is what we may call "free (or, variable) meter." In other words, the number of stresses may change from line to line without forming a regular or predictable pattern.

Rhythm refers to a certain flow in lines which is based on an ordered and repeated alternation of strong and weak beats. In English we perceive rhythm through stresses on certain words. Reading Edwin Markham's short poem "Outwitted" aloud gives us a feeling for what rhythm is (´ = strong beat or accent):

> He dréw a circle that shút me oút—
> héretic, rébel, a thíng to floút.
> But lóve and Í had the wít to wín:
> Wé drew a círcle that toók him ín!

In Hebrew, rhythm may also be described in terms of word stress. If a translation is sensitive to form or tries to maintain grammatical parallelism, a corresponding rhythm may be retained in the translation. A good example is the time poem from Ecclesiastes 3:

> For everything there is a season,
> and a time for every matter under heaven:
>
> a time to be born, and a time to die;
> a time to plant, and a time to pluck up what is planted;
> a time to kill, and a time to heal;
> a time to break down, and a time to build up;
> a time to weep, and a time to laugh;
> a time to mourn, and a time to dance . . .

In this rather literal translation from RSV, the reader can easily sense the balanced rhythm so typical of much of Hebrew poetry. This same point-counterpoint rhythm is often evident in Proverbs as well:

> Like a bird that strays from its nest,
> is a man who strays from his home. (Pro 27.8)

3.3.2 Alliteration

One of the most frequent sound devices used in Hebrew poetry is that of repeated consonants. This is called **alliteration**. English-speaking children learn this technique from age-old tongue-twisters: "Peter Piper picked a peck of pickled peppers" or "She sells sea shells by the seashore." But this device is a well-respected technique used also in serious English poetry to create a special effect. In his poem "The Meaning of Africa," the Sierre Leonean poet Abisoeh Nicol speaks of the "**r**ed **r**oad . . . , the **h**uddled **h**eaps of four mu**d** walls . . . ." . Repeated consonants do not occur only at the beginning of words. They may occur inside words and throughout a long passage. In the beginning of the book of Song of Songs, for example, the introductory lines are full of the sounds *sh*, *m*, *l*, and *r*:

shir	*ha-shirim*	*'asher*	*lishlomoh*
song-of	the-songs	which	to-Solomon

The Song of Songs, which is Solomon's

Words may imitate the actual sounds we hear in nature (this is called **onomatopoeia**). Thus a word like "wind" in Hebrew, *ruach*, sounds like the entity it refers to. In Judges 5.22 the words "galloping, galloping" *daharoth daharoth* sound like the event they refer to. In Hebrew, sets of repetitive consonants are often onomatopoeic. In Isa 10.14, as the prophet quotes the boastful speech of the king of Assyria ("I have gathered all the earth; and there was none that moved a wing, or opened the mouth, or chirped"), we hear the repetitive sounds *p* and *ts*, imitating the sound of a bird's chirping:

upotse	*pe*	*umtsaptsep*
and-one-opening	mouth	and-chirping

In the first poem in Ecclesiastes (1.4-11), the sounds of nature are evoked in a very effective way. In verse 6 we hear the rushing sound of the wind, with the fricative consonants: *s*, *sh*, *f*, *v*, *ts*, and *h*. In verse 7 the *h* and *sh* sounds continue, along with repetitive *m* and *l*, imitating the rolling and depth of moving waters:

(6)	*holek*	*'el-darom*	*wesovev*	*'el-tsafon*
	going	to south	and-turning	to north
	sovev	*sovev*	*holek*	*ha-ruach*
	turning	turning	going	the-wind
	ve'al	*sevivothaw*	*shav*	*ha-ruach*
	and-on	its courses	returning	the-wind
(7)	*kal*	*hanechalim*	*holekim*	*'el hayam*
	all	the-rivers	going	to the-sea

	vehayam	*'enenu male*
	but-the-sea	never full

'l meqom	*she-hanehalim*	*holekim*
to-place	which-the-rivers	going

sham	*hem*	*shavim*	*lalaket*
there	they	returning	to-going

While this device is extremely effective in the original language, a person not knowing Hebrew will not realize that alliteration occurs in a given text. Translators may learn this fact, however, from commentaries, translation manuals, or study Bibles.

3.3.3 Assonance

Like alliteration, **assonance** refers to repeated sounds, but in this case it is the vowels that are repeated. Such repetition may help to create a certain mood or express a certain attitude. For example, in Isa 6.3, when the cherubim call to one another, we hear the *a* and *o* sounds expressing the majesty of God:

> *qadosh, qadosh, qadosh Yahweh tseva'oth*
> *malo' kal ha-arets kevodo*

> Holy, holy, holy is the LORD of hosts;
> the whole earth is full of his glory.

Remarkably, in the English translation the repetition of the long **o** sound has a similar effect as in the original!

In the Song of Songs assonance is a frequent feature, expressing the two lovers' delight. At the climax of the Song (5.1), we hear a series of *i* and *a* sounds in words spoken by the young man. The parallel structures intensify the effect of the repetitive sound:

ba'thi	*legani*	*'achothi*	*kallah*
I-came	to-my-garden	my-sister	bride

'arithi	*mori*	*'im*	*besami*
I-gathered	my-myrrh	with	my-spice

'akalti	*ya'ri*	*'im*	*divshi*
I-ate	my-honeycomb	with	my-honey

shathithi	*yeni*	*'im*	*halavi*
I-drank	my-wine	with	my-milk

Like other features such as parallelism and inclusio, assonance can help us determine where significant breaks in a poem occur. In the example given above, on the basis of the feature of assonance, we can break the verse into two parts. After "I drank my wine with my milk," an *i-u* alternation begins:

'ikelu	*re'im*	*shethu*	*ve*	*shikeru*	*dodim*
eat	friends	drink	and	get-drunk	lovers

This break is confirmed by the shift in person and mood from "I" to imperative plural "you." Many scholars feel this last line is spoken by another person or group of persons, possibly the daughters of Jerusalem.

Again, the feature of assonance cannot be recognized by translators with no working knowledge of Hebrew. Nevertheless most commentaries will point out assonance in the original text if it is a prominent feature of a passage. Translators need to know when a given passage is marked with assonance, so they may recreate a similar effect in their translation (see chapter 4).

3.3.4 Rhyme

Along with assonance and alliteration, **rhyme** is an element which is usually not apparent in a translation. Formed by sound correspondences at the end of words, rhyme is a familiar feature of English poetry, as seen in the following lines from a poem by Robert Frost (Untermeyer, page 437):

> The woods are lovely, dark and **deep**,
> But I have promises to **keep**,
> And miles to go before I **sleep**,
> And miles to go before I **sleep**.

Rhyme is not so common in Hebrew, however, but is sometimes found at the end of lines. As in English, it serves to link two lines into one thought:

> *veyig'e kashachal tetsude**ni***
> *vetashov tithpala-**vi***

> And if I lift myself up, thou dost hunt me like a lion,
> and again work wonders against me. (Job 10.16)

> *Nachelathenu nehefkah leza**rim***
> *Bathenu lenak**rim***

> Our inheritance has been turned over to strangers,
> our homes to aliens. (Lam 5.2)

Rhyme is not limited to line-final position but may also occur within the line itself (**internal rhyme**). In English this is not frequent but it does occur. It can be seen in the following first line of "The Raven" by Edgar Allen Poe:

Once upon a midnight **dreary**, while I pondered, weak and **weary**,

This phenomenon does occur sometimes in Hebrew as well, but it is rare. Note how in Lam 5.2, above, the sequence *thenu* occurs internally in each line. When it does occur, it serves to link two phrases more closely together.

3.3.5 Wordplay

Wordplay is another dominant feature of Hebrew poetry as well as of other literary genres. In wordplay, technically known as **paronomasia**, two words with similar sounds may occur in the same context, or one word may be used with two different meanings. In English, wordplays or "puns" are mainly used for light humor, but in Hebrew they normally occur in serious or ironic contexts. One of the most famous wordplays of Scripture serves as the conclusion of the very moving "song of the vineyard" (Isaiah 5). By their meaning alone the final words in each pair of lines express a strong contrast. But in the original Hebrew the closeness in pronunciation between the words is even more striking. This expresses a very sharp ironic accusation:

> For the vineyard of the LORD of hosts
>   is the house of Israel,
> and the men of Judah
>   are his pleasant planting;
> and he looked for **justice** [*mishpat*],
>   but behold, **bloodshed** [*mispach*];
> for **righteousness** [*tsedaqah*],
>   but behold, a **cry** [*tse'aqah*]! (Isa 5.7)

Another famous prophet known for wordplay is Micah. At the end of chapter 1 (10-16), his message to each town of Judah is highlighted by a word play based on its name:

> Tell it not in **Gath** [sounds like "tell"],
>   weep not at all;
> in **Beth-le-aphrah** [means "house of dust"]
>   roll yourselves in the dust.
> Pass on your way,
>   inhabitants of **Shaphir** [means "pleasant"],
>   in nakedness and shame;
> the inhabitants of **Zaanan** [sounds like "come forth"]
>   do not come forth;
> the wailing of **Beth-ezel** [Beth = "house"]
>   shall take away from you its standing place.
> For the inhabitants of **Maroth** [sounds like "bitter"]
>   wait anxiously for good,
> because evil has come down from the LORD
>   to the gate of **Jerusalem** [sounds like "peace"].
> Harness the steeds to the chariots,
>   inhabitants of **Lachish** [sounds like "steeds"];

you were the beginning of sin
    to the daughter of Zion,
for in you were found
    the transgressions of Israel.
Therefore you shall give parting gifts
    to **Maresheth**-gath [means "heritage"];
the houses of **Achzib** [means "deception"] shall be a deceitful thing
    to the kings of Israel.
I will again bring a conqueror upon you,
    inhabitants of **Mareshah** [sounds like "conqueror"];
the glory of Israel
    shall come to **Adullam** [sounds like "their ornament"].
Make yourselves bald and cut off your hair,
    for the children of your delight;
make yourselves as bald as the eagle,
    for they shall go from you into exile.

By their frequency and irony these wordplays are meant to express the overwhelming judgment of God.

3.4 Stylistic features found throughout Hebrew literature

Along with his criticism of Lowth's three categories of parallelism, the modern scholar James Kugel also noticed something interesting about Hebrew poetry. He claimed that every feature found in Hebrew poetry is also found in narrative and other literary types. He even went so far as to say that the category "poetry" does not exist in Hebrew. While we cannot agree with this last claim, it is true that the features of Hebrew poetry can also be found in nonpoetic texts. For example, parallelism, or the tendency to balance structures, is certainly present in many works. In Jonah we note that the book is perfectly symmetrical, with the first two chapters (the Lord's call and Jonah's response) being balanced out by the last two (the Lord's call and Jonah's final response). Inclusios, or envelope structures, are a common feature in biblical books such as Esther, and in the prose opening and closing of the book of Job. Even alliteration can play a role in narrative text, as in Gen 3.1, where the serpent passage is conspicuously marked with hissing *s*, *sh*, and *h* sounds. Again, wordplay is a crucial part of many of the narrative books such as Genesis and Joshua, where proper names are often related to particular circumstances.

In this section we look at some other features which are not unique to poetry, but which do occur especially frequently in poetic contexts. As the density and variety of these features build up in a given passage, the text can be described as being more and more poetic.

3.4.1 Figures of Speech

Figures of speech occur in every language. They are used in every speech style, from slang ("he's a real rat!") to more literary forms ("a land flowing with milk and honey"). In poetry, however, figures of speech are especially frequent and rich. These concrete images serve to bring alive abstract thoughts. They are not the message, but they bring the message to us in terms we can understand, feel, and even visualize. In Isa 29.8, for example, the disappointment of the enemies of Jerusalem is spelled out in very down-to-earth images:

> **As when a hungry man dreams he is eating**
>   **and awakes with his hunger not satisfied,**
> **or as when a thirsty man dreams he is drinking**
>   **and awakes faint, with his thirst not quenched,**
> so shall the multitude of all the nations be
>   that fight against Mount Zion.

3.4.1.1 Similes and Metaphors

Traditionally figures of comparison are divided into two types: similes and metaphors. Similes contain an overt marker of comparison such as "like" or "as":

> Though your sins are **like scarlet,**
>   they shall be **as white as snow;**
> though they are red **like crimson,**
>   they shall become **like wool.** (Isa 1.18)

Metaphors are images where no such comparison word occurs. Two things appear to be equated:

> **The LORD is my rock.** (Psa 18.2)

> **The LORD is my shepherd.** (Psa 23.1)

> But **I** am **a worm.** (Psa 22.6)

Both these types of figurative expression are extremely frequent in Old Testament poetry, and both have three main components, whether explicit or implicit in the text:

(a)   the **object,** or topic of the comparison
(b)   the **image,** or what the object is being compared to
(c)   the **basis** of the comparison between the image and the topic

Each biblical figure of speech must be properly analyzed and understood before it is translated. Some of the difficulty in understanding figures of speech comes from the fact that the basis of, or reason for, the comparison is often left out. In what way, for example, is the LORD like a rock or a shepherd? How is the psalmist like a worm?

However, difficulties of interpretation may still arise when all three parts of the figure are explicit in the text. For example, even if we can understand that "the sins as red as scarlet will become white as snow," the translator still needs to go behind the expressions to determine what these different colors meant in a biblical setting. Certainly there are cultures where the symbolic meaning of red and whiteness is not understood, or where such colors may designate something other than what they did in biblical times. (See chapter 5 for a discussion of these problems.)

Figures can be extended for several lines. In Psalm 1, for example, an image of a tree planted by a stream continues over several lines. In the last climactic line of the unit, the meaning of the image is clearly stated:

> his delight is in the law of the LORD . . .
> He *is like a tree*
>   *planted by streams of water,*
> *that yields its fruit in its season,*
>   *and its leaf does not wither.*
> **In all that he does, he prospers.**

Such extended figures can appear throughout long stretches of speech. In Jeremiah 3, for example, Israel's infidelity to God is pictured quite graphically as an unfaithful wife in a series of images which extends through most of the chapter. Ecclesiastes 12, on the other hand, is a shorter but much denser passage, with so many images combined that it is difficult to grasp the meaning of each one (guards, grinders, almond trees, grasshoppers, and broken pitchers and wheels). Whether the meaning of each is perfectly understood or not, these images stick in our minds as symbols of the inevitability of approaching old age and death. Thus figures of speech evoke far more than their surface meaning and give to any poem a beauty and power not found in everyday speech forms. While most readers do not pause to figure out consciously the basis of the comparison, the pictures created by figures of speech stay in the mind and communicate in a deeper way than nonfigurative text.

Biblical figures of speech must also be analyzed from the viewpoint of their literary **context**. For example, in Psa 52.8 the psalmist declares:

> But I am like a green olive tree
> in the house of God.

The link of the "green olive tree" to its context is not very obvious, so we must go back through the psalm to see where this image comes from. In the preceding verses we see that evil people are being addressed (52.5):

> But God will break you down for ever;
>   he will snatch and tear you from your tent;
>   he will **uproot** you from the land of the living.

This is the first allusion to a tree within this psalm. The unrighteous person is uprooted from the land like a tree from the ground. Further, his very life will end ("uprooted from the land of the living"). This sets the scene for the contrast that comes further on in the poem. The righteous person is like a tree that is not uprooted. Thus the figure refers, at least in part, to stability, deep-rootedness, and permanence—the opposite of being "rooted up." The lot of righteous people is far better, because they are not only "in the land of the living" but "in the house of God."

Besides the link to the literary context, we must ask ourselves about the positive or negative connotations created by the figure. We must ask ourselves what Hebrew speakers thought about when they heard the word "olive tree." Perhaps they thought of greenness, of fruit, of oil, of abundance, of prosperity, and even blessing. The house of the LORD could refer to the temple, but here it seems rather to emphasize being in the community of believers in the presence of the LORD.

Poetic figures are very complex devices, with many overlapping meanings determined by the words, the literary context, and the cultural suppositions behind them. Translators must go beyond a superficial analysis (defining the topic of the comparison, the image it is being compared to, and the basis of the comparison), to understand the role of the figure in its immediate and even extended context. Confronted with one single image, "like a green olive tree" (Psa 52.3), translators may be tempted to replace this image by a functional equivalent, but when seen in its wider context, its role is important. Indeed, in the context of the entire book of Psalms, it can be considered a key image (see section 5.4.3).

3.4.1.2 Personification and anthropomorphism

Other kinds of figurative speech include **personification** and **anthropomorphism**. In both these figures abstract elements take on life and are often spoken of in human terms:

> The roads to Zion **mourn**. (Lam 1.4)

> Steadfast love and faithfulness will **meet**;
>   righteousness and peace will **kiss each other**.
> Faithfulness will **spring up** from the ground,
>   and righteousness will **look down** from the sky. (Psa 85.10-11)

> The sword shall **devour** and **be sated**,
>   and **drink its fill** of their blood. (Jer 46.10)

The Old Testament is filled with anthropomorphic expressions in which human attributes and activities are applied to God:

> O sing to the LORD a new song,
>   for he has done marvelous things!
> His **right hand** and his holy **arm**
>   have gotten him victory. (Psa 98.1)

> He who **sits** in the heavens **laughs**. (Psa 2.4)

3.4.1.3 Part-whole relationships

In other figures of speech, parts of elements may be used to refer to the whole. (This is known technically as **synecdoche**.) As seen above, when the psalmist says "his holy arm has gotten him victory," it really means God himself, or his strength, has made him victorious. We note the following very common part-whole relationships:

(1) Body parts often refer to the whole person:

> **My soul** clings to thee. (Psa 63.8)
> (my soul = I)

> **Lying lips** are an abomination to the LORD. (Pro 12.22)
> (lying lips = liars, people who lie)

> For the **mouths of liars** will be stopped. (Psa 63.11)
> (mouths of liars = liars)

The meaning of body parts can be extended even further. For example, "lying lips" may refer to lying people, but it may also refer to the lies themselves coming from those lying lips.

(2) One person can refer to all the descendants of that person:

> thou didst restore the fortunes of **Jacob** (Psa 85.1)

In this example, Jacob refers to all those who descended from him, that is, the whole nation of Israel.

(3) Names of cities, countries, or other locations can refer to the inhabitants of those places:

> Praise the LORD, **O Jerusalem!**
> Praise your God, **O Zion!** (Psa 147.12)

> (CEV: **Everyone in Jerusalem,**
> come and praise
> the LORD your God.)

> let **Ethiopia** hasten to stretch out her hands to God. (Psa 68.31)

> (CEV: make the **Ethiopians** . . . .)

> O sing to the LORD a new song;
> sing to the LORD, **all the earth!** (Psa 96.1)

(CEV: Sing a new song to the LORD!
Everyone on this earth,
sing praises to the LORD. . . .)

Part–whole figures may have several layers of meaning. For example, in the following line from Psa 87.2, there are many steps to understanding the meaning:

The LORD loves **the gates of Zion**

"The gates of Zion" stands for the walls that surround the city. Zion itself is a mountain, but the name usually refers to the city of Jerusalem. CEV renders this as "and he loves **that city** more than any other place in all Israel." Some may want to take the extension further and speak of the inhabitants of the city, or by further extension, all the people of God.

Part–whole relationships can be taken literally or figuratively. In Pro 14.11 house and tent may refer specifically to literal dwellings:

The **house of the wicked** will be destroyed,
but the **tent of the upright** will flourish. (Pro 14.11)

The homes of wicked people will be destroyed, but the homes of the righteous, however meager, will flourish. However, we could go beyond this literal interpretation to say that the people themselves are being discussed, their well-being, or even their very existence.

3.4.1.4 Standard figures

The list of figures in Old Testament poetry is indeed very great, but there is a stock of standard figures that occur throughout Hebrew literature. Most of these involve the device known as **metonymy,** the use of the name of one thing for that of another. Students of the Old Testament will be familiar with these, so we list just a few:

sword, bow, spear = war, aggression (Psa 46.9)
cup = punishment (Isa 51.17) or state of being (Psalm 23)
oil = prosperity, consecration (Psa 45.7)
wine = gladness, and sometimes love (Song of Songs)
lion, jackal = enemy (Psa 57.4; Psa 44.19)
green, flourishing tree = prosperity (Psa 52.8)
pit = death or Sheol (Psa 49.9)

It would be helpful for translators to keep a list of some of the most important biblical figures, along with their standard renderings, to ensure a more consistent translation (see section 5.4.3).

3.4.2 Rhetorical and leading questions

Rhetorical questions are very prominent in Hebrew literature. They are especially important in poetry and are found throughout the book of Job, the Psalms, the Song of Songs, and the prophets. In everyday speech, rhetorical questions (or questions that do not expect explicit answers) are used to express a wide variety of emotions and attitudes: confidence, joy, anger, sarcasm, distress, rebuke, or sadness. Because emotions are expressed so intensely in poetry, we are not surprised to find that rhetorical questions frequently appear in this context. In Psalms may they express the anguish of the poet (6.3; 22.1; 74.1, 10-11):

> Why dost thou stand afar off, O LORD?
> Why dost thou hide thyself in times of trouble? (Psa 10.1)

But they may be used to express the poet's confidence and feelings of trust as well:

> The LORD is my light and my salvation;
>   whom shall I fear?
> The LORD is the stronghold of my life;
>   of whom shall I be afraid? (Psa 27.1)

Rhetorical questions are also used in reasoning or teaching situations, when the speaker is trying to make a point. In the following example from Psa 94.9, the psalmist describes the character of God:

> He who planted the ear, does he not hear?
> He who formed the eye, does he not see?

Rhetorical questions are sometimes used in the context of self-reasoning; for example, when the poet is trying to convince himself of the Lord's faithfulness and love:

> Will the LORD spurn for ever,
> and never again be favorable?
> Has his steadfast love for ever ceased?
> Are his promises at an end for all time?
> Has God forgotten to be gracious?
> Has he in anger shut up his compassion? (Psa 77.7-10)

In the context of poetry we also often find what we could call **leading questions**, or questions that are followed by answers in the text. For example, in Jeremiah the prophet asks a question and then answers it himself:

> **Were they ashamed when they committed abomination?**
>   No, they were not at all ashamed;
>   they did not know how to blush. (Jer 8.12)

These questions often play a role in defining the structure of the poem. In Psalm 15, for example, a leading question in parallel form sets the theme for the entire poem, which in turn acts as the appropriate answer:

> **O LORD, who shall sojourn in thy tent?**
> **Who shall dwell on thy holy hill?**

> He who walks blamelessly, and does what is right,
>   and speaks truth from his heart;
> who does not slander with his tongue,
>   and does no evil to his friend . . . .

Similarly Psalm 121 begins with a thematic question: "I lift up my eyes to the hills. From whence does my help come?" and the rest of the psalm then concentrates on the answer to this question.

In Song of Songs the leading question is a very frequent, almost artificial device, which opens a poetic unit. For example, at 5.9 the daughters of Jerusalem ask two parallel questions that allow the young woman to take up a lengthy description of her lover's wonderful attributes (5.10-16):

> **What is your beloved more than another beloved,**
>   **O fairest among women?**
> **What is your beloved more than another beloved,**
>   **that you thus adjure us?**

> My beloved is all radiant and ruddy,
>   distinguished among ten thousand.
> His head is the finest gold;
>   his locks are wavy,
>   black as a raven. . . .

In the poetic sections of Ecclesiastes as well, a thematic question is often used to set the scene for critical observations that follow (1.3).

3.4.3 Hyperbole, irony and sarcasm

As noted above, there are a number of stylistic features in Hebrew which can occur in either a poetic or a nonpoetic context. These include hyperbole, irony, and sarcasm. Because they may be prominent in certain poems, we mention them briefly here.

Hyperbole is exaggerated speech, which is used for its dramatic effect. If someone says "I'm freezing to death," this does not mean that the person is literally dying. Rather the person is emphasizing through exaggeration how cold he or she is. Because poetry often deals with highly emotional subjects, hyperbole is sometimes used in this context. A good example is found in one of the psalms of David:

> I am weary with my moaning;
>> every night I flood my bed with tears;
>> I drench my couch with my weeping. (Psa 6.6)

Another example of hyperbole comes from Psa 91.7,

> A thousand may fall at your side . . . .

There are not literally one thousand enemies at the person's side, but the psalmist is saying that, no matter what happens, you should trust in God for deliverance.

Again, when people sang:

> Saul has slain his thousands,
> and David his ten thousands (1 Sam 18.7),

they did not really mean that David killed exactly ten thousand men, only that he killed very many (and many more than Saul!).

Irony and **sarcasm** are expressed when a person says one thing but means something else. Though ironic statements are sometimes humorous, they are more often biting and meant to ridicule or reprove someone. The poetry of Job is filled with sarcastic or ironic statements exchanged between Job and his friends, and even between Job and God. When Bildad speaks with Job, Job ironically answers:

> How you have helped him who has no power!
>> How you have saved the arm that has no strength!
> How you have counseled him who has no wisdom,
>> and plentifully declared sound knowledge! (Job 26.2-3)

Job's point is that Bildad has helped no one, certainly not Job himself. He says Bildad has "declared sound knowledge," but he means just the opposite! This usage is marked in the English text by the adverb "plentifully" (Hebrew "in abundance"). The effect of the irony is made stronger here, because Job speaks of himself in the third person as one who has no power, no strength, and no wisdom.

When God speaks to Job from the whirlwind, there is also sharp irony in his voice (Job 38.4):

> Where were you when I laid the foundations of the earth?
> Tell me, if you have understanding.

Rhetorical questions are a very common way of expressing strong irony:

> If I were hungry, I would not tell you;
>> for the world is mine and all that is in it is mine.

> Do I eat the flesh of bulls,
>   or drink the blood of goats? (Psa 50.12-13)

Again, ironical statements are not limited to poetic contexts, but they occur most frequently in this form of heightened speech.

3.4.4 Key words

Key words may occur throughout a poem, giving it a certain flavor and tying the work together as a whole. The repetition of the word "time" in the poem in Ecclesiastes 3 is a prime example. The repetition of the word "praise" in almost every line of Psalm 150, the final psalm in this collection, is most certainly intentional. In the Song of Songs, repetitive terms highlight themes that characterize this book. For example, references to "lilies," "fawns," "doves," "wine," and "myrrh" occur throughout the text. This helps us to see that, even though some parts of this book do not seem closely related, there is, in fact, an overriding unity in the work as a whole.

As noted earlier, key words may serve to indicate the boundaries of poetic units, as when an inclusio surrounds a passage (see 3.2.4). For example, a key term may serve as a link between units. Thus, in the last chapter of the Song of Songs (verses 8-10), there is a small unit dealing with a little sister. This unit ends with the Hebrew word *shalom*: "then I was in his eyes as one who brings **peace**." The following unit (verses 11-12) begins with a word that resembles *shalom*: *shelomoh*, or "Solomon." The repetition of this key root *sh-l-m* links these two sections together, if only superficially. The word *shelomoh* occurs at the beginning and end of verses 11-12, forming an inclusio which defines this section as a sub-unit.

3.4.5 Shifting persons

Another interesting if sometimes puzzling feature of Hebrew poetry is switching person in the middle of a passage. This occurs, for example, when the writer or speaker refers to himself or herself as "I," in the first person, but then switches to the third person, speaking of himself or herself as "he," or "she." Shifting persons has many functions, which include defining structure, signaling the beginning and end of a poem, and marking a climax.

In Psalm 23, for example, we note that the poem speaks about God in the third person at the beginning of the poem, then addresses him in the second person, and at the end, switches back to third person. The poet, who is speaking in first person, remains constant throughout the poem. This shift functions much like an inclusio (see section 3.2.4). The third person reference to the LORD provides an envelope structure around an intimate confession of faith, which is addressed to him:

> **The LORD** is my shepherd, I shall not want;   (third person)
>   **he** makes me lie down in green pastures.
> **He** leads me beside still waters;
>   **he** restores my soul.

He leads me in the paths of righteousness
    for his name's sake.

Even though I walk through the valley of the shadow of death,
    I fear no evil;
for **thou** art with me;   (second person)
    thy rod and **thy** staff,
    they comfort me.

Thou preparest a table before me
    in the presence of my enemies
thou anointest my head with oil,
    my cup overflows.

Surely goodness and mercy shall follow me
    all the days of my life;
and I shall dwell in the house of **the LORD**   (third person)
    for ever.

Note how the shift in person helps us to delimit the main parts of this poem. This same literary device is very common in the Psalms (19.7-14) and in other poems in the Song of Songs (6.4-10).

Person shift also indicates the beginning or end of a discourse. In Psalm 18, for example, the first line says "I love **thee**, O LORD, my strength!" but the rest of the Psalm goes on in the third person, talking about God and giving the reasons for this exclamation: "**The LORD** is my rock, and my fortress . . . . I call upon **the LORD**, who is worthy to be praised. . . ."

In Psalm 13 the psalmist begins by addressing God and continues on in this way through most of the poem: "How long, O LORD . . , How long wilt **thou** hide **thy** face from me?" The psalm ends, however, in the third person (like Psalm 23), with a resolution on the part of the poet: "I will sing to **the LORD**, because **he** has dealt bountifully with me."

We note that sometimes a psalm will end with a switch in addressee. For example, in Psalm 31, in the first part of the poem (verses 1-20), the poet addresses the LORD in the second person. From verse 21, the psalmist talks about the LORD in the third person: "Blessed be the **LORD**, for **he** has wondrously shown his steadfast love to me." But at the very end of the psalm, the poet turns to his fellow worshipers and says "Love the LORD, **all you his saints**!" Thus we see that person shifts are a frequent device for signaling the beginning and, even more often, the end of a poem.

Probably the most important function of shifting persons, however, is to highlight or emphasize a point. In Hebrew poetry the person may shift suddenly in one or two verses right at the climax of the poem. For example, in Psalm 18 we note that from verse 26 the LORD is addressed in second person, but in verses 29 and 30 there is a mixing of persons. In most languages this is not natural, but in Hebrew this signals the intensity of the poet's feelings—in this case, the strength of his confidence in the Lord (translation from NJPSV):

> 26 With the loyal, **You** deal loyally;
>   with the blameless man, blamelessly.
> 27 With the pure, **You** act purely,
>   and with the perverse, **You** are wily.
> 28 It is **You** who deliver lowly folk,
>   but haughty eyes **You** humble.
> 29 It is **You** who light my lamp;
>   **The LORD, my God** lights up my darkness.
> 30 With **You**, I can rush a barrier;
>   with **my God** I can scale a wall. . . .

This kind of mixing of persons often signals foregrounding in the speeches of God, as in the following example from Psalm 50. At the high point of the psalm (verses 22-23), God is speaking and refers to himself both in the third and first person. Note too that the structure of these verses is chiastic, with the third person ("God") appearing on the outside, and the first person ("I," "me") occurring internally:

> Mark this, then, you who forget **God**,
>   lest **I** rend, and there be none to deliver!
> He who brings thanksgiving as his sacrifice honors **me**;
>   to him who orders his way aright
>   **I** will show the salvation of **God**!

Shifting person also occurs when quotes are made with no markers of direct discourse. We hear the voice of God dramatically intervening, for example, in the middle of Psalm 46:

> Come, behold the works of the LORD . . . .
> He makes wars cease to the end of the earth;
>   he breaks the bow, and shatters the spear,
>   he burns the chariots with fire.
> **Be still and know that I am God.**
>   **I am exalted among the nations,**
>   **I am exalted in the earth.**
> The LORD of hosts is with us;
>   the God of Jacob is our refuge.

A similar strategy is seen in the Song of Moses in the book of Deuteronomy. Here the nation of Israel is personified as a person stuffing himself with food. The person is first described in the third person and then addressed in the second person in a very mocking tone. Very abruptly the discourse switches back to third person as it sums up his sin:

> But **Jeshurun** waxed fat, and kicked;
>   **you** waxed fat, **you** grew thick, **you** became sleek;

but **he** forsook God who made **him**,
and scoffed at the Rock of **his** salvation. (Deut 32.15)

One final context where there may be a shift is in moments of intimacy, when a shift in person seems equivalent to averting the eyes to express modesty or shyness. This may account for the rather curious first lines of the Song of Songs: "O that **he** would kiss me with the kisses of **his** mouth! For **your** love is better than wine. . . ." In the following example (7.6-8) the young man begins addressing his lover as "you," but changes to figurative or euphemistic language as the discussion becomes more intense:

How fair and pleasant **you** are,
O loved one, delectable maiden!
You are stately as a palm tree,
and **your** breasts are like its clusters.
I say I will climb the palm tree
and lay hold of its branches.
Oh, may **your** breasts be like clusters of the vine,
and the scent of **your** breath like apples . . . .

Thus shifting persons is an extremely common feature of Hebrew poetry, with many functions. It may indicate structure within a poem by marking the beginning, the end, or a high point of a poem. It can also convey a variety of attitudes, such as boldness, shyness, or mockery.

3.5 Poetic units

In narrative prose we know that long stretches of speech are divided into units called **paragraphs**. In poetry as well, certain lines may be grouped together into larger literary units. These are called **strophes** or **stanzas**. While some scholars use either word to designate a poetic unit, others consider strophes to be smaller groupings of lines, and stanzas to be groups of strophes.

3.5.1 Strophes

Strophes are groupings of poetic lines that are linked together by a similar thought, meaning, or structure (Reyburn, 1994). Though Psalm 121 is a very tightly knit poem based on the key root "keep," it can be divided into four separate strophes. These are separated by blank spaces in the following NRSV (New Revised Standard Version) rendering:

1 I lift up my eyes to the hills—
from where will my help come?
2 My help comes from the LORD,
who made heaven and earth.

3 He will not let your foot be moved;
he who keeps you will not slumber.

4 He who keeps Israel
   will neither slumber nor sleep.

5 The LORD is your keeper;
   the LORD is your shade at your right hand.
6 The sun shall not strike you by day,
   nor the moon by night.

7 The LORD will keep you from all evil;
   he will keep your life.
8 The LORD will keep
   your going out and your coming in
   from this time on and forevermore.

In this psalm the first strophe (verses 1-2) has a tight question–answer structure. It is tied together by the key word "help." The lines in the second strophe (verses 3-4) are linked by a common subject "he" ("the LORD"), the key words "keep" and "slumber," as well as the emphatic negatives appearing throughout the strophe. In the third strophe (verses 5-6) verse 6 provides greater detail about verse 5. Verse 5 tells us the LORD is a "shade." Verse 6 specifies that the LORD is a shade from the sun and the moon. The concluding strophe (verses 7-8) repeats the key word "keep" three times. Verse 8 further repeats and expands the promise in verse 7.

How do we know where one poetic unit stops and another begins? There are a number of features that can signal that a new unit in a poem is beginning. Some of these features are described below. The presence of one feature alone may not constitute enough evidence for claiming a break. But if several features combine together, then we can be relatively sure that a break is present and a new poetic section has started.

1. **A refrain**: At 2.7; 3.5; and 8.4 in the Song of Songs, we hear the refrain "I adjure you, O daughters of Jerusalem, by the gazelles . . . ." This signals the close of a unit. Thus the next lines must begin a new poetic unit.
2. **A change of scene or location**: Immediately following the refrain at Song of Songs 2.7, we seem transported to a new setting: "The voice of my beloved! Behold he comes, leaping upon the mountains . . . ." We can be fairly sure that a new poetic unit is beginning here.
3. **A change of participant**: At 3.1 in the Song of Songs, there is a shift from the lover, running like a gazelle on the rugged mountains, to the young woman, at night, lying alone on her bed. A shift in participant, scene, and time combine to let us know that a new unit is beginning.
4. **Leading questions**: We have noted above that leading questions often signal a new unit or the boundaries of poetic units. Note at 3.5 in the Song of Songs, the refrain, "I adjure you, O daughters of Jerusalem," ends a unit. At 3.6 a leading question ("What is that coming up from the wilderness . . . ?") opens a new unit.

5. **Change of address and/or speaker, often indicated by a vocative**: At the end of chapter 3 in the Song of Songs, the daughters of Jerusalem are being addressed (probably by the young woman). At 4.1 there is an abrupt shift of speaker and addressee. Obviously the young man is speaking to the young woman: "Behold you are beautiful, my love, behold, you are beautiful!" Here then is a clear break in the text. A new poem begins.

6. **Inclusio**: A word or group of words occurring at the beginning and end of a discourse may set off a group of lines as a distinct strophe or poem. At 5.10 in the Song of Songs, the term "my beloved" occurs both at the beginning (verse 10) and at the end (verse 16) of the young woman's striking description of her lover.

7. **Imperatives**: Combined with other features, such as inclusios, vocatives, changes in person, or other devices, imperatives can show that a new unit is beginning. In the Song of Songs, at 6.13, there is an abrupt shift marked by the imperative "Return, return." This imperative combines with a vocative, and probably a change in speaker, to signal the beginning of a new unit. (See also Isa 51.9; 52.1.)

8. **A change in person or addressee**: While the basic theme may remain constant, a shift in person may indicate a new strophe. In Psalm 30, for example, there is a clear break between verses 1-3 and 4-5. Verses 1-3 address the LORD, while verses 4-5 address "O you his saints."

9. **Repetitive expressions**: Certain lines or themes may reoccur, helping us to identify strophes within a poem. In Psalm 66, repetitive imperatives alternate and signal the beginning of new strophes. Three strophes, beginning at verse 1, verse 8, and verse 20, contain imperatives to praise God. The unit beginning at verse 16 also mirrors the beginning of an earlier strophe at verse 5:

> 1   **Make a joyful noise to God**, all the earth
> 2   sing the glory of his name . . . .
>
> 5   **Come and see what God has done:**
>   he is terrible in his deeds among men. . . .
>
> 8   **Bless our God**, O peoples,
>   let the sound of his praise be heard . . . .
>
> 16   **Come and hear**, all you who fear God,
>   and I will tell what he has done for me. . . .
>
> 20   **Blessed be God**,
>   because he has not rejected my prayer . . . .

10. **Figures of speech**: At times figures of speech, along with other features, may signal the beginning or end of a poetic unit. In the following examples similes occur at the beginning of the LORD's dramatic declaration:

> **You are as Gilead to me,**
>   **as the summit of Lebanon,**
> yet surely I will make you a desert,
>   an uninhabited city. (Jer 22.6)

> **For this is like the days of Noah to me:**
>   **as I swore that the waters of Noah**
>   **should no more go over the earth,**
> so have I sworn that I will not be angry with you
>   and will not rebuke you. (Isa 54.9)

In Jer 51.38-40, contrasting similes begin and end a poetic unit, while metaphorical expressions are found in the middle:

> **They shall roar together like lions;**
>   **they shall growl like lions' whelps.**
> While they are inflamed I will prepare them a feast
>   and make them drunk, till they swoon away
> and sleep a perpetual sleep
>   and not wake, says the LORD.
> **I will bring them down like lambs to the slaughter,**
>   **like rams and he-goats.**

11. **Special particles**: the *hoy* cry, or "woe" statement, usually signals the beginning of a new unit, as seen, for example, in the last parts of the book of Amos:

> **Woe** to you who desire the day of the LORD!
>   Why would you have the day of the LORD?
> It is darkness, and not light . . . (5.18).

> **Woe** to those who are at ease in Zion,
>   and to those who feel secure on the mountain of Samaria . . . . (6.1)

> **Woe** to those who lie upon beds of ivory,
>   and stretch themselves upon their couches . . . . (6.4)

This same particle *hoy* can be used in a positive way to begin a poetic unit:

> **Ho,** every one who thirsts,
>   come to the waters;
> and he who has no money,
>   come, buy and eat! (Isa 55.1)

Another particle, *'eyk* "how," often signals a new poetic unit as well:

56

> **How** Babylon is taken,
> the praise of the whole earth seized! (Jer 51.41)

Many scholars believe that the word *selah*, which appears over seventy times in the Book of Psalms and the book of Habakkuk, indicates a pause in the recitation or in the singing of a poem. At times this word appears at strophe divisions. In Psalm 66, for example, it occurs at clear breaking points, prior to cries of "come and see" (verse 5), "come and listen" (verse 16), or calls to praise the Lord (verse 8). However, this word does not always indicate strophe divisions. For example, in Psalm 57 *selah* occurs in what appears to be the middle of a strophe, perhaps marking a contrast between the fate of the psalmist and that of his enemies (57.3,4; NIV):

> He sends from heaven and saves me,
> rebuking those who hotly pursue me; ***Selah***
> God sends his love and his faithfulness.
>
> I am in the midst of lions;
> I lie among ravenous beasts—

Therefore this word should not be used as a sole indication of a strophe division. Other features should be present to confirm that there is indeed a breaking point in the poem.

12. **Artificial means**: Divisions in some poems are very clear because the poet has imposed a special organizing pattern on the poem. This is the case with the **acrostic** poems, those poems that are organized according to the sequence of the letters of the Hebrew alphabet. Thus it is very easy to see how the composer of Psalm 119 wanted his poem divided: every line in the first unit begins with the first Hebrew letter *'alef* (verses 1-8), in the second, with the second letter of the alphabet *beth* (verses 9-16), and so on until the final letter *taw* is reached (verses 169-176). Lamentations and several psalms (34, 37, 112) are built on a similar alphabetic pattern.

3.5.2 Stanzas

We noted above that some scholars analyze Hebrew poetry into **strophes** and **stanzas**. Stanzas are made up of strophes and represent major divisions in a poem. For example, we could say that Psalm 119 is made up of 22 stanzas, based on the Hebrew alphabet. But within some stanzas it may be possible to identify smaller units that can be called strophes. If we take the first unit *alef* in Psalm 119, we can subdivide the poem into at least two parts. In verses 1-3 the LORD is praised in the third person. This seems to serve as an introduction. Starting from verse 4 and through verse 8, however, the psalmist begins to address the LORD personally in the second person:

> 1 Blessed are those whose way is blameless,
> who walk in the law of **the LORD**!

> 2 Blessed are those who keep **his** testimonies,
>   who seek **him** with their whole heart,
> 3 who also do no wrong,
>   but walk in **his** ways.
>
> 4 **Thou** hast commanded **thy** precepts
>   to be kept diligently.
> 5 O that my ways may be steadfast
>   in keeping **thy** statutes!

It is important to note, however, that versions differ considerably as to how they handle strophes and stanzas. Most versions do not formally make any distinction between them. Usually divisions at any level are indicated by leaving a blank line between two units. Further, scholars differ in their opinion about where breaks occur in many poetic passages. However, it is important for translators to pay careful attention to the larger patterns in poetry, since these structures do affect one's understanding of the overall message of a given poem. For more discussion on the formatting of poems, see chapter 6.

3.6 Divergence from an established pattern

We have outlined many of the basic features of Hebrew poetry, including parallelism, word pairs, chiastic structures, refrains, and envelope structures.

Because so much of Hebrew poetry is regular and well-patterned, intentional shifts from the norm are surprising and effective. Expressions that we are used to hearing may be purposely changed to create a kind of shock. For example, in what is certainly the most moving passage of the prophet Amos' message, we are confronted by a series of similarly constructed parallel lines that build to a climax in the last two lines:

> Though they dig into Sheol,
>   from there shall my hand take them;
>
> though they climb up to heaven,
>   from there I will bring them down.
>
> Though they hide themselves on the top of Carmel,
>   from there I will search out and take them;
>
> and though they hide from my sight at the bottom of the sea,
>   there I will command the serpent, and it shall bite them.
>
> And though they go into captivity before their enemies,
>   there I will command the sword, and it shall slay them;
>
> **and I will set my eyes upon them**
>   **for evil and not for good.** (Amos 9.2-4)

The final and startling message stands out because the poet has purposely interrupted normal poetic patterns. He stops the rhythmic pattern (though they . . . there I will . . .). More important, he purposely reverses the normal order of the word pair "good" and "evil." Thus it is the combination of regularity and the lack of it which makes this poem successful.

Against the backdrop of the expected, the poet can express his or her originality. This may occur on a larger scale (seen above) or on a very small scale. In Isa 54.7, for example, when we read "for a small moment I abandoned you," we might expect a time expression paralleling "for a small moment," or else an opposing expression of time, "for a long time." What we get instead is a surprising focus on the great love and mercy of God, as seen in our own translation of the lines:

> For a small moment I abandoned you,
> but **with great mercy** I will gather you up.

The same pairing of "moment" and "everlasting love" reoccurs in verse 8. Thus, by using unexpected combinations of words, the poet's message is expressed in a much stronger and more touching manner.

We noted in our discussion of parallelism that a figurative line often occurs after a more general one. But this order can be reversed for special effect. In Psa 102.11 both lines contain figures of speech. But the first is more literary and very poetic. The second is so concrete and direct that it shocks us:

> My days are like an evening shadow;
> **I wither away like grass**. (Psa 102.11)

Shifting persons (section 3.4.5) is another way that Hebrew poets draw attention to a particular theme. We have seen that shifts in personal reference may help us determine the boundaries of strophes in a poem. However, when shifting persons occurs within a single strophe, there is a certain shock value. The reader or hearer pays particular attention to the unusual grammar. In Psalm 16, for example, the shifting of persons helps to define strophes. But in the middle of the poem (verse 5), the shift is so swift that it grabs our attention, as seen in the more literal rendering of NJPSV:

> **The LORD** is my allotted share and portion;
> **You** control my fate.

The emphatic form of the pronoun "you" in Hebrew, as well as the lack of parallelism in the verse, makes this line stand out in a special way.

At first glance, then, the common poetic devices of Hebrew poetry may seem rather rigid and confining, leaving little room for artistic freedom or creativity. However, just the opposite is true. Hebrew poets use unique combinations of sameness and difference to emphasize their point. When regular patterns are interrupted, the reader or hearer knows it is time to pay special attention. This is when the real creativity of the poet is exercised and a main point of his message is expressed.

Questions for Reflection

1. Reread the list of possible relationships which parallel structures can exhibit (section 3.2.1.3). Find one set of parallel lines within Biblical poetry which illustrates each of the listed relationships.

2. Look for four examples of biblical parallelism that show a development or progression: "A, what's more, B." Explain the nature of this development.

3. Study Psalm 113 in a more literal version (RSV, NIV, NJPSV), and try to identify as many features of Hebrew poetry as you can.

4. Study the last two verses of Psalm 13. What feature of Hebrew poetry is illustrated here? Compare a more literal version and a common language translation. In what ways are they the same or different? Can you explain why this is so and what purpose they serve?

5. Read Isa 1.4-8. What person is this passage written in? If you had to divide these verses into sections, how would you go about it?

6. Study the following passages from Song of Songs: 1.9; 2.2; 2.9; 4.4; 7.4; 8.1. In each case try to determine the basis of the figurative comparison that is used. (Note that for some of these even the scholars do not agree, so there may be more than one correct answer.)

7. Read Job 40.6-14. How would you characterize the emotive tone of this passage? What stylistic devices help to make this evident?

8. Study Amos 8.1-2 in several different versions and, if possible, a study Bible or commentary. Determine what stylistic device is used here and what its function is.

9. List five comparative figures of speech from any one book of the Old Testament. Identify the type of figure, and determine the topic of comparison, the image it is being compared to, and the basis for the comparison. Finally, tell how the figure helps to emphasize the intended meaning.

10. See if you can find an example of irony in any poetic book in the Old Testament. What purpose does irony serve here?

11. Study Psalm 22 in the TEV and note where the breaks (strophes or stanzas) occur. Then list some of the chief markers of these distinct poetic units.

Chapter 4:

Guidelines for Transferring Biblical Poetry into Target Languages

4.1 Introduction

In the first part of this book, we have given an overview of the life setting, genres, and principal features of biblical poetry. In this chapter we discuss two major questions involving the translation of Hebrew poetry: When should we attempt to render poetry in the source text as poetry in the translation? What features of Hebrew should we attempt to preserve in the translation? We believe that it is possible and even recommended to render poetry in the source text as poetry in the translation in certain well-defined contexts. This is because many features of Hebrew poetry can be maintained and appreciated by readers around the world.

4.2 When should poetry be translated as poetry?

Should translators attempt to translate every poem found in the Hebrew Old Testament as a poem in their own language? Before answering this question, translators must first understand the roles and functions of poetry in the Hebrew Bible (see chapter 2), and the roles and functions of poetry in their own culture. It is appropriate to render the source text as poetry in the translation when the function of poetry in Hebrew is closely matched by the function of poetry in the target language.

4.2.1 Matching subject matter and the goal of speaking

As we have seen in chapter 2, poetry in ancient Hebrew culture was used in many contexts or life settings. It was used in everyday experiences; for example, to express sadness at the death of a friend (2 Sam 1.19-27). But it was also used in more formal settings to praise God (Psalms 145–150) or to complain to him (Psalm 6, 10, 13; Job's speeches). Poetry was often composed for a particular occasion. Liturgical psalms (Psalm 2) were probably recited at the time the king was anointed. Marriage poems may have been recited or sung at his wedding (Psalm 45). Other hymns were sung as travelers made their way to Jerusalem for special feasts or festivals (Psalms 120 and following). Some poems are clearly memorial, serving to commemorate or celebrate some important past event. These types of songs or poems teach each succeeding generation about their history (for example, the Song of Deliverance in Exodus 15, and the Song of Deborah in Judges 5). Finally, religious, political, and social criticism could be communicated through poetry. The famous prophets of the Old Testament—Isaiah, Jeremiah, Amos, Micah, Habakkuk, among many others—used this form of speech to communicate their message.

Chances for a successful transfer of a poetic text in the Bible into poetry in the language of the translation are relatively high if the function of poetry in the target language is the same or similar to the function of poetry in the original. This means that the subject matter being addressed and the goal of speaking correspond very closely. We will see that, while there does not need to be a one-to-one correspondence, it is helpful if there is at least some overlap in function.

There are many features that are involved in the creation of a poem. These features vary from culture to culture and even within the poetic genres of a given language. These may include:

(a) **Individual vs. communal nature of the poem**: In some cultures poems are communal, even if one or a few individuals are responsible for composing them. The communal poem is not a poem of self-expression but an expression of the hopes, joys, fears, attitudes, or values of a group, even the entire nation. In Western cultures, however, most poems are individual. They usually reflect only one person's viewpoint.

(b) **Sexual differentiation**: In many cultures the composition and performance of certain poetic genres may be restricted to one sex. In some cultures laments may be restricted to women, for example, and praise of warriors restricted to men.

(c) **Professional status of the poet:** In some cultures only certain people are allowed to create a poem or sing songs. These people are professional artists who praise nobility or transfer traditional knowledge through song. There may be professional mourners who are paid to sing laments. In other cultures anyone with artistic talent may compose a poem or song.

(d) **Variability in the form of the poem**: In some languages poems are created and committed to memory or paper. They do not change over time, and each time they are recited or sung, they have exactly the same form. In other cultures, however, poems conform to a pattern which can be adapted according to the circumstances. Each time a song is sung or a poem is recited, slight variations may be introduced by the performer.

(e) **Public or private nature of the poem**: Some poems or songs are composed to be recited in public, while others are meant to be kept private. A poem can be composed for a formal or official occasion, or it can be created as a unique and private expression of an individual.

(f) **Mode of presentation**: There are many ways in which a poem may be presented. A poem may be recited or chanted by one person or several. It may be sung by an individual, a chorus, or a combination of both, with or without musical accompaniment. It may be acted out with gestures, dance, and other types of dramatic accompaniment. Besides its oral forms, a poem or song is often written. In America, for example, though there are public poetry readings within certain social contexts, a very common way to communicate poetry is through the written word.

In many European cultures, poems appear on posters, in greeting cards, or in magazines, but most often in a book of poetry which is purchased by a person wishing to read a particular set of poems. The other standard context for poetry is song, be it formal (national anthems, worship services) or informal (folk songs, contemporary music).

These factors as well as others may enter into the discovery, definition, and analysis of a given poetic genre. We need to consider them, along with subject matter and goal of speaking, when looking for matches between poetic genres.

4.2.2 Examples of possible poetic matches

Below we will consider several types of Hebrew poetry discussed in chapter 2 and show that matches do exist between them and poetic genres in other cultures. Note that a match between Hebrew and the language of translation may not be perfect, but whenever there is common ground in terms of form or function, there is a better-than-average chance that a poetic transfer will be successful.

4.2.2.1 Laments

We have seen that a lament is a dirge or funeral song, recited or sung at the occasion of a death. The most striking example of this genre is the poem David offers at the death of Saul and Jonathan (2 Sam 1.19-27), parts of which are cited below:

> 19 Thy glory, O Israel, is slain upon thy high places!
>   How are the mighty fallen! . . ,
>
> 23 Saul and Jonathan, beloved and lovely!
>   In life and in death they were not divided;
>   they were swifter than eagles,
>   they were stronger than lions.
>
> 24 Ye daughters of Israel, weep over Saul,
>   who clothed you daintily in scarlet,
>   who put ornaments of gold upon your apparel.
>
> 25 How are the mighty fallen
>   in the midst of the battle!
>
>   Jonathan lies slain upon thy high places.
> 26   I am distressed for you, my brother, Jonathan;
>   very pleasant have you been to me;
>   your love to me was wonderful,
>   passing the love of women.
>
> 27 How are the mighty fallen,
>   and the weapons of war perished!

We note the deep emotional tone of this poem, the figurative language, as in "swifter than eagles . . . , stronger than lions," and the repetitive line "How are the mighty fallen in battle." The poem begins as communal ("O daughters of

Israel, weep . . .") and becomes intensely personal ("I am distressed for you, my brother, Jonathan!"). Names of the deceased are mentioned throughout the poem, as are praise names: "the glorious ones of Israel," "the mighty," "the weapons of war." In this poem the focus is on the feats and moral character of the deceased, with no appeal to God or mention of him.

We have seen, however, that in a biblical context the lament genre is not restricted to the death of an individual. At some point in time this poetic form was extended to apply to any communal catastrophe or tragedy. Prophets often used these types of songs to lament over the physical and moral defeats of the people of Israel. They used many striking figures of speech, portraying Jerusalem (that is, their nation) as a caged lion, an unfaithful wife, an abandoned lover, or a ruined vineyard.

In many parts of the world, poetic laments exist, whether carefully written down for preservation or spontaneously rendered in song. We know there is unlikely to be an exact one-to-one correspondence between laments in Hebrew and those of other cultures. Indeed, within a restricted region or group of peoples, there may be great differences. In West Africa, for example, there is no single style for laments. In Muslim contexts there may be formal dignified songs sung by a professional *mallam*. In contrast, in Kru cultures there are repetitive, plaintive cries and sobs, as women go about the village in groups, shuffling to the beat of a rhythmic funeral dance. Within a given language group there may even exist several kinds of lament, to be sung for different types of people (chiefs or warriors, for example) or in different contexts (for example, upon hearing of someone's death, when the body is displayed, or when the body has been buried).

But with all these differences we may be surprised to find important points of similarity existing between Hebrew poetry and poetry in the language of translation. For example, these may include repetition of names, use of praise names, colorful imagery, slow rhythm, and emotional cries. The following Akan dirge sung by a mother for her son is certainly different from the one David sang for Saul and Jonathan, yet there is a close match in the goal of speaking. Both mourn the loss of a loved one:

> Grandsire Gyima with a slim but generous arm,
> Fount of satisfaction,
> My friend Adu on whom I depend,
> I depend on you for everything, even for drinking water.
> If I am not dependent on you, see what has become of me.
> Although a man, you are a mother to children,
> A man who takes another's child for his own,
> Who builds mighty but empty houses,
> Who is restive until he has fought and won,
> Osibirikuo, Gyane the short one,
> Dwentiwaa's husband, and a man of valor.
>
> (Finnegan, 1970: 153; Nketia, 1955:195)

Though the poetic form may differ, it is obvious that the Akan poem and David's lament over Saul and Jonathan serve the same purpose. Their goal is to express sadness, despair, and grief. Note that in each, positive qualities of the deceased are enumerated, and many names are used to refer to him. It would seem natural therefore for Old Testament translators in this language to attempt to render David's poem as poetry in their own language.

But what about the other Old Testament passages where lament genres are used to "mourn" national catastrophes? When translating we will have to ask ourselves if it is possible to extend the lament genre to other settings that are sad. If so, translators can try to adapt the style of their funeral dirges, not just in 2 Samuel, where a true lament is found, but also in Lamentations and parts of Amos, Ezekiel, and other prophetic books where the lament genre is used. In this way the strong feelings and connotations present in the original have a better chance of being expressed in the translation. Translators may want to explain in the introduction to Lamentations that this is a lament, or they may want to take the adaptation of a lament one step further and transfer the poem into song (see the first article in the Appendix, by Hope).

Given the universal feeling of loss at death and the desire to express this in song, it is very likely that laments in the Bible can be matched by poetic laments in the language of the translation.

4.2.2.2 Love poetry

Love poetry is another genre where there is likely to be a functional match between Hebrew and most languages. Though scholars debate the deeper meaning of the Song of Songs, few doubt that its first goal is to express the love felt by two individuals. The world over, we find expressions of the same feelings: longing for the presence of a loved one, and bidding the loved one to come from afar. We also find descriptions of the physical attributes and moral qualities of the loved one, along with descriptions of their mutual love.

Though translating the Song of Songs is no easy task, in most languages there will be a match in the goal of speaking between this Hebrew text and love poetry in the target culture. Indeed, there will probably even be a number of stylistic matches between the two.

In most love poetry around the world, figurative language is used to describe the loved one. Metaphors and similes often compare a loved one to natural elements (flowers, deer, and other graceful creatures) and to royalty (kings, queens, and princesses). Love itself is often compared to fire, the sun, or the wind. In the following excerpt from a Nyamwezi poem, we see a description of the loved one's positive qualities, including a comparison to a musical instrument (Finnegan, 1970: 254; Tracey, 1963: 20):

> My love is soft and tender
> My love Saada comforts me,
> My love has a voice like a fine instrument of music . . . .

Here we see several features similar to those in Hebrew poetry. The repetitive "my love" slowly unfolds the poet's feelings, much like a Hebrew parallelism. Similes such as "like a fine instrument" are also typical in Hebrew love poetry.

In the Biblical song of love, the young woman describes her lover's sweet smell:

> your anointing oils are fragrant . . . (1.3)

> My beloved is to me a bag of myrrh,
> . . . a cluster of henna blossoms (1.13, 14)

The young woman describes her lover's physical charms through a variety of figures of speech:

> My beloved is all radiant and ruddy . . . .
> His head is the finest gold;
>   his locks are wavy,
>   black as a raven,
> His eyes are like doves . . . .
> His lips are lilies . . . . (5.10-13)

In modern Lokpa love songs sung by village girls in the moonlight (Benin in the 1950's), the loved one is also praised for his sweet smell. In this case, however, the focus is on his modern rather than traditional qualities (Ouoro Madougou):

> . . . Call for me my love, ey!
> the one who has covered himself with perfume
> the one who wears shirts,
> the one who wears pants
> the one who wears hats
> Call for me my love, ey!
> Right now he'll be sitting on his chair
> with red kola in his mouth
> and a cigarette from his lips.

We are struck by the differences in content, but surprised at the basic similarities between this song and many poems in the Song of Songs. In Lokpa culture young women call to others, much as the young woman in the Song calls the daughters of Jerusalem. There is no doubt that this constitutes a very strong functional match between genres in the two languages.

In love poetry the world over, lovers call to each other just as they do in the Song of Songs (1.4; 4.8; 7.11). In the following lines from old Spanish literature, we find expression, form, and content that is similar to many passages in the Song of Songs. Parallel lines alternate in an *a-a-b-b* rhyming pattern. Here, too, the beloved is called by varying names. We note that the woman in this poem has the same forthright character of the woman in the Song of Songs, as she calls to her lover:

> *Amigo el que yo mas queria,*
> *venid a la luz del dia;*
> *amigo el que yo mas amaba,*
> *venid a la luz del alba.*

> Friend, my most cherished one,
>   come by daylight;
> friend, my most beloved one,
>   come by dawn.

Love poetry is one domain where hyperbole, or exaggeration, is common. Themes of desire, longing, and separation are often expressed through comparisons to sickness or even death. Note how the following Akan poem expresses similar themes to those in the Song of Songs (5.2-6). A brief narrative passage is followed by a deeply emotional one, as the lover awakens to find the loved one and is deeply moved ("I am dying")—a very good example of poetic hyperbole:

> I sleep long and soundly;
> Suddenly the door creaks.
> I open my eyes confused,
> And see my love standing by.
> Mother Adu, I am dying.
> Adu, kinsman of Odurowa,
> What matters death to me?
>   (Finnegan, 1970: 261; Nketia, 1963: 37)

Though certainly some of the imagery of the Song of Songs will be unfamiliar in the receptor culture and may have to be modified (chapter 5), a poetic rendering of this book will probably be appropriate and appreciated in almost any language.

4.2.2.3 Praise songs

Throughout the world the most well known and appreciated biblical poetry is found in the book of Psalms. Praise to God for his creation, his lovingkindness, and his help in time of trouble flow through line after line. In other parts of the Bible, we also find poems praising heroes, as when the women praise the heroic deeds of David (1 Sam 18.7).

In many cultures praise songs are used to celebrate the deeds of great ancestors, famous warriors, and respected chiefs. There are also languages where the supreme being or any number of minor deities are praised as well. In Old Sanskrit (India), for example, many poems glorify and call out to deities who are associated with natural phenomena (fire, wind, dawn). In the following poem dedicated to the god of fire, Agni, this deity is praised for his blessings and power. This is followed by a request for help in difficult times and for cleansing. The repetitive lines and striking images remind us of certain psalms:

> Scattering evil with light,
> Shine on us, Agni, powerfully,
> Scattering evil with light. . . .
> O God whose arms embrace the world,
> Agni, whose face shines on all sides,
> Scattering evil with light;
>
> Ferry us across the hostile waters,
> O God whose face shines on all sides,
> Scattering evil with light;
>
> Ferry us from sin to goodness,
> As a boatman ferries pilgrims over a stream,
> Scattering evil with light. (Aldan, 1969:14.)

Similarly in Yoruba (Nigeria), praise poems celebrate various deities. In the following poem the god Ifa is praised in a set of parallel lines (Finnegan, 192):

> Ifa is the master of today;
> Ifa is the master of tomorrow;
> Ifa is the master of the day after tomorrow;
> To Ifa belongs all the four days
> Created by Orisa into this world.

If such praise poetry exists in the language of translation, then it certainly will be appropriate to translate psalms of this nature and other praise poems as poetry in the translation. But in some cultures and in some contexts, poems expressing praise to God or the supreme being may simply be unknown. Does this mean that a poetic transfer of psalms of praise into the target language should not be attempted?

For example, the Dinka from Sudan have songs praising cattle, and the astounding imagery of their songs matches even the most complex imagery in the Psalms:

> My bull is as white as the silvery fish in the river;
>   as white as the egret on the river bank;
>   as white as new milk;
> His bellowing is like the roar of the Turk's cannon from the great river.
> My bull is as dark as the rain-cloud, that comes with the storm.
> He is like Summer and Winter;
>   half of him dark as the thundercloud;
>   half as white as sunshine . . . ,
>   (Finnegan, 1970:251-2; transcribed by Cummins, 1904)

Here we are far from a perfect match, in that the object of praise in the target language (a bull) is not the typical object of praise in the biblical text (normally the LORD). But we do have a significant match in function, since in both cases a poem is used to glorify something, even if it is not the supreme being. In this case it is very likely that a poetic transfer will be successful, because the poetic form is recognized and accepted as an expression of praise and glory. In other words, the principal goal of speaking is similar. Thus a poetic translation of Psalms should at least be attempted in this language, if only in a trial portion. There is every likelihood that such poems will be readily understood and appreciated.

This shift of praise from smaller deities to the supreme being has already occurred in various cultures in West Africa. Traditionally songs in Bete and Godie (Côte d'Ivoire), and Lokpa (Benin), were never addressed directly to God but rather to lesser deities. With the passage of time and the introduction of the Christian message, however, this has changed. Now Christian songs exist that praise God, and even in a secular context, songs now call to God or talk about him.

Of course, translators must be sensitive to public reaction to such poetic transfers. Some believers strongly object to using song styles associated with traditional religion and adapting them for translation of the Biblical message. In the Dida culture, traditional song forms were almost completely replaced by Western forms (Krabill, 1995). But in many cultures such objections are usually short lived. A later generation usually appreciates having songs composed in a form that is natural and pleasing in their language.

4.2.2.4 Proverbs

While in western cultures proverbs are not considered as poetry, in many languages they exhibit properties of this genre. Rhythm, balance, and terseness are usually characteristic of proverbs and poetry. In Hebrew this is even more true, since most proverbs exhibit tight parallel structures and the same stress patterns as poetic lines (section 3.3.1):

be'efes	*'etsim*	*tikbeh*	*'esh*
without	wood	goes-out	fire
uve'en	*nirgan*	*yishtoq*	*madon*
and-without	gossiping	lies-down	quarrel

> For lack of wood the fire goes out;
> and where there is no whispering, quarreling ceases.
>
> (Prov 26.20)

We have also seen how proverbs in Hebrew exhibit parallelism and word pairs, just as other poetic lines do.

Though Webster's Dictionary defines a proverb as a "brief popular epigram or maxim," this scarcely describes the Hebrew situation. Proverbs in Hebrew were the expression of a whole philosophy of life. Though perhaps popular in style, their main purpose was teaching, that is, to guide conduct, influence moral standards, and affect judgment, according to the norms set forth in the Law of Moses.

Though usually oral, the proverb in Africa has a similar goal. It embodies the essence of traditional wisdom. Proverbs enter into the most crucial discussions of life, such as debates, trials, or family councils. It is not just enough to know a proverb. A true sign of wisdom is applying it in just the right context. In Central Africa strings of proverbs are often used in judicial cases and debates. Within this setting there is a quick exchange of argument and response in the form of alternating proverbs, one countering the other, with the more skilled debater winning out. In literate African societies today, proverbs are brought to bear on the much wider concerns of politics and social issues, as they are sprinkled through newspaper articles, TV and radio shows, and popular novels.

In terms of function, then, there is an excellent match between Hebrew proverbs and African ones, and often there is a match in terms of style as well. The following Moore maxim, though shorter than most Hebrew ones, is concise and rhythmic. It has a point–counterpoint rhythm. Yet, unlike many Hebrew proverbs, it rhymes:

> *Sa yaa toogo*
> *ya noogo*

> The sky is stormy;
> tomorrow will be beautiful.

In Tsonga of South-East Africa (Schneider, 1986, 1987), proverbs have many features in common with Hebrew poetry. They may exhibit parallelism. They usually have the point–counterpoint rhythm of Hebrew proverbs, as well as their conciseness:

> *ku veleka*   *vukosi*
> to procreate   wealth

> *k'ambala*   *mavala*
> to dress   color

> To bear children makes you (truly) rich;
> To dress up (only) makes you colorful.

The following example from Tsonga shows antithetic parallelism ("to live"–"to die," as well as a positive–negative interplay):

> *ku hlwela ku hanya*
> it tarries to live

> *ku fa a ku hlweri*
> to die does not tarry

> To live takes time;
> To die does not!

This similarity to Hebrew proverbs is certainly not restricted to Africa. In Tagalog from the Philippines, proverbs also consist of two short rhythmic lines with the same number of syllables. In this language proverbs are considered poetry, since both lines typically have the same number of syllables and are often marked by rhyme at the end of each line (Dorn, 1994:306):

> *Nuti ang gumamela*
> *nula ang sampaguita*
>
> The hibiscus turns white;
> the jasmine turns red.

In Tamil from India, we find a "better than" expression that is almost identical in form to proverbs cited in Ecclesiastes (7.1-8):

> Better hatred than the friendship of fools.
> Better death than chronic illness.
> Better to be killed than soul-destroying contempt.
> Better abuse than praise undeserved. (Aldan, 1969:68)

Despite the fact that the match is often quite close between Hebrew proverbs and those in the language of translation, the task of translation is not always easy. Proverbs, though usually concise in form, include underlying presuppositions based on particular cultures. The hearer is expected to abstract a basic truth from a specific situation and then apply the same principle to numerous other parallel situations. Because the thought is brief yet complex, it is often very hard to recapture it completely in a translation. While the functional match between the goal of speaking may be extremely close between the source and target languages, translators in some languages may have to spend a great deal of time finding just the right words to express a certain biblical thought.

One important question arises concerning the substitution of indigenous proverbs for biblical ones. If a proverb in the language of translation means about the same thing as the biblical one, may we substitute this local form? For example, Pro 19.21, "Many are the plans in the mind of a man, but it is the purpose of the LORD that will be established," is freely rendered in the popular maxim "Man proposes but God disposes." Certainly the primary meaning is very close, but by substituting one for the other, some elements of meaning are lost. For example, here the biblical contrast between the "many" plans of humans and the sole purpose of God is lost. Thus it would be a rare case indeed where one proverb would be exactly equivalent to another. Further, proverbs often have more than one meaning, depending on context and social setting. In substituting a local proverb for a Hebrew one, we run the risk of introducing multiple meanings that were not intended in the original. If this is the case it will be better for translators to try to render a certain biblical proverb by using a proverbial style in the receptor language, rather than by substituting what seems to be a local equivalent.

Our discussion of proverbs leads to another important point. Like all types of poetry, proverbs are meant to be "savored," or reflected on. In many cultures a proverb is like a knot, meant to be untied. Its meaning is enhanced by its mysteriousness. Overtranslating, that is, making the meaning too explicit, may be a self-defeating exercise and should certainly be avoided.

4.2.2.5 Narrative and historical poetry

Narrative and historical poetry are literary forms that serve much the same purpose as prose. Though they use many stylistic devices similar to other types of poetry (for example, rhythm, rhyme, meter), their essential function is to tell a story. Epics such as the Iliad and the Odyssey fit into this category.

With very few exceptions, narrative or historical poetry is not found in the Bible, even though it does occur in related languages such as Ugaritic. As Alter notes (1985:27), Hebrew poetry is essentially nonnarrative:

> The Hebrew writers used verse for celebratory song, dirge, oracle, oratory, prophecy, reflective and didactic argument, liturgy, and often as a heightening or summarizing inset in the prose narratives—*but only marginally and minimally to tell a tale.* [Italics added.]

Even where biblical poems do make reference to historical events (Song of Deborah, Song of the Sea, Psalms 78, 105, 106), the purpose is not to inform people about what happened. They are rather celebratory, drawing attention to important aspects of events that were already known by the audience.

Many African languages also avoid poetry for narrative purposes. In Godie, poetry or song is not used to tell a story. For example, the history of a village may begin in a stylized way, with the genealogy of the speaker, but it will quickly shift to simple narrative storytelling, with dialogue, minimal character development, and straightforward descriptions of action, in much the same style as Hebrew narratives. Here, then, we note that there is a functional match in the use of prose rather than poetry for a given literary domain.

Just as Hebrew literary style allows poetry to occur for dramatic purposes in the middle of a narrative (Adam's poem, Gen 2.23; Lamech's poem, Gen 4.15), poetic inserts occur in languages around the world. In Africa it very common for folktales to be interrupted by songs. Indeed the westerner is often shocked to find a congregation initiating choruses in the middle of sermons, at the audience's own discretion! In an African context these "song inserts" reinforce the story theme, allow the audience to participate, and perhaps give the story teller a short rest. In the Hebrew examples we have, we do not know if these poetic inserts were ever sung by the audience. They often occur at the high point of a story, expressing the intense feelings of a main character or foregrounding an important theme. Even if they are not identical in use, these switches from prose to poetry may be far less surprising in many cultures than they are in a western setting.

Note that it is possible for there to be a complete mismatch between two literary traditions. While Hebrew does not use poetry to relate narrative or historical events, some languages may prefer this style. For example, in Fula and in some related languages, long epics are used to relate historical as well as mythical events, such as the origins of certain peoples. Epic poems provide an effective teaching device. They are pleasing to hear and easy to remember. In such situations translators may be faced with a more puzzling dilemma: should they translate Hebrew prose as prose, or should they rather conform to the standards of the language, and translate biblical prose in the book of Genesis, for example, as poetry? This would be pushing the notion of dynamic equivalency to the limit, but it is a question that needs to be asked in cultures where such oral poetry is a major means of communication, and where people expect certain types of information to be conveyed in a particular genre.

4.2.2.6 Prophetic poetry

We have seen cases where poetic transfer has every chance to succeed, and further, where prose in Hebrew can be matched by prose in a translation. In some cases, however, the transfer between genres may not be possible, or if possible, it will not produce what would be considered a successful or natural translation.

Old Testament prophecy, for example, is almost always transmitted in poetic form, and this poetic form served a particular purpose. Its use is probably linked to the oral nature of the original message. But more importantly the form (or genre) and the content of the message were especially suited to each other. Hebrew prophecy often consists of exhortations, warnings, predictions, or indictments. As Alter notes, Hebrew parallelisms often have a kind of building up or crescendo effect which is very intense. They serve to highlight or "zoom in" on the inevitable retribution to be carried out by an all-powerful God (1985: 53, 73, 76).

But parallel verse may not be the proper vehicle for communicating prophetic messages in every language. For example, readers in English today may have trouble understanding the historical background of such a text and its complicated figures of speech. They may spend time trying to figure out who is speaking to whom. Readers may not get the message of a given prophetic passage, simply because they are overwhelmed by the complex poetic structure and imagery. Indeed, is this not why we often feel less pleasure in reading the poetry of the Prophets than when we read the Psalms? Without a functional match between genres, we do not feel the real impact of the original text and are, at times, left feeling slightly disoriented.

Translators must ask themselves if the message of a particular stretch of Hebrew poetry will be properly represented by poetry in the translation. For example, in translating the vision passages of Amos (locusts, fire, plumb line, basket of fruit), some versions have rendered these in prose rather than in poetry. This is especially true of common language versions such as TEV and the French common language version (FRCL). Many readers of English and French can appreciate this, because a more straightforward style of language enables the hearer or reader to concentrate on the meaning of the vision, rather than trying to figure out the meaning of the poetry. And because the visions involve dialogue between God and the prophet, a prose rendition will seem more natural in many languages.

However, TEV often translates even the most moving passages in ordinary prose (Amos 9.1b-4, for example). In these instances the sensitive reader may find poetry more appropriate, even though prophetic messages—or their modern functional equivalent, preaching—are not normally conveyed in this genre. Because of the intense emotional message, FRCL switches to a poetic form at this point. Even if the other visions do not lend themselves to poetry, this final dramatic vision of the LORD standing by (or, on) the altar is somehow different. Mere humans do not dare to answer back here! This is the ultimate vision, the ultimate destruction, the unrelenting rhythm of a God who will not be turned away from carrying out his decision. Here a poetic rendition seems especially fitting.

On the other hand, while prophetic poetry in the biblical sense does not seem to be a standard feature in many oral traditions, some African translators (in Baoule from Côte d'Ivoire, Ditammari and Lokpa from Benin, and Tonga from Zambia) report that songs may be used to give hidden warnings to listeners, even expressing at times impending judgment. In Central Africa divinatory oracles are commonly expressed in poetic form. In Kenya and Burkina Faso it is not uncommon to express strong political comment in poetic form. Songs were used for this purpose also in Zambia in pre-independence days. In these languages translators will certainly want to consider the possibility of retaining or adapting a poetic style when translating prophetic utterances.

But in other cases where there is not a functional match between the use of poetry in the two languages, we may have to avoid translating in this genre. Perhaps a heightened form of prose can be used instead. Or we can resort to a solution that some translations use, that is, to set out part of a prophetic message in poetic format and another part in prose (FRCL, NIV, CEV, and others). This means converting one biblical genre into two different genres in the target language. This solution is not without difficulty, however, because translators will have to determine which parts of prophecy can be communicated well by poetry and which parts can not.

4.2.2.7 Wisdom or didactic poetry

We have already discussed the translation of proverbs, which are an important part of wisdom literature. Now we turn to some other examples from this type of writing.

In the book of Ecclesiastes we find a mixture of poetry and prose. Before translating we must ask an important question: Is poetry used in the target language in teaching contexts? Are proverbs and poems ever cited by teachers in the target culture to illustrate points being made? If so, then it is advisable to translate the poems found in chapters 1 and 3, as well as the proverbs, in poetic or proverbial form. This may require adding an introductory clause or phrase to let the readership or audience know what is happening, "As it is said in the poem . . . ," or by using special formatting (see chapter 6).

The book of Job is certainly one of the most difficult books in the category of wisdom literature. It contains two main genres: prose and poetry. While the prologue and epilogue are in prose, the bulk of the book (chapters 3.3–42.6) is a series of long poems. But these poems are of different types. There are laments, praise songs, poetic rebukes, and collections of proverbs. There are argumentative passages filled with irony, sarcasm, and rhetorical questions. And we find divine proclamation as well. The goal of speaking is also hard to define. Though the main purpose of Job seems to be didactic, it is also a kind of drama that was certainly meant to entertain its audience.

These various features present translators with a number of problems. Most versions translate the genres in the form in which they appear in the original. The prose sections are rendered as prose, and the poetic sections as poetic, or at least in poetic format. But translators need to ask: Does this sort of didactic poetry exist in their language? Is it possible to include dialogues between friends, or between a person and God, in poetry? Are dramas with alternating speeches known in the culture? In what context do they occur?

Surprisingly there may be some matches of poetic form between Job and the language of the translation. For example, in Tagalog of the Philippines, there is a special genre called *balagtasan*, which is a debate in poetic form. There are two debaters and one "middleman" (like Elihu!) who serves as referee and judge. All speakers must express themselves in accepted forms of Tagalog poetry (Dorn, 1994). In Kuna, a language spoken in Panama, there is a complex system of "turn-taking" between two speakers (Sherzer, 1983)—a form that may be utilized when trying to translate the book of Job.

In Lokpa of Benin, the task of translating Job was particularly challenging. Though counsel or criticism may actually be given through poetic form in song, long poetic interchanges similar to those in Job do not occur. The translator is faced with difficult choices: If the major portion of Job is to be understood as a series of dialogues, the translation must be cast in indirect speech. But when this approach is taken, the text becomes more prose-like and less poetic. Nevertheless, for reasons of naturalness and comprehension, an indirect style was adopted.

However, there were points in Job where both the translator and the consultant wished the translated text could conform to a more poetic style. These include Job 3, which is clearly a lament. In its first draft this passage was rendered by indirect speech in the third person, and the result was hardly poetic: "Job said that the day should perish on which he was born." Third person can be changed to first, but as the translator noted, "Yes, but then it would be a 'song' (that is, a 'poem')." Such a song of lament is a perfect functional match between Hebrew and Lokpa. A man in serious difficulty, one who feels he has undergone an undeserved fate, would lament just as Job is doing. But in the biblical context this lament is made in the presence of friends, and in chapter 4 it is answered. The translator faced the choice of preserving the poetic, song-like nature of the lament, or of making this lament part of the dramatic scene—a speech that would have to be answered.

As noted above, translators must be flexible and open to innovation. That is, they must be sensitive and creative enough to discover where the target language has room for the adaptation of literary genres. It was noted that in the case of Psalms it would be easy for a culture with praise poetry to adopt praises to God, even though this exact literary form never existed previously. If laments are sung or spoken for individuals, their range may be extended to communities in distress, for example. In the case of Lokpa, although the translator felt compelled to present the major portion of Job as dialogue, he compromised by keeping a poetic format and as many poetic stylistic features as possible. He thus extended the domain of the literary genre open to him.

4.2.3 Summary of proposed method of translating poetry

To sum up, rendering the biblical text in poetic form should be a conscious decision made by translators and their coordinators, project advisers, and consultants. It must first be determined that a poetic transfer can be made, based on thorough research of the available functional matches between the source and target languages. This means that no blanket statements can be made; no neat rules can be written. It means that for every book (or even parts of each book), translators, coordinators, and consultants must agree how each text will be treated in order to express its message faithfully.

Before beginning the translation of the Old Testament, translators should spend a significant amount of time studying the role of poetry in their own culture. They should try to categorize poetic types and analyze what functions each type has. Then, when it is time to approach a biblical text such as Psalms, Job, or the Prophets, they can see if there is a functional match and to what degree this occurs. If the goal of speaking or the subject matter of poetry in Hebrew overlaps significantly with that of poetry in their own language, a poetic transfer may be successful. By understanding the limits and potentials of poetry in their own languages, translators will also be able to see how those limits can be stretched or adapted, hence utilizing the resources of their language to the fullest degree. This may include certain innovations that could enrich, rather than detract from, the literary quality of the translation.

Translators also have the option of publishing sample texts in a poetic style early on, to see how their translation and the various innovations in literary style are accepted, and where certain revisions perhaps need to be made.

4.3 Preserving the poetic flavor of the original

Along with the question of the conditions needed for poetic transfer to be successful, we come to the very delicate issue of how far translations should go in attempting to preserve or reproduce formal features of the original. How far should we go in trying to preserve the stylistic flavor of Hebrew poetry? What we would like to suggest is that it is usually possible and helpful to integrate at least some of the features of Hebrew poetry into a translation.

It is important to remind ourselves that, when important selections of world literature are translated, poems are not usually translated as prose, but as poems. Further, if the translation is well done, the reader or hearer will in some way experience the essence of the poem in the original language (see chapter 1). In Japanese, for example, there are brief, delicate poems called haiku. Below are examples of translations of two of these poems into English:

Voices
Above the white clouds:
Skylarks.

(Kyoroku; Lewis, 1965)

Stillness:
The sound of the petals
Sifting down together.

(Chora; Lewis, 1965)

Note that this is not a normal style or format in English poetry but, through translation and the skilled use of format, we may experience this form of foreign beauty. The translation may not be perfect, but this attempt at preserving the stylistic flavor of the poem is certainly more effective than rendering it in pure prose. In the same way, we hope that some of the richness and texture of Hebrew poetry may be carried over into our translations.

In the following section we would like to demonstrate that many poetic features in languages throughout the world match, to varying degrees, certain features of Hebrew poetry. If such functional and stylistic matches do exist, we should at least make some effort to render poetry as poetry. In so doing we may be able, in some measure, to preserve the poetic flavor and effect of the original biblical text.

4.4 Stylistic matches

We have seen that there are a number of functional matches in literary genres between biblical Hebrew and contemporary languages around the world. What is even more encouraging is that there are many cases where poetic style and structure are similar. In chapter 3 we discussed a number of stylistic devices which characterize Hebrew poetry. In the following discussion we will show that these devices are not unique to Hebrew. By first identifying a stylistic device in Hebrew and then matching it with one from the language of translation, translators have a better chance of making a successful poetic transfer.

4.4.1 Matches in structure

As we have seen, Hebrew poetry is characterized by very formal structures, including many types of parallelism, chiastic structures, inclusios, and refrains. In many languages throughout the world, similar poetic devices are often used.

4.4.1.1 Parallelism

The building block of Hebrew poetry is paired, or related, sets of parallel lines (section 3.2.1). But parallelism is not an unusual structure, unknown in other parts of the world. On the contrary, it is a basic part of much of the world's poetry. Therefore we need to investigate similar patterns in the target language which may be useful for translating. In chapter 3 we have seen that the types of parallelism in Hebrew and the relationships between parallel lines can be quite complex. Here we will concentrate on two types of parallelism: (i) syntactic or grammatical parallelism and (ii) what we could call "developmental parallelism," which roughly corresponds to Kugel's formula: "A, and what's more, B."

Grammatical parallelism

Grammatical parallelism involves the use of similar grammatical structures with varying vocabulary. For example, in Psa 47.6 the sentence structure of each line is identical. In the first line "God" appears, while in the second line this is replaced by "our King":

> Sing praises   to God,   sing praises;
> Sing praises   to our King,   sing praises.

We have seen that this is a very common feature in Hebrew poetry, occurring throughout the Psalms, the Song of Songs, Proverbs, Job, and the Prophets. Translators should study poetry in their own language to see if such grammatical parallelism exists. Looking back to the love poems and songs that have been discussed (section 4.2.2.2), we see that syntactic or grammatical parallelism characterized the old Spanish love poem:

> Friend, my most cherished one,
> come by daylight;
> friend, my most beloved one,
> come by dawn.

It occurred as well in the modern Lokpa love song, in the lines:

> the one who wears shirts,
> the one who wears pants,
> the one who wears hats.

Grammatical parallelism is an extremely common feature of poetry in languages around the world. In a popular Yoruba song honoring the mayor of a city in Nigeria (Finnegan, 1970; 275), parallel figurative comparisons emphasize the message of the entire poem:

> I am greeting you, Mayor of Lagos
> Mayor of Lagos, Olurum Nimbe,
> Look after Lagos carefully.
> **As we pick up yam pounder with care,**
> **As we pick up grinding stone with care,**
> **As we pick up a child with care,**
> So may you handle Lagos with care.

Note that in the example above, when the series of parallel lines stops, the main message of the poem is highlighted: "So may you handle Lagos with care." We have seen that parallel lines leading up to a significant statement is a device that is also found in Hebrew poetry (section 3.2.1.4). Indeed, it is found in languages around the world. In the following Hindi poem a father laments that his daughter has not found a husband. The first two sets of lines are grammatically parallel. The last line breaks the pattern and provides some significant information: apparently it is at fairs that young men and women meet or are betrothed (Aldan, 1969: 119; Thakur Prasad Singh):

> Yes, all the older girls were married,
> and all the younger, too, were married.
> Each found an answer to her prayer;
> Each wore the flowers in her hair;
> **But fairs have ended for the year.**

Often this sort of grammatical parallelism in the original text is carried over into the translation used as a base (for example, English, Spanish, or French). If so, translators can recognize this and preserve the syntactic parallelism in their own translation. For example, most translators intuitively translate the time poem in Ecclesiastes following the Hebrew's parallel syntactic structures without even realizing it. This is true in English:

> a time to kill and a time to heal,
> a time to break down and a time to build up

Note that in the second line, even though there is a single verb root in Hebrew, RSV has made the effort to match the verb plus preposition ("break down . . . build up"), creating a perfect balance in English. The repetition of the "b" at the beginning of each verb adds to the poetic effect. Translators who recognize syntactic or grammatical parallelism in the source text and who are creative with the stylistic devices in their own language will generally be able to successfully render grammatical parallelisms as poetry in their translation. If there are two or more ways to express a line of Hebrew poetry, the translator should choose the one that most closely reflects the form of the original.

Developmental or dynamic parallelism

We have seen that many parallel lines can be characterized as "A, and what's more, B." Some scholars refer to this as "seconding." It is interesting that this kind of parallelism also is found around the world. Among the Kuna people of Panama, for example, such patterns are typically used in healing rites and in magical spells (Sherzer, 1983, 128-129). Two lines are almost identical, but in the second, usually one word changes, as illustrated in the following example about catching a dangerous snake:

> He is **cutting** small bushes.
> He is **clearing** small bushes.

> The specialist **moves a little**.
> The specialist **advances**.

> His (the snake's) hooks open and close.
> His (the snake's) hooks open and close **repeatedly.**

In the second of each line, there is a repetition, but we learn something more. The snake "specialist" not only cuts the bushes, he clears them. He doesn't just move, he advances. The snake's mouth opens and closes repeatedly.

Similar if not identical devices abound on the African continent. Note that in the beginning section of a Dinka hymn to the divinity Deng, we find a pattern much like the Hebrew's "A, what's more, B" (Finnegan, 1970):

> Great DENG is near, and some say 'far' . . . .
> The creator is near, and some say 'he has not reached us'.

Note that, though the lines are similar in form, the second line tells us something more than the first. Great DENG is here referred to as "creator," an exchange of divine names much like the one found in many psalms (section 3.2.1.3). The poet further defines "far" in the next line by telling what far means: the divinity has not reached down to them. The concept is personalized: "he has not reached us." This movement from abstract to personal is typical of Hebrew poetry as well. Note also the rhythm and the point–counterpoint balance within each line, which is similar to that seen in the time poem from Ecclesiastes.

Even if languages do not have the tight syntactic parallelism so loved by the Hebrews, certain texts may illustrate a progression of thought that is similar. In the following Bete (Côte d'Ivoire) lament over a deceased husband, we find repetition and the slow unfolding of grief. The lines of both stanzas mean much the same thing, but the second stanza is sadder, as the expressions become more specific and more tender. Finally an isolated line breaks the pattern, again a climactic stylistic device similar to the one found in Hebrew:

> With the setting of the sun, you fell.
> The new day comes, the sun shines.
> You do not come.

> With the setting of the sun, you fell.
> The sun, it goes, it comes.
> Father of Gbokoya, you do not come.

> And there is no echo.

Bete is a language with no written poetry, but one can imagine that if the Old Testament were to be translated, speakers of this language might well appreciate the repetitive and slowly unfolding movement of formal parallel structures found in the Hebrew Scriptures.

In an Ambo hunting song from Zambia, repetitive structures and a slow buildup lead to a kind of climax. It is only in the last word that we discover what is causing so much emotion (Finnegan, 1970:229):

Nafwa mitima kubamba
Pakusanga silimakene.
Nafwa mitima kubamba
Pakusanga silimakene,
Pakusanga silimakene **nama**.

Heavens, my heart is throbbing,
While I see them standing
Heavens, my heart is throbbing
While I see them standing
While I see them standing, **the game**!

In modern Spanish poetry as well, syntactic parallelism may build to an unexpected conclusion. In the following poem by Manuel Macahdo, a poet of the 1930's, there is a movement from the purely physical to the abstract: "my body," "my soul," "my heart," "my life." The repetitive syntactic parallelism gives way to a repetitive word *el mar*, "the sea," which leads to the surprising conclusion of the poem:

Para mi pobre **cuerpo** *dolorido,*	a
para mi triste **alma** *lacerada,*	b
para mi yerto **corazon** *herido,*	a
para mi amarga **vida** *fatigada*	b
¡el mar amado, el mar apetecido,	a
el mar, el mar, y no pensar en nada!	b

For my poor and aching **body**,
for my sad and hurt **soul**,
for my rigid and wounded **heart**,
for my bitter and tired **life** . . ,
the beloved sea, the much desired sea,
the sea, the sea, and not having to think about anything!

Despite the break in the final line, we observe that the poem is held together by an alternating rhyme scheme: *a-b-a-b-a-b*.

Many more examples could be given, but the point is that in many cultures poems progressively move forward in meaning, in emotional intensity, and in communicative effect. Alter describes this movement in Hebrew poetry as one of ". . . intensification, focusing, specification, concretization, dramatization," and he notes that in many cases there is a kind of "crescendo development" (1985:22, 29). This movement from one line to another seems to be a major means of poetic expression in many languages. Such languages will be able to imitate the syntactic parallelism as well as the dynamic forward movement from line to line, ending in a climax that is present in many biblical poems.

Stairstep parallelism

In section 3.2.1.1 we saw examples of stairstep parallelism, where one element from the first line is repeated in the second, which serves to focus on some significant added information:

The LORD is **a stronghold** for the oppressed
a stronghold *in times of trouble* (Psa 9.9)

Similar structures exist in languages around the world. This can be seen, for example, in the following love lament from Chopi (Finnegan, 1970: 253; from Tracey, 1948):

I am most distressed
I am most distressed *as my man has gone off to work*
And he does not give me clothes to wear,
Not even black cloth.

Note too that, besides the obvious stairstep pattern, there is a kind of rhythmic envelope around the poem. The poem begins and ends with very short, sad phrases.

In the example cited earlier from Yoruba, the last word of one line is taken up in the next. This is a common strategy in many African poems:

I am greeting you, **Mayor of Lagos**
Mayor of Lagos, Olurum Nimbe,
Look after Lagos carefully.

If this kind of patterned repetition is popular in poetry of the language of translation, it may be possible to use it in rendering biblical poetry. Translators must determine, however, what the function of this type of structure is before automatically applying it to various biblical genres. For example, in English, stairstep parallelism is often used in children's nursery rhymes. Indeed, in some languages this structure may create a fairy-tale flavor. If there is a formal match between poetic devices, translators must make sure that the moods and connotations conveyed by the stylistic technique match as well. Otherwise a translated poem may be interpreted in an incorrect way, or the poem may convey the wrong feeling or impression.

4.4.1.2 Inclusios and refrains

We have seen that envelopes, consisting of repeated elements at the opening and closing of a unit, are extremely frequent in Hebrew poetry. But this device is actually quite common the world over. A simple envelope surrounds the following Acholi lament sung for a dead brother (Finnegan, 1970: 150; from Okot, 1963). This short poem shows many other poetic features as well: multiple names for the deceased, images, evocative sighs, and repetition.

I wait on the pathway in vain.
He refuses to come again.
Only one, beloved of my mother oh,
My brother blows like the wind.
Fate has destroyed chief of youth completely.
I wait on the pathway in vain.

Since this kind of envelope occurs very frequently in the Psalms (8, 135, 147–150) to mark off a distinct poetic unit, a direct transfer of inclusios in the Acholi translation would certainly be quite natural.

In Bobo, a language from Burkina Faso, an inclusio surrounds a working song sung by women in the fields (Maurice Sanou):

Oh! Men are traitors!
Men are traitors! They are not worth it.
If I decide to find myself another man,
they will say I am an immoral woman.
Oh! Men are traitors!

Repetitive lines may also be used as refrains at the end of poetic units. In a Gujarati poem from India (Aldan, 1969; Sundaram), the first stanza of a poem has an envelope structure:

I'll come as a flower to you.
A child you may be, wet and small, playing under a tree,
I'll drop on your head with a gentle tap,
and drink the innocent wonder in your eyes;
Picking me up you will toy with me,
You may tear out my petals and scatter them to winds,
I care not.
I'll come as a flower to you.

This envelope sets the stage for the entire poem. In the four stanzas that follow, every one ends with the refrain "I'll come as a flower to you."

Even more common than envelopes, refrains are a sign to readers or hearers that the passage they are hearing is stylistically set apart or, in most cases, coming to an end. When this literary device is present in the Hebrew original, it can be easily imitated. In some languages refrains are more common than in Hebrew. If this is the case it would be permissible for translators to introduce refrains where they do not occur in Hebrew. It must first be determined, however, that the content of the refrain adds no new information and in no way changes the focus of the poem. By adding such refrains, translators can add naturalness and poetic flavor to their translations (see section 5.3.1.2).

4.4.1.3 Chiastic structures

We have seen that chiastic structures involve parallels in an X, or crossover, pattern, **a-b-b'-a'** (section 3.2.2). For example, in Job 40.10 God challenges Job:

Adorn-yourself-now   (with) glory and splendor
(with) and honor and majesty   you-clothe-yourself

Deck yourself with majesty and dignity;
With glory and splendor clothe yourself.

In Hebrew this device is less common than the normal parallel structure and serves special purposes, such as tying the discourse together, shifting to a new topic, and signaling the climax or peak of a poem. Though chiastic structures exist in other languages, they seem to be less frequent and to play a less important role than in Hebrew. In Tsonga some proverbs are chiastic (Schneider, 1987:107):

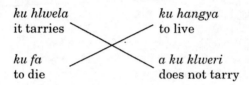

ku hlwela   *ku hangya*
it tarries   to live

ku fa   *a ku klweri*
to die   does not tarry

Living takes time; dying does not.

Examples of stairstep parallelism, which can also be seen as a partial or incomplete X-structure, are somewhat more frequent. In the example already cited from Yoruba, "you" of line a is further identified ("Olorum Nimbe"):

I am greeting you,   a   **Mayor of Lagos,**   b
Mayor of Lagos,   b'   Olorum Nimbe   a'

In some languages an **a-b-b'-a'** pattern may be superimposed on a poem. In the following Agni war song sung to a colonial administrator in Côte d'Ivoire (Finnegan, 1970: 208; Delafosse, 1900;), the first and last lines match, as do the second and next to the last. This chiastic structure marks the beginning and end of the poem, exactly as was the case in the time poem of Ecclesiastes 3 (see section 3.2.2).

Give me some powder and some guns; I will leave tomorrow.   **a**
I want to cut off their heads; I will leave tomorrow.   **b**
They have women with much beauty; I will leave tomorrow.
They say they have gold; I will leave tomorrow.
Today I need to make my bullets; I will leave tomorrow.
Today I must offer a sacrifice; I will leave tomorrow
I want to cut off their heads; I will leave tomorrow.   **b'**
Give me some powder and some guns; I will leave tomorrow.   **a'**

Besides the envelope and **a-b-b'-a'** pattern, we note the refrain "I will leave tomorrow." The song becomes a chant, and this repetition seems to express the growing eagerness of the war party. It also seems to evoke the inevitability of war. Despite its differing subject matter, this poem has some similarity to Psalm 136, with its repetitive and rhythmic "for his mercy endureth forever." Here again there is a partial match of style but not of subject matter. Despite this difference the poem shows that translators in Agni have many stylistic devices at hand which are basically the same as those in Hebrew. Not only would they be able to imitate many of the poetic features of Hebrew, but their rendering would probably preserve a good deal of the flavor and function of the original.

4.4.2 The use of sound effects

As we have already suggested, here is one place where poetic transfer is extremely difficult. Due to the very nature of language, exact rhymes, alliteration, assonance, and other sound effects will almost never match. However, certain languages may use similar devices in their songs, and this can be exploited in translating Biblical poetry.

4.4.2.1 Alliteration and assonance

We have seen that in Hebrew the repetition of consonants and vowels can evoke a particular feeling or a similar sound (section 3.5). Poets throughout the world use this device. For example, a Nigerian poet, Isaac Olaleye, uses it in almost every line as he describes in English the singing of people in his village (1995):

> They sing about **cr**awling **cr**eatures
> In the **d**eep, **d**ark rain forest
> About **b**abbling **b**irds in the **br**illiant **bl**ue sky
> And monkeys **tatt**ling in the **tr**ees.

Indeed a good place for a translator to attempt such poetic transfer is in the introductory poem of Ecclesiastes. Here we find a very effective use of alliteration. In 1.7 words contain fricative sounds (*h*, *s*, *sh*, and *v*) evoking the rushing wind, while 1.8 contains words with liquid and resonant sounds (*l* and *m*), evoking the flow of rivers or the ebb and flow of the sea. Though the match between sounds may not be identical, translators can seek out sounds in their own language that evoke the sound of running water. Psalms is another place where alliteration or assonance can be used to evoke a certain mood. For example, a Chichewa (Malawi) translation of Psa 1.4 takes advantage of the techniques of assonance and alliteration to express the emptiness of the wicked:

> *Kunena iwo, **angonga gaga***
> As for them, they are like chaff.

Translators should study sounds in their own languages and determine what these sounds evoke in various settings. Then they can profitably apply this knowledge when translating biblical poetry.

4.4.2.2 Rhythm

Though some languages may not have accent patterns similar to those found in Hebrew (section 3.5.1), many do have a point–counterpoint rhythm so typical of this language. For example, in Moore from Burkina Faso, such rhythm is a primary feature of both proverbs and poetry (Yibuldo, 1971: 2,3). Proverbs are balanced and sometimes rhyme:

Sa yaa toogo	*yaa noogo*
The sky is stormy	Tomorrow will be beautiful

A point–counterpoint rhythm results from the repetitious pattern of sets of parallel lines, as seen in the following work song sung by young women pounding millet (note that *to* is a kind of porridge eaten with sauce):

My co-wife cooked *to*	and didn't invite me
Me too, I cooked *to*	and didn't invite her
She named her dog	"Don't invite your neighbor"
My dog's name is	"The one who took the initiative."
The master's dog (is named)	"Don't make me ashamed!"
The bachelor's dog (is named)	"Give me it all—
There won't be anything left"	
Come and get it	"Give me it all"
Heh! Come and get it	"Give me it all—
There won't be anything left!"	

Note that, as often happens in Hebrew, a Moore poem built on a point-counterpoint rhythm abruptly changes that rhythm at the end of the poem (as seen in the lines in bold).

In speech communities that appreciate this type of balanced, rhythmic line, it may be possible to capture the rhythm inherent in the source text of the time poem in Ecclesiastes, for example. Even if this kind of rhythm were restricted to a given genre (such as a work song, for example), it is possible that the style may be successfully introduced into other genres. The translator must exercise caution, of course, not to use a style that connotes the wrong feeling. A lament translated into the rhythm of a work song, for example, may not be an acceptable transfer.

4.4.2.3 Rhyme

We have seen that rhyme plays only a minor part in Hebrew poetry (section 3.5.4). In other languages as well, rhyme may not be a major feature of poetry. In Africa, for example, where there are many tone languages, tonal melodies may be more important than rhyme. In some languages, however, rhyme may be an essential feature of poetry. This is especially true of early poetry in Romance languages such as French, Spanish, Italian, or Portuguese, and in Germanic languages such as German or English. In the Philippines rhyming is a distinctive feature of poetry. In the following first lines of a modern Tagalog poem, there is a typical **a-a-b-b** pattern (Dorn, 1994:304):

*Nabaghan si Tata Gus**tin***	a
*isang umaga nang kanyang mapan**sin***	a
*na may mga anay na nama**hay***	b
*sa haligi ng kanyang ba**hay***	b

Daddy Gustin was surprised
one morning when he noticed
there were termites residing
in the support-posts of his house.

In languages where such rhyming schemes are common, translators should attempt to use rhyme while translating poetry. For the book of Psalms, for example, if praise poetry in the target languages uses rhyme, it would be appropriate for translators to use this device in their translation, even though it does not occur in the original. This is because adding rhyme would convey the same message to the readers or listeners as the original did: "This is poetry. This is beautiful language used to glorify or speak to God." Of course translators must be careful not to distort the message of the original. If rhyme is considered childish or sets a mood other than the one found in the original poem, it should not be used.

4.4.2.4 Wordplay

Wordplay (section 3.3.5) is one of the poetic devices that is very difficult to imitate. Most often translators must resort to explaining significant wordplays in footnotes. Some common language translations put meanings of such words in parentheses or add the meaning in the text. However, wordplay does exist in many languages. In the following Moore proverb, for example, a change in one vowel brings out an important change in meaning:

Wend kota	*wend keta*
The God who lives	is still living

Taking advantage of this device in his language, the Moore translator has been able at times to render wordplays in the translation. For example, in 1 Sam 25.25 there is a play on words between the name "Nabal" and the Hebrew word *nabal* "fool." In the Moore translation it is said of Nabal that he is *nabd bala* "plain stupid."

In several translations the wordplay in Amos 8.1-2 between "summer fruit" (*qayits*) and "hour of doom" or "end" (*qets*) has been effectively communicated. In some African languages the prophet says he sees a basket of "*ripe* fruit." The Lord then states that "the time is *ripe* for my people Israel (to be destroyed)."

In most languages the wordplay in Gen 2.23 ("she shall be called 'woman' (*'ishshah*) because she was taken from man (*'ish*)," goes by unnoticed by the reader or hearer. But when translators are made aware of the wordplay, they are sometimes able to replicate a similar wordplay in the translation. In San, a language of Burkina Faso, for example, a talented translator–song writer composed the following:

Look! (expression of joy) This is another "myself"!
She is a part of my body.
They will call her "second of man,"
because she was taken from man.

(In this language an idiomatic expression for "woman" is "second of man.")

In languages where plays on words are appreciated, translators are certainly free to try rendering those in the original by wordplays in the translation. In the above cases none of the translators knew Hebrew, but they were informed of the wordplays in the original through footnotes in translations used as base texts.

4.4.2.5 Ideophones

In some cases the target language may have stylistic devices based on sound which do not occur in the source text. Ideophones are well known for their descriptive and emotive effect. They consist of repetitive sounds or syllables which evoke some state, event, or feeling. In Godie the sound *prrrrr!* evokes the shining moon. In Chichewa the sound *biliwiliwili* evokes fresh greenness of new vegetation. In many cases the impact of an ideophone is similar to that of a vivid metaphor or some other type of graphic figure of speech. They often stand in the place of adjectives, adverbs or even verbs.

Some African poets writing in English have incorporated English-based ideophones into their poems, as in the following "Laundry by the Stream" (Olaleye, 1995: 26):

Women and children stream
To the stream
To do their laundry.
In heavy wooden bowls
They scour the clothes,
And beat them **flap-flop, flap-flop**
On rocks, and in the bowls.
They pound the clothes **thwack-thwack, thwack-thwack** . . . .

If ideophones are well-attested in poetic contexts in the language of the translation, then there is no reason why a translator cannot use this poetic device in attempting a poetry-to-poetry transfer. In Chewa, for example, an ideophone was successfully used in Psa 1.3 to express the greenness of the tree growing by the stream:

*Onse masamba ali **biliwiliwili!***
All of its leaves are **shiny green**!

In Gbaya from Cameroun, translators very effectively use ideophones in Psa 115.5-6 to express the uselessness of false idols (Noss, 1976: 116-117):

> the gods have mouths, but they say words not *mgbukum*
> (there is no response when one speaks to them)
> they have eyes *zal zal* (that should see clearly)
> but they see things not *tamtudum* (the darkness of blindness)
> they have ears, but they hear things not *mgberem* (deaf)
> they smell scent things with nose them not either

As with other sound effects, however, the translator must take care to verify that in adding a descriptive ideophone, the original tone of the biblical poem is maintained. Overuse in some cases may make the poem sound childish or humorous, when the original is not.

In languages where no ideophones exist, onomatopoeic words may be used in a similar way. They can be added to the translation if they are considered poetic and do not distort the meaning of the original.

4.4.3 Rhetorical and leading questions

We have seen that questions figure prominently in Hebrew poetry (section 3.4.2). The most common type of question is rhetorical, that is, questions that expect no answers but imply an emphatic statement. The question itself implies its own answer. In the Old Testament this type of question expresses a wide range of emotions and attitudes. They may express wonder and awe:

> When I look at the heavens . . ,
> What is man that thou art mindful of him? (Psa 8,4)

Or they may express depression and despair:

> My God, my God, why have you forsaken me? (Psa 22.1)

In biblical Hebrew and in many other languages, rhetorical questions are the debater's key tool: prodding, rebuking, and pushing the listener to reflection and a change in thinking or attitude (Job 21; 27.8,9; 30.1). Many times in the Psalms the poet addresses himself, chiding, encouraging, complaining, or just despairing.

Rhetorical questions are apparently found in every language. In laments and love songs from around the world, we find rhetorical questions that remind us of those used in Hebrew poetry. This can be seen in the following love poem from Somalia (Finnegan, 1970:254, Tracey, 1963):

> Woman, lovely as lightning at dawn,
> Speak to me even once.
>
> I long for you, as one
> Whose dhow in summer winds
> Is blown adrift and lost,
> Longs for land, and finds—

Again the compass tells—
A gray and empty sea.

If I say to myself 'Conceal your love!'
Who will conceal my tears?
Like a tall tree, which, fallen, was set alight,
I am ashes.

My heart is single and cannot be divided,
And it is fastened on a single hope;
Oh you who might be the moon.

Note that the rhetorical question in bold print functions much like those in the monologues or "interior dialogues" of the Psalms. Stylistically it is also similar: rhythmic, repetitive, with a kind of play on words ("conceal . . . conceal"). It very poignantly expresses the poet's deep emotion. Note as well that, like rhetorical questions in Hebrew, this question helps to define the structure of the poem by dividing it into two parts. The question allows the reader to pause before the second and more intense part of the poem.

In the following Dinka hymn, which we cited earlier in part, the point-counterpoint rhythm typical of a Hebrew psalm is coupled with pleading cries to the divinity. Note how close in form and function the repeated rhetorical question is to many lines from the Psalms ("Why dost thou stand far off, O LORD?" Psa 10.1). As do some psalms, this poem ends in quiet resignation:

Great DENG is near, and some say 'far'
O Divinity
The creator is near, and some say 'he has not reached us'
Do you not hear, O Divinity?
The black bull of the rain has been released from the moon's byre.
Do you not hear, O Divinity?

I have been left in misery indeed,
Divinity, help me!
Will you refuse [to help] the ants of this country?
When we have the clan-divinity DENG
Our home is called 'Lies and Confusion'.
What is this all for, O Divinity?
Alas, I am your child.

In the following Chinese lament over old age, rhetorical questions are scattered throughout the poem, and then in the final line a rhetorical question sums up the poet's sense of disorientation (Claves, 1986: Kao ch'i, 134):

. . . Now I've returned to the eastern garden,
and sigh with grief that plants and trees die out.
Living in retirement, **who pays attention to me?**

> Only sadness follows me everywhere.
> Most people of the world are happy within,
> still not tired of the pleasurable banquet.
> But I alone must feel this sadness;
> vacillating—**what shall I do now?**

Even in languages without extensive written poetry, rhetorical questions may figure prominently as the climax to a sad song or poem. This is the case in Godie from Côte d'Ivoire. In a typical two-line lament, the first states the situation: "My friend, you have gone off walking, oooh" (on a trip or, by figurative extension, have died). The line is repeated slowly and melodically and then is followed by a staccato rhetorical question that seems to stop in midair: "When will you come back?" The cycle is repeated several times. This song, though made up of just a few words, expresses immense sadness, through both rhythm and the very effective use of the rhetorical question. Its simplicity heightens rather than diminishes its poetic force.

Many African languages use such questions in the same contexts as biblical poetry—as a teaching, rebuking, or argumentative device. In his poem "The Meaning of Africa," the Sierre Leonean poet Abisoeh Nicol (Hughes, 1968) questions Africa as if he were reproaching a person:

> . . . Now you lie before me passive
> With your unanswering green challenge.
> **Is this all you are?**
> This long uneven red road, this occasional succession
> Of huddled heaps of four mud walls
> And thatched, falling grass roofs . . . .

It is very likely that rhetorical questions do appear in poetry in the language of translation, and that they can be used effectively in rendering Hebrew poetry. But before beginning systematically to replace every rhetorical question in a biblical passage with one from the target language, translators should make a thorough survey of the rhetorical questions found in their language and determine their function. How are they used? Positively or negatively? What emotions or attitudes do they express? Are they frequent or rare? Do they occur in poetry? If so, do they occur throughout a poem, or only in the middle or at the end? Then for each biblical poem translators must analyze the rhetorical question in context, to see if its usage coincides in terms of situation, meaning, and function with those found in their own language.

Translators may find that their language uses rhetorical questions in poetry more often than the Hebrew poets did. In this case the translator is free to use them even where they do not appear in Hebrew, if they express the emotion and emphasis intended in the original.

We have also seen that leading questions frequently appear in the Psalms, the Song of Songs, and Ecclesiastes (section 3.4.2). They are structure-defining devices, usually beginning a section and leading into a kind of answer that is developed in the rest of the poem. We saw this strategy at work in Psalm 15, for example:

Lord, who may dwell in your sanctuary?
Who may live on your holy hill? (NIV)

These two questions introduce and set the theme for the rest of the poem, which serves as the answer: "He whose walk is blameless . . . ." Similar structures may appear in the target language. In the following Yoruba poem about a battle, the poet asks a question and then answers it in the rest of the poem (Finnegan, 1970):

What about a great fight that was fought at Ofa?
Is there anyone here who witnessed a bit of it?
Although the trees that saw it here all shed their leaves,
And the shrubs that saw it were all steeped in blood,
And the very stags that saw it grew fresh horns while the hunters looked on,
Yet I saw every bit of it, for it was fought where I was born. . . .

This example shows clearly that the same device is used both in Yoruba and Hebrew poetry. It is a major feature of the famous English love poem by Christine Rosetti as well (Untermeyer, 1966):

How do I love thee? Let me count the ways. . . .

This stylistic device may be found in languages the world over. In such languages a direct translation of psalms and other poems with the question–answer structure may be quite acceptable. But the translator must be careful to make sure that, if the question–answer format is maintained, the tone of the poem remains the same as in the original. For example, if the first lines of Psalm 15 are translated as a question that sounds sarcastic or implies a negative answer (Who can? No one!), then this form must be avoided. The translator may have to utilize a completely different strategy in this case: "O LORD, here is the kind of person who can stay in your tent, who can dwell on your holy hill: It is the one who walks blamelessly . . . ."

4.4.4 Figurative language

All languages use figures of speech in the form of metaphors, similes, and personification. Figurative language occurs in everyday conversations, but it is usually denser and richer in poetry. Some scholars feel that imagery is the key that unlocks the meaning of a poem. Indeed, a poem can be based entirely upon a single metaphor, as seen in the following Mohawk poem by Glenn Lazore (Sharpe, 1985:1):

My face is a mask I order to say nothing
About the fragile feelings hiding in my soul.

Translators should ask themselves which figures of speech are preferred in their language: metaphors (as seen above), or the explicit comparisons we have seen in African poetry?

In the Nyamwezi love poem, for example, the voice of the loved one is compared to the sound of a musical instrument. In the Dinka praise song we find line after line of striking simile: "My bull is **as white as** the silvery fish in the river; **as white as** the egret on the river bank; **as white as** new milk . . . ."

It is not enough to simply recognize figurative language in the source text. Translators must study their own languages to determine the frequency, type, and context of images. Are there genres where metaphors and similes always occur? Are there genres where they never occur? Are images used once and then dropped, or are there cases of extended metaphor, where an image may dominate several lines or a whole poem? Are the bases of comparison made explicit, or are they more likely to be implicit in the text?

Some genres seem to have much more figurative language than others. We have already seen that, in love poetry, imagery often plays a key role. In the following poem "Ancient Feeling," by the Chinese poet Wu Wei-yeh (Claves, 1986: 373), varying images occur in every line. There is not one global image but many smaller ones: a loom in the process of weaving, a tree in the process of blossoming, flowers woven into a robe, and flowers blowing in the wind:

> Beloved, you are like thread in the loom
> woven into a flowering tree of love!
> I am like the flowers on your robe:
> the spring wind blows but they won't drop off.

Some languages may associate certain metaphors or similes with certain genres or themes. For example, the theme of the loved one being part of one's garment seems to be very common in Chinese love poetry. In the Manyoshu we find a similar image: "My very soul, it seems, has stolen into every stitch of the robe you wear." In such a language it will be easy to retain much of the imagery in the Song of Songs, while in others the imagery of the original text may be too dense or unfamiliar and may have to be reduced or simplified.

Another genre where we would expect a great deal of imagery is in religious poetry. In cultures the world over, deities (or personified natural forces) are compared to compassionate human beings, be they male or female. In Hebrew poetry God is often compared to a father and a husband. In Zuni, an American Indian language, we find a song from a corn ceremony comparing the rain to a mother:

> Nicely, nicely, nicely, away in the east,
> the rain clouds care for the little corn plants,
> **as a mother cares for her baby.**

In the Rig Veda, from ancient India, the wind is portrayed as a doctor and as a father. The poet then calls upon the wind to be a brother and a friend (Aldan, 1969.16):

.Delighter of men's hearts is the wind,
a good doctor, a giver of long life.
Grant us life, O wind our father!
Be to us brother and friend.
To your secret cave, run! Fetch immortal honey.
Feed us, O wind!

In many languages similes will be preferred over metaphor in the translation because they are easier to understand. Metaphors should not be automatically transformed into similes, however. Metaphors are clearly more powerful than similes and should be retained if at all possible.

Some languages may enjoy personification, in which case this type of biblical imagery can be retained. One such language is Chinese, where metaphors and similes based on personification abound. In the following lines from two different poets, mountains are personified in a most beautiful way:

White clouds like a scarf enfold the mountain's waist . . .
(Claves, 1986; Shen Chou, 172)

Rains pass, the mountain's face is washed;
clouds gather, the mountains enter dreams.
(ibid; Yuan Mei, 458)

Languages like Chinese, with a tendency toward dense or complex imagery, would welcome the figurative language of the Hebrew without too much modification. However, if languages do not use dense figurative language often, then translators should be careful when handling each biblical image. Personifications will have to be expressed through other means. Metaphors may be better understood as similes, and some images may have to be dropped altogether (see section 5.4.2-4)

4.4.5 Word order

Another stylistic device that is frequently used in Hebrew poetry is change in word order. The most intricate shifts in ordering is observed in complex chiastic structures (section 3.2.2). In the poetry of many languages, the order of words does not reflect what would be called natural word order. For example, in his poem "Stopping by Woods on a Snowy Evening," Robert Frost deliberately shifts the normal order of the first line for poetic effect (Untermeyer, 1966: 437). He reverses the sentence, "I think I know whose woods these are," to a more poetic line. One of the outcomes of this shift is that it highlights the alliteration "whose woods." It also allows the verb "know" to occur at the end of the line, where it is made to rhyme with "though" and "snow":

Whose woods these are I think I know.
His house is in the village though;
He will not see me stopping here
To watch his woods fill up with snow.

In English this is what we call poetic license. Rules governing how words should be arranged in sentences do not always apply in a poetic context. Though Hebrew poets used this device, normally it will be impossible for translators who do not know Hebrew to recognize special word orders in the source text (other than chiastic orders, which are quite evident). Even if we do have access to the original and can recognize word order shifts, we would not necessarily want to imitate these in our translation. Translators should study changes in word order which occur in poems and songs in their own language. They can determine how frequently this device is used and what effect changed word order has on a given line. If this is a typical feature of poetic texts in the target language, as is the case in Chichewa (Malawi), for example, such shifts can make the translation sound more natural and distinctively poetic.

4.4.6 Shifting persons

We have noted that in Hebrew poetry there may be abrupt shifts between third and second person, third and first, or first and second. For example, we saw in Psalm 23 how shifts in person form an envelope around this poem. The psalm begins with a third person reference to the LORD, goes into second person address, and ends in third person reference again. Though shifting persons may present serious problems in some languages, it may be quite natural and well understood in others. In many African languages, and especially in the context of religious poetry, shifting persons seems to be a common feature. In Yoruba, poems about Ifa (also named Ela) talk about this divinity and, with no transition, address him directly (Lasebikan, 1936: 46):

> **He** made the 'Odundun' King of leaves
> And the Tete its deputy;
> **He** made the Sea King of waters,
> And the lagoon its deputy;
> Still **Ela** was accused of the mismanagement of the world,
> Whereupon, **Ela** grew angry,
> And climbed to heaven with a rope.
> **Come back to receive our homage,**
> **O Ela!** (Finnegan, 1970: p. 199.)

Translators must study their own languages, to see if shifting persons occur in poetic or other texts and, if so, for what purpose. In many Kru languages, for example, narrators may interrupt the story line to openly rebuke the person they are talking about, addressing her or him in the second person, even if that person is not present. If shifting persons is a standard device in the target language, translators should determine what role this device plays (sections 3.4.5; 5.5) and decide if it is appropriate to render shifting persons found in the source text literally in their translation. Alternatively, where shifting persons is not accepted, other devices may be used as a functional substitute. For example, where shifting persons occur at boundary markings, they may be harmonized, with blanks left to show the divisions in the poem (see section 5.5).

4.5 Concluding remarks

We have suggested a few guidelines for determining when poetic transfer is possible and when it should be avoided. We have surveyed a number of variable features which can be examined, including the situational context, goal of the text, and several stylistic devices. The more matches shared by the source text and the target language, the greater the chances are for success in poetic transfer.

By citing many examples from poetry around the world, we have stressed that there are a number of stylistic features shared by Hebrew poetry and poetry from other cultures and literary traditions. Translators should use the tools at hand in their own languages to make their translations poetic. To do this, of course, they must know what poetic devices exist in their language, as well as their functions, and then use them at appropriate points in the translation.

Following these guidelines may give different results. Some translators will want to use those poetic features in their language which match the Hebrew ones. In this case the result will be a translation which is poetic and which retains many features of the Hebrew original. Some translators, however, may wish to go farther, using every poetic feature available in their language, whether it is frequent in Hebrew or not. Such translators may, for example, use features such as rhyming or ideophones to make their translation conform to poems in their own language. Some may take biblical material and translate it into poetic genres found in their own language (see Bliese in the Appendix). Whichever approach is taken, translators will have made a conscious effort to render poetry in the Bible by some poetic form. In this way, some of the beauty of the original will be transferred, either directly or indirectly, into the translation.

Questions for Reflection

1. Begin a notebook where you can collect poems and songs in your language. After you have a good collection, try to determine what literary genres exist in your language. For each genre try to write down some defining characteristics. Try to make a chart using words from your language to designate the genres. Be sure to devise some sort of a simple reference system so that your examples may be easily found and cited. For example:

GENRE	DISTINGUISHING CHARACTERISTICS
folktale	prose style two main characters lots of dialogue
proverbs	limited to two lines often negative–positive rhythmic

love poetry	always eight lines always parallel lines some rhetorical questions
praise songs	sung for warriors and rich people various "praise names" used very repetitive

2. Consider genres in the Bible. Do you think that there are some important matches between genres in your language and those in the Bible? Would it be appropriate to use these genres in your translation? Why or why not?

3. Does parallelism exist in poems or songs in your language? Give examples. How frequently does this device occur? In what ways is it like Hebrew poetry? In what ways is it different? Answer the same questions for features such as chiastic structures, envelopes, and refrains.

4. Is rhyme used in the poetry of your language? Give examples. Does rhyme occur only at the end of lines or internally as well? Are there structural patterns based on rhyme? If so, what are they? Give examples.

5. Is rhythm used in the poetry of your language? Are there special stress patterns? meter? Does tone play a part in poetry? If special patterns exist, describe the different types commonly found.

6. Does alliteration (repetition of consonants) exist in your language? If so, what sounds are frequently repeated? Do these sounds have certain connotations or evoke certain emotions? (for example, in English **sl** evokes slippery, slimy elements)

7. Does assonance (repetition of vowels) occur in the poetry of your language? If so, which vowels occur most often? Which vowels occur together? What emotions do these sounds evoke? Sadness? Pleasure? Anger?

8. Do you have ideophones? What notions do ideophones express? Natural phenomena? Feelings? In what context do you find ideophones? In everyday conversations? In both poetry and prose? Only in poetry or only in prose? Do they sound childish? Are they always funny? Do only the elders use them? Are they appropriate to include in a biblical poem? Give some examples to justify your answers.

9. What sounds or words would you use in your language to describe or evoke:
(a) the wind
(b) the ocean, rivers, rain
(c) thunder
(d) lightning

(e) disaster, sadness, anger
(f) happiness, pleasure, joy

10. Do wordplays exist in your language? If so, give three examples. Can you make any generalizations about when they are used? In which social setting? In what literary genre?

11. Do rhetorical questions occur in the poetry or songs of your language? If so, what emotions or attitudes do they express? Make a list of the attitudes they convey, and give an example of each (rebuking, awe, despair, or others). Are rhetorical questions restricted to certain parts of the poem? The opening? The closing? Or may they occur anywhere? Do leading questions occur at the opening of poems? Is this a common device?

12. Is the word order in your language fixed or is it free? Can word order be shifted for poetic effect? If so, give some examples and try to explain what effect the shift in word order has.

13. How do you know where to divide a poem in your language? Are strophes long or short? Are the boundaries marked in any special way? If so, tell how.

14. Study the follows lines taken from a translation of Lamentations 1 by Tim Wilt:

A lone! Once thriving with people, thriving among the nations,
Our city now sits like a widow:
Once a princess, now a prisoner.

B itterly she weeps in the night, tears upon her cheek.
Once loved by many, now none to comfort her.
All her suitors have betrayed her, enemies now.

C aptured, unable to escape from those hunting her down,
Judah, exiled, enslaved, miserable,
Sits among foreigners, with none to care for her.

How is this poem organized? Would you be able to do a similar translation in your language? Why or why not? What would be the effect on the readers or hearers? Can you find a psalm or other text that is organized in this way?

15. Study the following poem (Olaleye, 1995: 30) and pick out poetic features. Would you be able to imitate these features in your language? If not, what replacements can you suggest?

Rainy Season

In the rainy season
The sky is gray
Like a dirty curtain.
The days are grim;
The clouds are mourning,
For weeks the rain drizzles
Day and night.

The rain bathes and bends
A billion blades of grass.
The fields lie quiet and peaceful,
And trees, cold but clean,
Quietly pray
For the sun to come.

16. For the following biblical passages, try to identify what stylistic devices are being used in the original. (Remember, for this exercise a common language version should not be used!) Consider a translation in your language. Will you be able to retain these features in your translation? If so, would their function be the same? If not, why not? How might you compensate for their loss?

(a) Song of Songs 2.10
(b) Psalm 13
(c) Psalm 131
(d) Habakkuk 3
(e) Job 28

Chapter 5:

Some Problems Related to the Translation of Poetry

5.1 Introduction

Up until now we have presented various features of Hebrew poetry (chapters 2 and 3) and suggested criteria for deciding when it is appropriate to translate biblical poetry in poetic form in the target language (chapter 4). In this chapter we will deal with specific problems that translators face when they attempt to make this transfer. We will begin with a discussion of problems encountered when translating word pairs and parallelisms, and continue with a discussion of difficulties relating to repetition and ellipsis. Next we will discuss problems involving poetic language: word choice and the translation of unknown items, key terms, and difficult metaphors. We will also include a brief presentation on how to handle shifts in person. Finally we will discuss the advantages and disadvantages of some basic approaches to translating biblical poetry.

5.2 Problems relating to parallel lines

We have seen that parallel lines are the basic building blocks of all Hebrew poetry. We have noted that the second line is often more specific, more intense, more colorful, or more focused than the first one (section 3.2.1). But there is also a sense in which the second line repeats or confirms the idea in the first line, saying essentially the same thing but in different terms. This feature of Hebrew poetry raises many problems for translators.

When confronted with parallel lines, translators need to ask the following question: should the parallel lines in question be rendered as two lines as they are in the original, or should they be modified in any way? Because of repetition or other problems of translation, should two lines be rendered as one? If we examine different versions we note that different approaches are taken. In more literal translations such as RSV, NJB, NIV, and NJPSV, great care is taken to preserve parallel lines. These versions follow the original text closely and thus preserve the flavor of the original Hebrew poetry. Translations such as TEV, CEV, and common language versions in other languages often take the liberty of reducing two lines into one. For example, NRSV retains the parallel lines of Psa 85.3:

> You withdrew all your wrath;
> · you turned from your hot anger.

> Your fierce anger is no longer aimed at us.

In general we recommend that translators try to preserve parallel lines in translation. This is to ensure that the intended message is communicated in terms of the closest natural functional equivalent, along with its original emphasis. In this way as well, the beauty of the Hebrew text can be appreciated by the listeners and readers of today. In most languages parallelism, or at least repetition, is not an unnatural feature of poetry. So this is an option most translators have.

However, there are a number of situations in which translators may be led or even forced to collapse the two lines into one. Sometimes rendering parallel lines literally will lead to too much repetition in the translation. Often different vocabulary items are not available to make translation of both lines possible. A t other times adjustments must be made if the meaning of the lines is to be understood. In the following discussion we will look at several problems involving parallel lines and will try to provide some guidelines for translators.

5.2.1 Problems relating to word pairs

We have noted that one of the major features of Hebrew parallelism is the presence of word pairs (section 3.2.1.2). Hundreds of word pairs have been identified in Hebrew literature, especially in a poetic context. Many of these word pairs are naturally related pairs, and these may occur in any language. F or example, most languages will have terms for "sun" and "moon," "night" and "day," "dark" and "light," "father" and "mother ." These can be easily rendered in translation.

Sometimes when dealing with Hebrew word pairs, we may need to substitute functional equivalents for the original pair. For example, in many translations "summer" and "winter" are replaced by "rain time" and "dry time." "Sky" and "earth" may be rendered as "up above" and "here below" or similar expressions. Such substitutions are usually straightforward and raise few problems for translators.

Sometimes word pairs in Hebrew do not correspond to word pairs in the target language. Yet, because of their related meanings or because of associations established in the text, such pairs will be easily understood. There is a natural link in meaning, for example, between pairs like "orphan"-"widow ," "water"-"oil" and "people"-"nations." Biblically-specific pairs such as "Sodom"-"Gomorrah" or "Moses"-"Aaron" are frequently encountered in the text and become familiar to the reader. Such pairs are not a problem for translation.

Sometimes, however, while one part of the word pair is commonly known and easily translated, its counterpart is not. F or example, most cultures know "rain" but not all know "snow." This becomes a problem, for example, when translating Pro 26.1:

> Like **snow** in summer or **rain** in harvest
> so honor is not fitting for a fool.

Transliterating the word for "snow" and putting it in the glossary or a footnote is hardly an acceptable solution. Trying to explain "snow" with a long descriptive phrase would affect the balance of the lines and lead the reader away from the real message of the text. Leaving the word out altogether would rob the text of its point-counterpoint rhythm. A better solution is to substitute an equivalent image; for example, "hail." One translation team found a related image that made sense in their culture and preserved the meaning and balance of the lines:

> Honors given to a fool
> are as out of place
> as cold in hot season,
> or rain in harvest time.

There are also cases where the target language does not have synonyms to render a Hebrew word pair. For example, a language may not have two separate words for the word pair "plans"-"purpose," found in Pro 19.21:

> Many are the **plans** (*machashavoth*) in the mind of a man,
>   but it is the **purpose** (*'atsath*) of the LORD that will be established.

If only one word exists for these concepts, translators may have to use the same word or word root twice. The result may be repetitive, but understandable and acceptable in the language:

> People make all kinds of **plans**,
>   but it is the LORD's **plan** that will be done.

Note that even though we have reduced the word pair to one single item, the plural-singular contrast present in the original (the **plans** of a man and the **purpose** of the Lord) is maintained.

However, in some languages noun forms corresponding to these ideas may not exist, and one or both lines must be rendered with verbs:

> People may **plan** all kinds of things,
>   but the LORD **determines** what will be done.

In some cases translators will be able to preserve paired expressions by using a little creativity. For example, in English we do not have two different words to translate the Hebrew word pair referring to gold (*zahav-paz*). Yet this pair has been rendered dynamically in English by "gold"-"fine gold" and is now considered quite beautiful and poetic:

> More to be desired are they than **gold** (*zahav*),
> even much **fine gold** (*paz*) . . . . (Psa 19.10)

But certainly, for every word pair that finds a natural expression in the translation, there will be many others that may not ("heart"-"liver," "ox"-"ass," and others). Translators should try to find creative substitutes for word pairs, but if the result is unnatural, difficult to understand, or would misrepresent the biblical world, there is no point in maintaining them.

5.2.1.1 Ordering of word pairs

Sometimes word pairs exist both in Hebrew and in the target language, but the favored order of the words is not the same. Languages have their own fixed orders for pairs such as "black" and "white," "night" and "day," "light and "dark," or "good" and "evil." Translators are free to change the order found in the biblical text if necessary. For example, in Psa 55.10 we read that "day and night" evil people prowl around the walls of the city. In some languages this may be more natural as "night" and "day." If parallel lines are built on such a pair, as in Psa 19.2, it may be preferable to reverse the order of the words, or even of the lines in which they occur.

While translators are free to reverse the order of word pairs when this makes for a more natural translation, it is important to remember that Hebrew writers sometimes intentionally reverse the expected order of word pairs in the original (see section 3.6). For example, in Hebrew the normal order for the words "good" and "evil" is positive-negative:

> For God will bring every deed into judgment, with every secret thing, whether **good** or **evil** . (Eccl 12.14)

But the prophet Amos purposely reverses that order to express the terrible judgment at hand (9.4):

> and I will set my eyes upon them
> for **evil** and not for **good**.

Thus translators must determine whether a word pair appears in its natural order, or in an unusual or emphatic order, so that the proper impact can be preserved in the translation.

5.2.1.2 Weighing the importance of word pairs

Translators must continually weigh in their minds whether it is important to preserve a word pair or not. Hebrew often has word pairs that are simply not relevant in the target language. Forcing these into translation may make the text sound heavy and unnatural. It may pull the reader's attention away from the message being communicated, rather than helping in its transmission. In some languages "silver" and "gold" are not a natural set. Silver may simply be "white gold," and speakers may not see any natural relationship between the two. In many languages there is no distinction between "hand" and "arm," and the same word is used for both, so it is pointless to attempt to render this word pair. In translating such lines as "with a strong hand and an outstretched arm," the word pair cannot be maintained. In these cases it is better to concentrate on translating the intended meaning of the pair rather than trying to maintain the poetic form. In this last example translators may want to say "God delivered them with his strong and mighty arm," or even "his powerful strength." If "heaven(s)" and "earth" is not a natural word pair, instead of saying:

> His glory covered the **heavens,**
> and the **earth** was full of his praise (Hab 3.3),

we may say:

> His glory and praise are so great,
> they fill the whole wide world,

or, more simply, "His glory and praise fill the whole world." Note, however, that flattening out the parallelism robs the text of its rhythm, balance, and beauty.

One factor that should be taken into consideration is the frequency of the word pair in the Old Testament, as well as the frequency of each item of the pair. The pair "plans"-"purpose" is not very frequent. So if it is lost in the translation, the overall translation will not be greatly affected. On the other hand, words like "Zion" and "Jerusalem" occur very frequently, both as a word pair and separately. Thus most versions maintain this word pair, even though for many readers little meaning is lost if it is reduced. In Isa 2.3, for example, RSV chooses to retain the word pair, while CEV eliminates it:

> RSV: For out of **Zion** shall go forth the law,
> and the word of the LORD from **Jerusalem.**

> CEV: The LORD will teach us his Law from **Jerusalem**
> and we will obey him.

Note that in CEV the word pair "law [torah]–word of the LORD" is also reduced to "Law." This reduction seems unfortunate, however, since it may give the impression that the prophet is speaking only about a set of commands rather than the Word of the LORD itself.

Another factor that needs to be considered is the importance of the word pair to the overall message of the text. For example, some word pairs are considered key terms because they express ideas that are fundamental to Old Testament theology. Among the most well-known are "righteousness" (*tsedeq*) and "justice" (*mishpat*):

> But let **justice** roll down like waters,
> and **righteousness** like an everflowing stream. (Amos 5.24)

Another such pair is "love" (*chesed*) and "faithfulness" ('*emeth*):

> I will give thanks to thee, O LORD, among the peoples,
> I will sing praises to thee among the nations.
> For thy **steadfast love** is great above the heavens,
> thy **faithfulness** reaches to the clouds. (Psa 108.3-4)

Because of their importance in the Old Testament, translators should try their best to find nominal or verbal pairs which express these notions. If such pairs cannot be found, translators must find equivalent expressions to replace them. According to the principles of functionally-equivalent translation, key terms should be rendered according to the context in which they occur. However, in the case of important word pairs, it is advisable to pick some fixed expression in the target language which can be used each time the word pair occurs in the original. This is because these pairs signal theological themes that are basic to the message of the Old Testament. Just as "heaven and earth" express a certainly totality, the word pair "righteousness"-"justice" together sum up how God expects his people to live in this world. The word pair "steadfast love"-"faithfulness" (or "truth") expresses the very essence of the character of God. Thus translators need to be especially careful in finding equivalent words or expressions for these key theological terms.

5.2.1.3 Cultural considerations

There may be times when certain factors in the target culture may lead us to condense certain word pairs into one expression. For example, in Pro 1.8 we read:

> Hear, my son, your **father**'s instruction,
> and reject not your **mother**'s teaching.

CEV has reduced this word pair to a more general statement:

> My child, obey the teachings
> of your **parents**.

In a modern western society this is a more natural, though clearly unpoetic, way of speaking. It may reflect a changing American culture, where one-parent and blended families are as common as the traditional type. It appears that translators of the CEV reduced the parallel lines and eliminated the word pair in order to express this concept in a simple, straightforward way, as might be more expected in a modern American setting.

On the other hand cultural factors may lead us to expand rather than to reduce certain parallel lines. For example, in Psa 144.12 "sons" and "daughters" are referred to:

> May our **sons** in their youth
> be like plants full grown,
> our **daughters** like corner pillars . . . .

However, in most Kru languages spoken in Côte d'Ivoire and Liberia, it is much more common to speak of "children" than "sons" and "daughters." The word for "children" is a simple root, but to distinguish sons from daughters, speakers have to resort to long compound words: "male-children" and "female-children." In such cases it may be helpful to start with a generic expression using the most common term:

> **May our children be blessed.**
> May our sons in their youth be like plants full grown;
> our daughters like corner pillars . . . .

By signaling the two main topics of the verse, "children" and "blessing," the two specific examples come out more naturally, though of course the comparisons may need to be given a dynamic rendering as well; for example, by reversing the reference of the imagery, so that "youth" relates to "pillars," and "daughters" refers to "plants."

5.2.1.4 Final tips on word pairs

We have pointed out several difficulties that word pairs may present to translators. Several principles should be kept in mind when trying to find solutions to problem pairs:

(1) If the words that make up the word pair are more or less synonymous, one solution is to keep the parallel lines and introduce the same word or word root twice. This solution can be effective if the target language appreciates repetition.

(2) If the terms that make up the word pair express a totality ("heaven"-"earth"), a dynamic equivalent ("the whole wide world") can be substituted.

(3) If a member of the word pair is unknown or unfamiliar in the target culture (for example, "ox"-"ass" in a tropical rain forest setting), there is no reason to preserve the pair.

(4) Translators must evaluate how frequent and how important individual word pairs are. "Snow" and "rain" may be a frequent word pair in the Old Testament, but preserving it will have little impact on the message of Scripture. On the other hand, "Jerusalem" and "Zion" are so frequent that translators may wish to preserve this word pair, perhaps indicating somewhere (in a footnote or glossary) what the relationship is (see section 5.2.2 below). Pairs like "righteousness" and "justice" are essential to the message of the Old Testament, and translators should make every effort to find equivalents for such terms.

5.2.2 Guidelines for collapsing pairs or lines

We have noted above that translators basically have two options when encountering word pairs and parallel lines: they may maintain what is found in the original, or they may choose to modify the text in some way. As a rule of thumb it is best to try to preserve the original, but for a number of reasons, translators may be forced to adapt the lines in some way.

5.2.2.1 Collapsing for style and naturalness

Sometimes for reasons of style and naturalness in the target language, certain versions choose to collapse and combine parts of parallel lines. For example, in the beginning lines of Psalm 70, a set of parallel lines refer to God in two ways:

> Be pleased, **O God** (*'elohim*), to deliver me!
> O **LORD** (*Yahweh*), make haste to help me!

In this context in Hebrew the use of two different names emphasizes the desperation of the psalmist; he is crying out to God and begging for help. However, in similar circumstances speakers of English might not use two different names. English style often tends to avoid long repetition and tends to come directly to the point. Thus CEV, which is attempting to express biblical ideas in naturally-spoken modern American English, puts the two names together and reduces the length of the verbal expressions:

> Save me, **LORD God**!
> Hurry and help.

This rendering changes the look of the parallel lines, but it does not significantly change the meaning. Indeed it expresses the anxious mood of the psalmist in modern terms.

Thus, in deciding how to translate such lines, translators must weigh various options. While on the whole it is advisable to maintain the two lines and thus preserve the flavor of the original, this may not always be the best solution. If the message is communicated more naturally and can be better understood in a different form, we may wish to modify some of the parallel lines in our translation, as CEV has done here, as long as poetic style can be maintained.

5.2.2.2 Collapsing to avoid misunderstanding

Sometimes the retention of parallel lines leads the reader to misunderstand the meaning of the verse. If this is the case the translator should try to adapt the verse to make the sense clear. For example, in Isa 48.14 a set of parallel lines makes reference to Babylon and to the Chaldeans (NRSV):

> he shall perform his purpose on **Babylon**,
> and his arm shall be against the **Chaldeans**.

Many readers will not understand that "Babylon" and "the Chaldeans" are related, and that the word pair is referring to the same people. Babylon is the place where the Chaldeans lived. Though many versions retain the two names (RSV, NIV, Revised English Bible [REB], New American Bible [NAB], NJB), many common language versions collapse these two lines into one and make reference to only one name (TEV, CEV). FC maintains the parallelism but uses "Babylonia" in one line, and "Babylonians" in the next. This solution is quite effective. Another possibility is to put the word "Chaldeans" in the glossary, or to add a footnote, stating that Chaldea and Babylon are names for the same place.

Whatever solution is chosen, it is important to apply it in other biblical books using the same vocabulary.

In Isa 48.12 we find a similar though slightly more complicated example:

> Hearken to me, O Jacob,
>   and Israel, whom I called!
> I am he, I am the first,
>   and I am the last.

In the first two lines the people of God are referred to in two ways, "Jacob" and "Israel whom I have called." Here again some readers may be confused. First, they might think that individuals rather than peoples are being referred to. Secondly and more importantly, they might think that "Jacob" and "Israel" are two separate groups, when in fact these are variant names for the same people. That is why many modern versions choose to collapse these two lines into one, retaining one name and omitting the other. In the CEV rendering, seen below, "Israel" has been retained as the more common name, and the notion of "people" is made explicit:

> Israel, my chosen people,
>   listen to me. . . .

There may be ways, however, to retain parallelism and still avoid misunderstanding. For example, in the following lines from Psa 105.5, 6, the people of God are referred to by another set of names:

> Remember the wonderful works that he has done,
>   his miracles, and the judgments he uttered,
> **O offspring of Abraham** his servant,
>   **sons of Jacob**, his chosen ones!

One possibility is to introduce a vocative "you," which would show that the psalmist is talking to the same group of people (Bratcher and Reyburn, page 8):

> You who are descendants of Abraham,
> You, people of Jacob . . . .

or:

> You who are descendants of Abraham
> and sons of Jacob . . . .

TEV has gone even farther by rendering "offspring" and "sons" with the same word, "descendants":

> You descendants of Abraham, his servant,
> you descendants of Jacob, the man he chose . . . .

Note that this solution allows us to maintain the parallelism while insuring that the message is being communicated. In some circumstances translators can change the way the two names occur in context, and can bring them together on the same line with some kind of brief marker such as "namely" or "that is to say":

> Descendants of Abraham, that is to say, descendants of Jacob

However, in most languages this wording may not be natural and is certainly not poetic, and so it may not be the best solution.

To sum up, we can establish this important guideline: when the meaning of the text will not be correctly understood, the form of the text should be modified in some way. This can be done by eliminating one line or one name, by bringing the two names or two key terms together with a linking word ("namely"), or by adding information, such as the use of the vocative "you." If we do not wish to modify the text, but there is a potential for misunderstanding, then we must resort to a footnote or an entry in the glossary. If a given problem occurs only once or twice in Scripture, then a footnote may be a good solution. If, however, it is a more common problem, then an entry in the glossary is better.

If translators are forced to eliminate one line or one name, it is always best to retain the name that is the most well known in the community. For example, most modern readers will be more familiar with the name "Babylon" than with the name "Chaldea." So in the example from Isaiah, it is better to retain "Babylon" in the translation. Most readers are familiar with the name "Israel" referring to the people of God, more so than with "Jacob." For this reason "Israel" should be maintained and "Jacob" omitted in the example given above. As in all translation problems, this basic principle is at work: when there is a problem of comprehension, the translator must give priority to meaning over form.

5.2.3 The misleading "and" connection

Another reason why parallel lines are misunderstood concerns the interpretation and translation of the Hebrew conjunction *waw*. Many versions consistently translate this word as "and," when in fact it has many meanings: "and," "but," and "yet," among others. In other words, *waw* signals many different kinds of logical relationships. At times it may simply introduce a repetitive sentence. If a translator indiscriminately translates every "and" (or *waw*) in the source text as "and" in the target language, the reader may be confused. For example, in Isa 2.3 we read:

> For out of Zion shall go forth the law,
> **and** the word of the LORD from Jerusalem.

In this instance, the word "and" can mislead readers into thinking there are two distinct events taking place. In reality there is only one. Translators must be able to discern that this verse is not talking about two different events or entities (the **law** coming from Zion and the **word** of the LORD coming from Jerusalem). Neither is it talking about two different places. The "law" and "the word of the LORD" refer to the same entity, just as Zion and Jerusalem are the same place. In this context the Hebrew conjunction *waw* (translated as "and") does not signal consecutive actions but simply links the two clauses in a very superficial way.

To avoid this serious misunderstanding, the TEV translators remove the "and" but retain the parallel statement (though giving it a more dynamic form). They have brought the agent "LORD" up from the second line and placed it in a more prominent position in the first line. But they have chosen to retain the important word pair "Jerusalem"-"Zion":

> For the LORD's teaching comes from Jerusalem;
> from Zion he speaks to his people.

CEV, on the other hand, has removed any reference to Zion, so there is no chance whatsoever that a misunderstanding could occur. They make "the LORD" the subject of the finite verb "teach" and substitute a more natural "us" for "his people." Simplicity of speech may also have been a motivation here for collapsing the two lines into one:

> The LORD will teach us his Law
> from Jerusalem.

In this translation we no longer see or hear the Hebrew parallelism, but we do understand the message. Note, however, that there is some loss, since the notions "people of God" and "the word of the LORD" are missing from this translation. Furthermore, the text no longer sounds poetical at all.

Another possibility is to bring together the words referring to the same entity:

The Law, yes, the word of the LORD, will come forth from Zion in Jerusalem.

But this has the disadvantage of creating a line that is too long and complicated to be poetic. Translators will need to work with such passages creatively to find equivalent expressions that retain at least some poetic feeling and forcefulness.

Many translators fall into the trap of "two instead of one," even when the *waw* conjunction is left out of the translation serving as a base. Pro 23.34 is one verse that translators invariably interpret as referring to two distinct events rather than to one:

> You will be like one who lies down in the midst of the sea,
> like one who lies on the top of a mast.

Many translators see this as two images, one with the person out in the middle of the sea on a raft, and the other with the person inside the boat. TEV does away with the parallelism and renders this verse in prose. The image, however, is unified and clarified. There is only one action:

> You will feel as if you were out on the ocean, seasick,
> swinging high up in the rigging of a tossing ship.

CEV reduces even more:

> You will feel tossed about
> like someone trying to sleep
> on a ship in a storm.

Generally, then, when dealing with parallel lines, translators must always ask if there are two referents or one, two events or one. If there is an "and" (*waw*), they must always ask whether it is tying two different things together, or simply linking two identical things in a parallel construction.

Sometimes translators will need to do research on a particular passage to determine how many entities or actions are being referred to. For example, in the Song of Songs we find what appears to be a reference to three mountains (4.8):

> Depart from the peak of **Amana**,
> from the peak of **Senir** and **Hermon** . . . .

But looking into the matter more closely we discover that Senir was another name for Hermon (Deut 3.8-9). Thus the "and" that joins "Senir" and "Hermon" in Hebrew is better rendered as "even" or "that is to say." Most versions do not make this notion explicit (RSV, TEV, NJPSV). Even though this does not affect the major thrust of the poem as a whole, a careful translation should correctly express the meaning of the original.

To sum up, if a parallelism will be misunderstood as referring to two persons or two actions when only one is intended in the original, translators must adapt their translation. In extreme cases it may be necessary to collapse the two lines into one.

5.2.4 Problems of temporal ordering

At times parallel lines may not present items in exact temporal order. This may be due simply to the poet's manipulation to balance rhythm or to create some special effect. Whatever the reason, in some languages it will be helpful for readers if translators rearrange events in a natural order.

For example, in Isa 1.6 we read that the wounds of Israel are not "pressed out, or bound up, or softened with oil" (TEV: "Your wounds have not been cleaned or bandaged. No ointment has been put on them"). In many languages this order does not make sense. Surely ointment would be put on wounds before bandaging them. Translators are free to change the ordering of these expressions to make these lines more understandable.

Another difficult passage for translators is Job 3.3, when Job refers to his birth before his conception:

> "Let the day perish wherein I was born,
> and the night which said,
> 'A man-child is conceived.'. . ."

We can only speculate on why the poet chose to express himself in this way. Maybe the writer felt compelled to follow the normal order of the word pair "day"-"night." Possibly in that culture birth was associated with day, and conception with night. Or, does the second line express the poet's point with more intensity or emotion? Whatever the motivation for the verse as it stands, there seems to be no real reason why translators should not switch the order here (putting "be conceived" before "being born"), thus making the verse conform to real world expectations.

5.2.5 Parallel lines with the "for" conjunction

So far we have noted two problems dealing with relationships between parallel lines. In the first case translators may assume that two parallel lines refer to separate events, when in fact only one event is taking place (sections 5.2.2; 5.2.3). We have also seen that sometimes temporal actions occur out of order in parallel structures and can, if necessary, be turned around (section 5.2.4).

In this section we discuss another problem that translators often face, the translation of the conjunction "for." In more literal versions such as the King James Version (KJV) or even RSV, this conjunction often occurs at the beginning of parallel lines:

> For a dream comes with much business,
> and a fool's voice with many words. (Eccl 5.3)

Most often this "for" conjunction is a translation of the Hebrew word *ki*. Translators must be very cautious each time they see a "for" conjunction in such a context. Like the Hebrew conjunction *waw* ("and"), *ki* is ambiguous. In some contexts it signals the reason for a preceding statement. For example, in Psa 56.12-13 the psalmist tells the reason he will give thank offerings to God:

> My vows to thee I must perform, O God;
> I will render thank offerings to thee.
> **For** (*ki*) thou hast delivered my soul from death,
> yea, my feet from falling . . . .

In Psa 16.9-10, the statement introduced by *ki* ("for") tells why the psalmist is rejoicing:

> Therefore my heart is glad, and my soul rejoices;
> my body also dwells secure.
> **For** (*ki*) thou dost not give me up to Sheol,
> or let thy godly one see the Pit.

113

Sometimes, however, *ki* has an affirming function, meaning something like "indeed" or "truly." It may even be rendered as an emphatic "Yes!" This use can be seen in Psa 25.3, where *ki* is rendered as "yea":

> **Yea** (*ki*), let none that wait for thee be put to shame;
> let them be ashamed who are wantonly treacherous.

Yet in several versions used as a base text (such as RSV), the word *ki* is sometimes translated literally and indiscriminately as "for" in places where there is no logical relationship of reason. For example, in the NRSV and RSV rendering of Psa 18.27, *ki* is translated by "for," but what follows is not a reason. It is rather a confirmation or summing up of the preceding lines:

> 25 With the loyal thou dost show thyself loyal;
>   with the blameless man thou dost show thyself blameless;
> 26 With the pure thou dost show thyself pure;
>   and with the crooked thou dost show thyself perverse.
> 27 **For** (*ki*) thou dost deliver a humble people;
>   but the haughty eyes thou dost bring down.

In the verses following those cited above, however, *ki* has been correctly rendered by an affirming word "yea":

> 28 **Yea** (*ki*), thou dost light my lamp;
>   the LORD my God lightens my darkness.
> 29 **Yea** (*ki*), by thee I can crush a troop;
>   and by my God I can leap over a wall.

By studying the logical relationship between verses 26 and 27 and the relationship between verse 27 and the following verses, we can determine that in verse 27 *ki* probably has an affirming function as well, rather than signaling a causal relationship. Many versions recognize this (NIV, NJB, NAB, REB, CEV, TEV) and indicate the affirmation implicitly by eliminating the "for" conjunction in this verse.

Parallel lines beginning with "for" should therefore always be carefully examined before translating them. Translators should ask themselves whether the relationship with the immediate context is one of reason or of affirmation. By consulting many versions (especially common language ones) they may be able to see how other translators have understood the "for" (*ki*) conjunction. Then they can make a choice as to its meaning and find an appropriate equivalent in their language. If the "for" is taken as reason, they can use conjunctions like "because" or "since." If the "for" is rather to be interpreted as an affirming word, they can use equivalents like "really," "indeed," or "yes."

Sometimes it is very difficult to decide which meaning is intended. Translators may have to consult translation manuals and commentaries to try to determine what the exact relationship is between the line or lines containing preceding passage. For example, in Psalm 84 two *ki* statements occur toward the end of the poem:

> Behold our shield, O God;
> > look upon the face of thine anointed!
>
> **For** a day in thy courts is better
> > than a thousand elsewhere.
> I would rather be a doorkeeper in the house of my God
> > than dwell in the tents of wickedness.
> **For** the LORD God is a sun and shield;
> > he bestows favor and honor.
> No good thing does the LORD withhold
> > from those who walk uprightly.
> O LORD of hosts,
> > blessed is the man who trusts in thee!

Many versions render one or both of the *ki* conjunctions as "for" (RSV, NRSV, NIV, NAB, and NJB). Thus they interpret the lines beginning with this conjunction to explain some reason, perhaps why people who trust in God are blessed. However, other versions seem to take both *ki*'s to be noncausal and omit the "for's" (CEV, TEV, REB), as seen in the REB text:

> Better one day in your courts
> than a thousand days in my home;
> better to linger by the threshold of God's house
> than to live in the dwellings of the wicked.
> The LORD God is a sun and a shield;
> grace and honour are his to bestow.

Here the first "for" is interpreted as the marker of a final conclusion, which in English does not need to be indicated by any sort of conjunction.

The preceding example shows that silence or the lack of a conjunction can mean something in a given language. In English, for example, either a reason relationship or an affirming relationship may be implied by the lack of a conjunction. In the above example the statements by themselves are enough to affirm a thought. In the same way, leaving the *ki* conjunction untranslated can also convey a reason relationship. For example, in Psa 54.1-3 some versions translate *ki* as "for," while others simply leave it untranslated:

> (RSV) Save me, O God, by thy name,
> > and vindicate me by thy might.
> Hear my prayer, O God;
> > give ear to the words of my mouth.
>
> **For** insolent men have risen against me,
> > ruthless men seek my life . . . .

115

(REB)   Save me, God, by the power of your name,
        and vindicate me through your might.
        God, hear my prayer,
        listen to my supplication.
        Violent men rise to attack me,
        ruthless men seek my life.

In English the logical relationship of reason is still present, whether it is marked by an overt conjunction or not. Note, however, that the causal relationship is a little less obvious and is certainly not highlighted in the REB text.

To sum up, each time translators are confronted with the conjunction "for" at the beginning of lines in a base text, they should avoid automatically rendering it by a similar conjunction in the translation. They need to consult several versions and study the text to see which logical relationship—reason or affirmation—is present in the original text. Then they must decide which conjunction or particle (if any) is needed to express this relationship clearly in their language.

5.2.6 Further guidelines for collapsing parallel lines

We have seen that, for reasons of style, lack of vocabulary, or ambiguity, translators may be led to collapse or combine parallel lines. There are some limits, however, as to how far translators should go.

We have already noted many examples of reducing two lines into one. Here we will consider a slightly different case of two sets of parallel lines (four lines) which could be collapsed into one set (2 lines). In Psa 118.8-9 two "better" statements are made (NRSV):

> It is better to take refuge in the LORD
>   than to put confidence in mortals.   } A
> It is better to take refuge in the LORD
>   than to put confidence in princes.   } B

With the exception of the last word in each verse ("mortals," "princes"), these two sets say exactly the same thing. Translators may be tempted to collapse the two into one. It would be wrong, however, to collapse the four lines into a simple "It is better to take refuge in the LORD than to trust people." We note that there is an important relationship between the first and second sets. The second set of lines goes further than the first. It adds something significant: the word "princes," which contrasts with the term "mortals." Thus the meaning is "it is better to trust the Lord than to trust anyone—no matter who they are" or "—no matter how great they are." This is a case of Kugel's pattern, "A, what's more, B."

If for some reason we wish to collapse such sets, then we must be sure to capture the particular emphasis found in the original. CEV does this very thing in its translation:

> It is better to trust the LORD
> for protection
> than to trust anyone else,
> including strong leaders.

Perhaps "even strong leaders" (instead of "including") would be a better rendering of the Hebrew original.

Here we see an important principle for combining parallel lines. Though we may set a goal to preserve parallelisms in most cases, we may sometimes be obliged to collapse them for a specific reason. If we do, however, we must be very careful to remain faithful to the text. Special attention must be given to those parallelisms where there is a focusing or intensification in the second line or set of lines. We should not simply assume that these lines are repetitions, but must ask ourselves what their function is. This is part of the meaning of the original text which needs to be expressed in our translation.

5.3 Repetition and ellipsis

Repetition is one of the main characteristics of poetry in any language, and this is especially true in Hebrew poetry. We have seen the importance of repetitive sounds, grammatical structures, and meanings. Besides being able to recognize repetition in the source text, translators must determine how much repetition is acceptable in their languages and how it is used. As they translate they must judge whether their translation is too heavily burdened with repetition or does not contain enough repetition to be understood.

5.3.1 Too much repetition in the source text

In many languages, if Hebrew poetry is translated literally, the translation will seem unnaturally heavy. Consider, for example, the RSV rendering of Psa 28.3-5:

> 3 Take me not off with **the wicked**,
> with those who are **workers of evil**,
> who speak peace with their neighbors,
> while mischief is in their hearts.
> 4 *Requite them* according to **their work**,
> and according to **the evil of their deeds**;
> *requite them* according to **the work of their hands**;
> *render them* their due reward.
> 5 Because they do not regard **the works of the LORD**,
> or **the works of his hand**,
> he will break them down and build them up no more.

For the average speaker of English this translation is too repetitive (see especially those phrases appearing in bold and in italics). Translators must ask themselves if any part of the message or the feeling of the poem will be lost if the repetition is eliminated. In this passage repetition is used to emphasize the poet's anguish and his wish for justice to be done. If this kind of repetition is not natural in the target language, the translator may find other stylistic means for expressing the insistence and emotion of this passage. This may be done, for example, through focus constructions, emphatic particles, or ideophones, for example.

For languages that do not appreciate repetition, Psalm 136, with its repetitive refrain "for his steadfast love endures for ever," presents a particular challenge:

> O give thanks to the LORD, for he is good,
> **for his steadfast love endures for ever.**
> O give thanks to the God of gods,
> **for his steadfast love endures for ever.**
> O give thanks to the Lord of lords,
> **for his steadfast love endures for ever.**

In some languages a condensed version may sound more natural:

> O give thanks to the LORD, for he is good.
> O give thanks to the God of gods, the Lord of lords,
> **for his steadfast love endures for ever.**

Certainly, as this psalm unfolds from verse 10 onward, some will consider the refrain to be disruptive, especially if it is read silently rather than heard:

> to him who smote the first-born of Egypt,
> **for his steadfast love endures for ever;**
> and brought Israel out from among them,
> **for his steadfast love endures for ever;**
> with a strong hand and an outstretched arm,
> **for his steadfast love endures for ever;**
> to him who divided the Red Sea in sunder,
> **for his steadfast love endures for ever;**
> and made Israel pass through the midst of it,
> **for his steadfast love endures for ever;**
> but overthrew Pharaoh and his host in the Red Sea,
> **for his steadfast love endures for ever . . . .**

Some languages may prefer putting the sequence of events together rather than breaking them up with a repetitive refrain. For example, we may group the events together and then use a repetitive refrain at the end for emphasis:

> The Lord delivered his people from the Egyptians!
> With his powerful might, he divided the Red Sea in two,
> And Israel walked through the middle, untouched!
> But the Egyptian king and his great army were utterly destroyed!
> **It is true: God's love and loyalty never fail!**
> **Yes, very true, God's love and loyalty never fail!**

As noted in chapter 4, translators must feel free to adapt the form of a poem to make the translation poetic according to standards in their own language. Note, however, that when the repetitive refrain is removed from this psalm, the function of the poem changes. Psalm 136 certainly had a liturgical use. In all likelihood a lead singer sang the first lines, with the congregation joining in on the refrain. If we remove the repetition, the poem can no longer function in this communal way.

Repetition of key terms and key phrases is another important issue translators must face. In Hebrew poetry key terms can occur repeatedly within a passage. For example, in the time poem of Ecclesiastes, the word "time" is repeated twenty-nine times in the space of eight verses! As we have seen (section 3.3.4), the expression "a time to . . ." creates a rhythmic beat. The word "time" in Hebrew (*'eth*) makes a repetitive tapping sound throughout. In addition the repetition of the word "time" seems to drive home the message and theme of the poem. Most versions maintain this repetitive word, but in some languages it may be more effective to retain only one occurrence of the word "time" per line ("a time to find and to lose") rather than to follow the Hebrew lines exactly ("a time to find and a time to lose"). In this case a reduction of some of the repetitive "time" words should not take away from the overall message of the poem.

5.3.2 Not enough repetition in the source text

On the other hand, in many languages translators will want to introduce even more repetitive material into the translation. They are free to repeat elements to help create rhythm and poetic effect. Unless repetition draws unnecessary emphasis to some parts of a poem, translators may insert words or even complete lines to render the translation more natural or more aesthetically pleasing. For example, while translating part of the "Woe" sections in Amos (6.1), translators of one language decided it would be much more poetic in their language to repeat the initial "woe to you" at the end of the passage as well. This allowed for a proper conclusion to be made. It in no way changed the meaning of the text, but it rather heightened the condemning tone, which is a main component of the prophet's message.

In Psa 80.1 the TEV translators inserted a repetitive "hear us" that is not in the original text. This is done to balance out the second line, which has been adapted because of specific translation problems (see section 5.2.2). We can compare, for example, the NRSV rendering with the TEV:

> Give ear, O Shepherd of Israel,
>   you who lead Joseph like a flock! (NRSV)

> Listen to us, O Shepherd of Israel;
>   **hear us**, leader of your flock. (TEV)

Again, this insertion does not affect the meaning in any significant way and makes the translation sound more poetic.

5.3.3 How to deal with ellipsis

Ellipsis, a very frequent strategy in Hebrew poetry (section 3.2.1.1), is the reverse, so to speak, of repetition. At times biblical poets purposely left out words to create or maintain a certain rhythm and balance, or to give themselves space to include more ideas in the second line of a parallelism. In Isa 1.3, for example, the ellipsis of the verb "know" in the second line allows the prophet to add "its master's crib." This intensifies the message of the passage. An ox knows its owner, and knows where its food comes from. In contrast, Israel does not know its owner, God, the one who provides everything for them:

The ox	**knows**	its owner,
and the ass	*****	its master's crib;
but Israel	**does not know**,	
my people	does not understand.	

Sometimes the silence created by an ellipsis is poignant, meant to convey a deep emotion. In Lam 5.2, for example, through the emptiness of the second line, we feel the finality of total loss:

Our inheritance	has been turned over	to strangers,
our homes	*****************	to aliens.

Whatever the reason for an ellipsis, translators must often fill in its implicit information because of the grammatical patterns in their language. In many languages it would be impossible to translate the above passage without inserting the missing verbs. However, inserting missing elements can ruin the rhythmic balance in a verse. Translators must then somehow make adjustments to ensure that the resulting lines still sound poetic and that the deep feeling of the line is expressed.

In some poems ellipsis may be quite extensive. Sometimes words or even complete lines are at some distance from their grammatical contexts. In Psalm 136, for example, a significant ellipsis occurs. The missing element "give thanks" appears for the last time in verse 3:

> **O give thanks** to the Lord of lords,
> for his steadfast love endures forever; . . .

What follows is a long list of descriptive phrases qualifying God (verses 4-16), beginning with:

> to him who alone does great wonders, . . .
> to him who by understanding made the heavens . . . .

In many languages it will be good or even necessary to insert "give thanks" in appropriate places, as seen below in bold print:

Give thanks to the one who smote the first-born of Egypt,
and brought Israel out from among them,
with a strong hand and an outstretched arm.
Give thanks to him, for his love is forever.

Give thanks to the one who divided the Red Sea in sunder,
and made Israel pass though the midst of it,
but overthrew Pharaoh and his host in the Red Sea.
Give thanks to him, for his love is forever!

Sometimes ellipsis can be confusing, and in such cases translators may be obliged to move quite far from the original form to catch the meaning and mood of a verse. In the opening lines of Psalm 126, the chiastic wording in verse 2 is brief and moving. The word-for-word rendering in the Hebrew is seen below:

1   When the LORD restored the fortunes of Zion,
we were like those who dream.

2   Then filled   laughter   our-mouth

     and   *********   our-tongue   shouts-of-joy

RSV turns the chiastic structure into a parallel one but does not fill in the gap:

Then our mouth   was filled   with laughter,
and our tongue   *********   with shouts of joy.

This verse is poetic and rhythmic in English, but we note something unusual. While mouths can be "filled" with something such as laughter, tongues can not be "filled." We need a verb for the second clause, but it is difficult to determine which one. TEV deals with this by providing two short clauses. Despite a form very different from the original, this translation succeeds in capturing some of the intended emotion:

When the LORD brought us back to Jerusalem,
it was like a dream!
How **we laughed**, how **we sang for joy**!

Translators need to recognize ellipsis and determine what its function is. Sometimes they may have to add missing elements to make the sentence sound grammatical in their language, while at other times they may have to restructure the verse completely, as TEV has successfully done here.

5.4 Problems with poetic language

In chapter 1 we noted that poetry is different from everyday speech in that the language itself is highlighted. This means that words and expressions have been picked with special care by the poet to evoke certain moods and feelings. Part of what makes the translation of poetry so difficult is trying to find the right words to express what is present in the original. Metaphors and other comparisons may be difficult to understand and to convey in the language of translation. In the following discussion we will give suggestions for dealing with some of these issues.

5.4.1 The importance of word choice

One way translators can enhance their translations of poetry is to be very selective in their choice of words. For example, in Psalm 51 there is the well-known line (verse 5):

> True, I was born guilty,
> a sinner, even as my mother conceived me. (NAB)

In English another way to say "conceive" is "to get pregnant." In a historical narrative it is quite natural to say, for example, "Sarah got pregnant." But this expression would seem out of place in many poetic and religious contexts such as the Psalms. Some sort of euphemism or indirect expression would be necessary. Translators must therefore consider which words are available in their language, and then choose them to fit the context.

Another example of how word choice can affect a translation comes from the first chapter of the Song of Songs (verse 13). We read from RSV:

> My beloved is to me a bag of myrrh,
> that lies between my breasts.

Note, how the word "bag" stands out in the verse and causes some confusion to the reader. The word itself evokes different images in English: a grocery bag, or even the colloquial "old bag" (a derogatory name for a bothersome old woman). The word itself seems out of place in a love poem. REB, NAB, and NJB use the word "sachet," which suggests a small bag that is sweet-smelling. Even if this is a harder word to understand, it is appropriate to use it in this passage and include a footnote if necessary. The footnote would comment on the use of a sachet. It could say, for example, "This was a small bag (or, container) filled with good-smelling spices that was worn around the neck to perfume the body."

TEV takes another approach, removing the image of the perfume bag, but rendering the meaning in a dynamic way:

> My lover has the scent of myrrh
> as he lies upon my breasts.

The metaphor is lost, but the image of the sweet-smelling lover is evoked. At times, then, when our word choices are limited, we may have to concentrate on the meaning rather than giving a simple literal rendering. However, whenever possible we should use the most poetic language available.

5.4.2 Translating exotic or unknown vocabulary

As the above example demonstrates, we may encounter certain culturally-specific items and vocabulary that are foreign to modern readers. This causes many problems for the translator.

Translators are often confronted with a simile or metaphor where the object to be compared is known but the basis of comparison is not. In Pro 3.15, for example, we read that wisdom is more precious than "coral" (Traduction œcuménique de la Bible [French ecumenical translation of the Bible], and Brown, Driver, and Briggs). Actually there is a debate over the exact meaning of this word. Versions differ widely as to how they translate it. NIV and NJPSV translate "rubies," while FRCL has "precious pearls." When confronted with this word, many translators look for an equivalent for "rubies," "coral" or "pearls" in their own language. Since many languages do not have specific words for such items, they may end up transliterating one of these words from English, Spanish, or French. The passage then loses not only its beauty but its meaning as well.

When dealing with a comparison that is unknown or will probably confuse the reader, it is better to concentrate on the intended meaning. In such cases we normally look for a general or culturally equivalent expression to substitute for the unknown item. In a poetic context we should be especially careful to find a poetic expression that will fit neatly and rhythmically into the line. RSV seems to have taken this approach by saying very simply "She is more precious than jewels, and nothing you desire can compare with her."

Sometimes poets use words more for their sounds and connotations than for their meaning. Thus, in the Song of Songs, there is a whole atmosphere created by the use of special exotic terms. The greatest number designate sweet-smelling flowers and spices: "myrrh" and "henna" (1.13, 14), the "rose of Sharon" and "lilies" (2.1, 2), "apple trees" and "fig trees" (2.3, 13), "pomegranates," "nard," "saffron," "calamus," "cinnamon," "frankincense," and "aloes" (4.13-14), to name only a few. We also hear about precious jewels: "silver" and "gold" (1.11), "ivory," "sapphires" (lapis lazuli?), and "alabaster" (marble) (5.14, 15). All these terms are used to create an atmosphere of luxury, symbolic of the pleasure that the young lovers enjoy in each other's arms.

Normally, when confronted with items not known in the target culture, translators have several options:

(1) they may transliterate the term as is;

(2) they may transliterate the term and add a footnote explaining it;

(3) they may adopt a general term such as "spice" or "perfume";

(4) they may adopt a general term and add a description or comparison such as "a spice called cinnamon," "a sweet-smelling spice like cinnamon" or "a sweet spice used to season food";

(5) they may use a close equivalent from their language which does not conflict with the biblical setting.

When choosing a solution, however, we need to consider the function of the word in its context. In the Song of Songs we are not dealing with a historical narrative listing products brought into Solomon's court by some royal official. If this were the case, we might opt for the description mentioned in (4). Rather, we are dealing with poetry, so the usual solutions proposed for translating unknown cultural items should be modified or used with caution here.

For example, toward the end of chapter 4 in the Song of Songs, the poet is paving the way for a climactic moment in the poem ("I come to my garden, my sister, my bride") by speaking about his lover and all her delights. He uses metaphors from a sweet-smelling and fruitful garden to describe her (4.12-15):

> [You are] a garden locked, a fountain sealed.
> Your shoots are an orchard of pomegranates
>   with all choicest fruits,
>   henna with nard,
> nard and saffron, calamus and cinnamon,
>   with all trees of frankincense,
> myrrh and aloes,
>   with all chief spices—
> a garden fountain, a well of living water,
>   and flowing streams from Lebanon.

If the translator stops to explain each spice, as we may do in a historical passage, the resulting text will be anything but poetic. It would sound more like a dictionary:

> You are like henna, the sweet-smelling flower used to dye hands and feet,
>   like nard, an expensive perfume made from a plant.
> You are like saffron, a wonderful aroma in cooking,
>   and calamus, a sweet-smelling cane, and cinnamon, a spice used in
>   anointing oils and to perfume beds . . ,

In this rendering it is the exotic spices that are in focus and not the young woman. Thus this kind of translation undermines the purpose of the poem, which is to evoke all her wonderful qualities.

In such cases translators must ask themselves several questions: Does the target language have words for some or all of these spices? If they are known, are they considered positively, that is, as sweet-smelling? Do they fit the context? If so, these words can certainly be used. If some are known and others are unknown, we may emphasize those that are known and generalize the rest for maximum effect:

> You are as sweet as henna and cinnamon,
>   as fragrant as the most wonderful spices on earth!

We can take another approach and ask if the speakers of the target language will appreciate just the sound of all the exotic words in this text. In this case we can consider transliterating the terms and putting footnotes in the text. But this puts a heavy burden on the reader, who may stumble over or be distracted by all these foreign terms. In the end this may detract from the real meaning the author intended. What the translator wants to do is somehow to evoke the overall mood that the author wished to create: sumptuous, sweet-smelling, exotic luxury.

Another example of a similar problem comes from the book of Psalms. Psalm 119 is certainly one of the most beautiful poems in the Bible. As a means of praising God's law, the poet uses numerous synonyms. There is the word "law" (*torah*) itself (119.1), but then a host of others, depending on the version consulted: "instructions," "teachings," "ways," "paths," "precepts," "commandments," "judgments," "ordinances," "decrees," "promises." Though every attempt should be made to find equivalents for each distinct word in the original text, there are not many languages that will have enough vocabulary items to do so here. Instead of cluttering the poem with lengthy, non-poetic descriptions or definitions, it is probably wiser in this context to let there be some overlap. Translators may not be able to maintain every exact distinction in the original, but the meaning and emphasis of the text can still be preserved.

Again, when dealing with unknown geographical regions, context and genre play an important role. In narrative texts, place names are crucial, and translators often make explicit, by means of a general or classifying word, whether a given name refers to a country, city, river, or mountain. Including such information helps readers to keep track of the vast number of unknown names that occur in a narrative context. However, in a poem such additions may be disruptive to the poetic line. These place names often have an evocative or figurative function rather than a historical one. Poets may have included the words just for the sound of them, for some wordplay, or to evoke some mood or attitude which in our day may escape us. In such cases it may be best simply to use the transliterated name and supply a footnote.

In 1.14 of the Song of Songs, we read (NRSV):

> My beloved is to me a cluster of henna blossoms
> in the vineyards of En-gedi.

As translators we can ask why the poet mentioned this particular place. Is it significant? First, if we look at the Hebrew, we see that there may be some rhyming or assonance intended, as "En Gedi" rhymes with "my beloved is to me," found in the context. Second, if we try to identify the place, we find it described in a footnote by the New Jerusalem Bible as "a fertile oasis of vines and palms on the desolate west shore of the Dead Sea." Including such a footnote is an acceptable solution that we may choose to adopt. It is better than using a complicated description of the place within the poem itself. However, another approach is to utilize one short, evocative term such as "lush" or "fertile" to suggest what the author intended: "You are like flower blossoms from the gardens of lush En-Gedi." This will give at least some clue as to the reason for the inclusion of the name in the poem, without needing to add a footnote. If a term for "oasis" exists, we may also be able to introduce that: "My lover is like a lovely flower blooming in a desert oasis."

5.4.3 Identifying and retaining key figures

Another important task for translators is determining which terms are especially important in a given passage. Key terms or expressions may occur in one part or throughout a poem. They may express a main theme, an important biblical concept, or may serve to set the scene for the poem itself. It is important that these key elements be retained in the translation wherever they occur.

A major working procedure is that all key terms must be identified in a poem (or in a poetic book) before translation begins. Otherwise translators may substitute synonymous or dynamic terms for a word that has important links later in the text. For example, in Psalm 9 we note a kind of wordplay based on the word "gate":

> 13 Be gracious to me, O LORD!
>   Behold what I suffer from those who hate me,
>   O thou who liftest me up from **the gates** of death,
> 14 that I may recount all thy praises,
>   that in **the gates** of the daughter of Zion,
>   I may rejoice in thy deliverance.

If the translators have not studied the poem in its entirety, and if they mechanically translate line by line, they will most certainly render "gates of death" by a more generic expression, "from death," or by a more dynamically equivalent form, "from the jaws of death" or "from the hands of death." However, such a translation misses the significant contrast found in the following verse ("gates of death" contrasted with "gates of the daughter of Zion"). Translators may deliberately choose to leave out the reference to gates in both verses, as TEV has done. This version speaks more directly of God rescuing his people from death. However, this should be a conscious choice on the part of the translator and not an oversight.

Some of the richest beauty of Hebrew poetry comes from metaphors that extend over larger stretches of the discourse. In the beginning section of Isaiah 28, for example, there is a remarkable intertwining of images which begins in verse 1:

> 1 Woe to the proud **crown** of the drunkards of Ephraim,
>   and to the fading flower of its **glorious beauty**,
>   which is on the **head** of the rich valley of those overcome with wine! . . .
> 3 The proud **crown** of the drunkards of Ephraim
>   will be trodden under foot;
> 4 and the fading flower of its **glorious beauty**,
>   which is on the **head** of the rich valley,
>   will be like a first-ripe fig before the summer;

> 5 In that day the LORD of hosts will be **a crown of glory,**
>   **and a diadem of beauty** . . . .

Part of the problem for translators is actually understanding what lies behind these images. When confronted with such difficult passages, translators must first consult commentaries and translation manuals to understand the meaning of the Hebrew metaphor. For example, in this case commentators inform us that the capital city of Samaria is being ironically compared to a crown of flowers on someone's head (Watts, 1985:362). The city itself stood on top of a hill overlooking a fertile valley. The image is one of condemnation: here the crown is on the head of foolish drunkards. The flowers are drooping; the beauty of the place has faded.

This image is vividly contrasted with a future day when God himself will appear as "a crown of glory, a diadem of beauty," bringing justice and strength (verse 5). Thus there is a crucial link between verses 1 and 5.

Common language versions such as TEV and FRCL try to make some of the figurative language more understandable. For example, TEV uses the better-known name "Israel" for "Ephraim" and identifies it as a kingdom. They preserve the important link between verses 1 and 5 by keeping the expression "crown of flowers" the same in both places:

> 1 The kingdom of Israel is doomed! Its glory is **fading like the crowns of flowers** on the heads of its drunken leaders. . . .
>
> 5 A day is coming when the LORD Almighty will be like a **glorious crown of flowers** for his people . . . .

Some translations such as CEV try to make the text more intelligible to modern readers by naming the city of Samaria. The figure of drooping flowers is made very explicit and understandable. But we note that, by making the text much clearer and more straightforward, CEV loses the striking contrast between the crown on the head of drunkards (verse 1) and the LORD as the glorious crown for his people (verse 5):

> 1 The **city of Samaria**
>   above a fertile valley
>   is in for trouble!
>   Its leaders are drunkards,
>   who stuff themselves
>   with food and wine.
>   But they will **be like flowers**
>   that dry up and wilt. . . .
>
> 5 When this time comes,
>   the LORD All-Powerful
>   will be a **glorious crown**
>   for his people who survive.

Here we see a good example of the tension translators face. If the metaphor found in the original is maintained as is, most readers will probably not

127

understand it. If the meaning is made clear, the important thematic and poetic link between verses 1 and 5 is lost.

Translators should pay special attention to frequently occurring images and thematic elements that dominate a whole poem. For example, in the Song of Songs certain key figures are repeated throughout the book. These include the images of royalty and nature, and the important wine-love metaphors. These may present serious problems for translators. Perhaps vines are not grown in the target culture, or wine is not known. Translators may be tempted to simply omit these images. However, to do away with them completely would affect the entire book and destroy much of its imagery. If necessary an explanation may be included in the glossary or in an introduction; for example:

> In Israel, fruit growing on vines was cultivated to make a fermented drink called "wine." In this poem about the love between a young man and woman, the woman is compared to the field where these vines grow. Their love is compared to sweet-tasting wine. As in many cultures around the world, the feeling of love and happiness felt by a young couple is compared to the pleasant sensation given by this intoxicating drink.

At least in this way the imagery will be better understood in the context of the poem and its cultural-historical setting.

5.4.4 Creatively adapting figures of speech

Very often, when figures of speech are translated literally, they have little or no meaning for the reader. They only create confusion instead of comprehension. But translators with a good knowledge of their language and a little creativity can adapt figures of speech in such a way that the basic image is preserved and still understood.

For example, in one language, translating literally the metaphor "your eyes are doves" (Song of Songs 1.15) led to a sentence with no meaning. Not only is it difficult to understand how the woman's eyes were like doves, but more importantly, in this culture doves are not considered beautiful but rather stupid! The translator could have concentrated on rendering the meaning, "you have such beautiful eyes," but another possibility was to substitute a real object of beauty in the culture, "your eyes are like the eyes of a deer," though this takes us quite far from the original.

Sometimes just changing one word will make a certain metaphor or simile understandable. For example, in Nahum 3.12 we read:

> All your fortresses are like fig trees
>   with first-ripe figs—
> If shaken they fall
>   into the mouth of the eater.

For one translation team, translating the second set of lines literally gave an unacceptable image. However, when "hands" were substituted for "mouth," the image became clear and the figure of speech regained its effectiveness.

In Micah 7.17 the prophet says that the nations will "lick the dust like a serpent, like the crawling things of the earth." However, in many languages snakes do not "lick the dust." In one language, when the word "eat" was substituted for "lick," the metaphor became acceptable and comprehensible. Thus the striking image of the lowliness of the snake was preserved.

Translators are encouraged, then, to try to save biblical figures of speech by adapting them in little ways that will make them sound more natural in their language.

5.4.5 Eliminating figures of speech

There are times, however, when a figure of speech has no meaning, or even has the wrong meaning, when it is translated literally. In such cases it is acceptable to eliminate the figure of speech in order to preserve the intended meaning. For example, in Lam 2.1 we read (NJPSV):

> The LORD . . . has cast down from heaven to earth
> The majesty of Israel.
> He did not remember His Footstool
> On his day of wrath.

In many cultures there is no such thing as a "footstool." Even if there is such an item, if this verse is translated literally, the meaning of the verse may not be understood. In other contexts we see this image of God's footstool applied to the earth (Isa 66.1) and to the temple (Psa 99.5). It is the latter meaning that applies here. Thus, rather than trying to translate literally or to provide a detailed explanation of what a footstool is, the best solution in most cases is to drop the image altogether and to render the sense of the passage. Thus TEV substitutes the intended meaning for the figure:

> . . . Its heavenly splendor he has turned into ruins.
> On the day of his anger he abandoned even his Temple.

To give another example, in one language translators translated literally Nahum 2.7:

> its mistress is stripped, she is carried off,
> her maidens lamenting,
> mourning like doves, and beating their breasts.

But then the translators themselves realized that, from their perspective, doves do not make a mourning sound, and the figure of speech made no sense and even seemed ridiculous. However, in this culture people do "beat their breasts in sorrow." So it was felt that not much was lost if the figure of speech was eliminated. In the resulting translation the maidens lamented, cried, and beat their breasts. This was sufficient to communicate the sorrowful message of the text.

To sum up, translators must identify all extended metaphors and determine how to handle them. When dealing with limited cases, it may be necessary to sacrifice a few poetic effects in order to preserve the overall meaning of the passage. In longer passages with many references to the same figure of speech, however, translators should do their best to maintain the original imagery. When an image is especially significant, either due to its frequency ("vineyard" and "wine" in the Song of Songs) or to its theological importance (the virgin daughter in Isaiah, the unfaithful wife in Jeremiah 3), it is crucial to search for solutions that allow us to maintain the biblical image throughout the text.

5.4.6 When the meaning of a figure is uncertain

When translators have problems identifying the meaning of a figurative image, they may consult commentaries, study Bibles, dictionaries, and translation manuals. Sometimes, however, biblical metaphors can be quite obscure, and commentators either disagree or freely admit that the meaning is unclear. For example, in Isa 5.18 we find a mixture of metaphor and simile that is very difficult to understand:

> Woe to those who draw iniquity with cords of falsehood,
> who draw sin as with cart ropes.

Does the expression "those who draw iniquity with cords and cart ropes" picture people who strain and work hard to do evil? Or are they somehow bound by the evil they do? Or are lies ("cords of falsehood") leading them deeper into sin? Is there an indirect reference to an idol being pulled about the streets, as was the custom in biblical times (Watts, 1985:62)?

With so many interpretations and options available, translators may be simply overwhelmed. There are several ways to approach the problem. Translators can do one of the following:

(1) Simply give a literal rendering of the original figure of speech
(2) Give a literal rendering of the figure and add a footnote explaining the possible meaning
(3) Keep the figure but try to render it more meaningfully
(4) Eliminate the figure and adopt one possible meaning, trying to render this dynamically in the text
(5) Carry out (4) but add a footnote with a literal translation or another possible meaning

In the case of this verse, most English versions opt for the first and easiest solution (RSV, NRSV, NIV, NJB). This has the advantage of preserving the original figure and lets readers try to puzzle out for themselves what the meaning is. In some ways this is not a bad solution, since metaphors are pictures that we form in our minds. They often lose their impact if they are deciphered and made explicit.

On the other hand, if the image is so foreign as to have no sense for the modern reader or suggests a wrong meaning, translators should probably opt for one of the other solutions. For example, a cultural note may be added to a literal translation to say that idols were often drawn on carts for public display. CEV tries to retain the image but personalizes it and gives a dynamic rendering:

> You are in for trouble! The lies you tell are like ropes by which you drag along sin and evil.

TEV, on the other hand, chooses to do away completely with the details of the image—the cart, the ropes—and concentrates on one possible meaning:

> You are doomed! You are unable to break free from your sins.

In terms of readers' ease of understanding, both the CEV and TEV solutions are acceptable. Note, however, that when we take the dynamic approach, we are forced to decide on one meaning and put that in the text. This underlines another tension that translators face: whether they should preserve images, even if they are hard to understand, or choose one likely meaning, and thus rob the reader (or hearer) of other possible meanings. If images are translated literally and are somewhat accessible to readers, perhaps it is best to retain them. However, when no meaning or a wrong meaning is communicated, translators have no choice but to eliminate the figure and give the most supported rendering. Footnotes may then be used to give literal or alternative readings.

5.5 Problems with shifting persons

We have seen that a basic characteristic of Hebrew poetry is shifting persons (section 3.4.5), and that this feature poses a major problem for translators. We have also seen that these shifts have many functions. They may indicate stanza breaks, they may signal the beginning or end of a smaller poetic unit, or they may be used to highlight an important message. Shifts may also indicate an attitude such as discreteness, timidity, or boldness.

Taking Psalm 23 again as an example, we note that most versions maintain the shifting of persons present in Hebrew. Verses 1-3 refer to God as "he"; verses 4-5 address him directly as "you," while the final verse (6) refers back to "he," as seen in the following NJB version:

> 1 **Yahweh** is my shepherd, I lack nothing.
> 2 In grassy meadows **he** lets me lie.
>
>   By tranquil streams **he** leads me
> 3   to restore my spirit.
>   **He** guides me in paths of saving justice
>   as befits **his** name.

4 Even were I to walk in a ravine as dark as death
  I should fear no danger, for **you** are at my side.
  Your staff and **your** crook are there to soothe me.

5 **You** prepare a table for me
    under the eyes of my enemies;
  you anoint my head with oil;
    my cup brims over.

6 Kindness and faithful love pursue me
    every day of my life.
  I make my home in the house of **Yahweh**
    for all time to come.

This version follows the Hebrew text quite closely and shows how shifting persons helps to divide the poem up into smaller units. The preservation of the third person for God allows us to see the structural envelope around the poem, the powerful and beloved name "Yahweh."

CEV, on the other hand, takes an entirely different approach. It does away completely with the "he"–"you" shift, maintaining "you" throughout. This personalizes the poem and makes it more accessible to modern readers. Note that despite this change the inclusio "LORD" is maintained:

    You, LORD, are my shepherd.
      I will never be in need.
    You let me rest in fields
      of green grass.
    You lead me to streams
    of peaceful water
      and **you** refresh my life.

    You are true to **your** name,
    and you lead me
      along the right paths.
    I may walk through valleys
    as dark as death,
      but I won't be afraid.
    You are with me,
    and **your** shepherd's rod
      makes me feel safe.

    You treat me to a feast,
      while my enemies watch.
    You honor me as **your** guest,
    and you fill my cup
      until it overflows.

> **Your** kindness and love
> will always be with me
>   each day of my life,
> and I will live forever
>   in **your** house, **LORD**.

Translators have basically two options when dealing with such passages. They may choose to maintain the persons as in the original, or they may harmonize the passage (make the references the same, as CEV has done in the example above). If the forms of the original are maintained, good formatting techniques can help the reader understand who is speaking (see chapter 6). Sometimes footnotes may be appropriate (see RSV, Song of Songs 1.1).

However, there are times when it definitely seems better to harmonize a passage. For example, when shifting persons indicates strong emphasis in the original text, it may be better to use other signals in the translation to show that emphasis. In Psa 50.22-23, shifting persons indicates God's boldness and the certainty of his message:

> Mark this, then, you who forget **God**,
>   lest **I** rend, and there be none to deliver!
> He who brings thanksgiving as his sacrifice honors **me**;
>   to him who orders his way aright
> **I** will show the salvation of **God**!

In English, shifting persons does not normally indicate boldness, so CEV does away with this device. The message from God is direct, as it would be in a context of accusation, threat, or promise:

> You have ignored **me**!
>   So pay close attention
> or I will tear you apart,
>   and no one can help you.

> The sacrifice that honors **me**
>   is a thankful heart.
> Obey **me**, and I, **your God**,
>   will show **my** power to save.

Note that this version has captured the insistence in God's voice by combining "I, your God." This is a faithful rendering of the tone of the original.

To sum up, we can suggest a general procedure for handling passages with shifting persons. Translators should:

(1) Identify cases of shifting persons in the biblical text
(2) Determine the function of the shifting persons in this context
(3) Decide whether a literal translation would confuse the reader or be extremely unnatural

(4)   Look into how common language versions deal with the problem
(5)   Choose a solution that will best communicate the meaning and goal of
      the text

There are several ways this problem can be solved. Translators may:

(a)   Maintain the shifting persons, with the possibility of an explanatory
      footnote
(b)   Harmonize the persons in a given poem, or part of a poem

If the second approach is taken, they may adopt some other stylistic means to convey the discourse function of the shifting person.

Common language versions such as TEV, FRCL, and CEV can serve as good models for how to handle this difficult but very frequent translation problem.

5.6 Basic approaches to translating poetry

Many people believe that there is no such thing as a true translation. As noted in the Preface, many feel "there is always something lost in the translation." If this is true for narrative texts, how much more so is it for poetic ones! Translators have a number of options, however, to help them through the more difficult problems.

5.6.1 Footnotes

If we look at translations of poetry world-wide—for example, Japanese, Chinese, or Indian poetry—we find that secular translators often resort to footnotes to explain certain images or facts that readers do not know or may overlook. As suggested throughout this book, Bible translators can also make use of footnotes. However, translations of the Old Testament will need to include footnotes referring to textual problems, and most will include notes explaining important social or historical facts. With all these notes being necessary, it does not seem very practical to introduce additional footnotes explaining poetic characteristics of the original. However, footnotes should be maintained when there is a prominent or meaningful wordplay. Certainly if we are preparing a study Bible, we should consider including some footnotes about prominent stylistic features.

5.6.2 A more literal approach

Many translations being done today are common language translations. This means that translators consciously choose to translate the meaning of the text in a dynamic and natural way, rather than to follow the literal form of the original text. However, this can result in a totally flat translation. According to this procedure poetry is not differentiated from narratives or historical texts in any way. One approach is for translators of common language versions to consider poetry as a special genre that demands a more literal translation. That is, translators may want to use principles of dynamic translation when translating historical books, but apply a more literal approach when dealing with poetry. This means that the form of a poem will be left more or less intact, so that the reader can interact with the original images in the poem.

For example, consider the following Chinese poem from the Ming dynasty, "A Lady Picking Flowers" by Shen Chou (Chaves, 172):

> Last year we parted as the flowers began to bloom.
> Now the flowers bloom again, and you still have not returned.
> Purple grief, red sorrow—a hundred thousand kinds,
> and the spring wind blows each of them into my hands.

From the context we know that the poet is making a connection between the emotions he feels and the flowers he sees around him. We note two outstanding expressions, "purple grief" and "red sorrow." Normally emotions do not have colors, but here the poet has assigned them some. This is part of the poet's technique and a mark of his creativity. Beside the fact that emotions have been assigned a color, there is another surprise: the colors assigned do not correspond to what we expect in our English-speaking culture. Purple and red do not usually indicate grief and sorrow. Rather, we would think of gray or black. But here the English-speaking translator has respected the Chinese poet's choice of words. In other words, he has not sought to substitute culturally relevant expressions. He has given us a more literal translation. Yet even though the resulting product is somewhat foreign, we may understand the poet's intent and his emotion, and we are touched.

Some translators of poetry may wish to follow the same approach to translating Hebrew poetry. If translations of poetry are a little more literal than other nonpoetic texts, readers have a chance to come into more direct contact with the poet and the poem. They are encouraged to appreciate the flavor of the culture behind the poem.

Another reason for taking a more literal approach is that poems often have multiple meanings. In the following poem a Chinese poet from the Ch'ing Dynasty, Fu Pao-shih, writes about Wu-ling Stream, which is lined with peach trees and leads to a lost land, Peach Blossom Spring (Chaves, 416):

> At the mouth of Wu-ling Stream,
> petals bright like clouds;
> in a boat I follow them,
> more and more inspired.
> Then return to my little home—
> the feeling still with me:
> brushtip filled with springtime rain
> I paint this flowering peach.

In this poem the poet goes on a journey (real or unreal?) and comes home inspired. Then, with "brushtip filled with springtime rain," he "paints a flowering peach." Is this last line literal or figurative? Is the poet actually painting a picture of a peach blossom? (We know that many Chinese poets painted alongside their written work.) Or is he talking in a figurative way about

135

the very poem he is writing? Both ideas come to us, and we may conclude that the author really intended both meanings. For this reason it seems right to translate literally, to give the reader the chance to see the two possibilities.

Thus, in translating biblical poetry, one option is to be more conservative, keeping poetic images as they are in the original. The purpose is to allow readers to figure out the poem for themselves, feel the impact of unusual language, and interpret as many meanings as they can find.

5.6.3 Freer approaches: "re-creation"

While some translators may decide to take a more literal approach to translating poetry, still others choose to have a freer hand. One such approach is "re-creation" (Wendland, 1993; Sterk, 1994). In this method the translator first studies the poem, trying to understand all the poetic devices in the original poem as well as its intended message. Then, with much more freedom, translator-poets re-create, in their own words and with their own literary genres, a poem that is functionally equivalent to the original. The goal is to write a poem that has the same purpose and the same content, and which also conveys the same impact and emotions. For example, the following is a genuine genre-for-genre translation of Psa 22.1 in Chichewa:

> *Haa! Mulungu'anga, mwandisiyiranji?*
> *Mulungu wanga, mwanditaya kodi?*
> *Nanga kukhala kutaliku n'chiani?*
> *Kundithandiza kwakanikadi zedi!*
> *Ine kubuula mwanu m'khutu sikumveka.*

> Aagh! M'God, why have you deserted me?
> My God, have you really cast me aside?
> What else could this aloofness mean?
> To help me you have flatly refused!
> This groaning of mine in your ear is not being heard.

For this method to work, however, the translator must have considerable poetic talent, and the consultant must be very vigilant to make sure that no ideas are added, overemphasized, or left out. This approach can be successful only when translator-poets understand the limitations of faithfulness to the content that is placed on them by the biblical text.

5.6.4 Final suggestions

Whether a team takes a more literal approach or a freer one will depend on the translation team itself and the community for whom they are translating. Are there poets available who can re-create a poem? Are there time constraints on when the translation must be finished? What kind of translation do the readers want or expect?

Indeed, translators may have to combine approaches, at times sticking very closely to the original language, and at others being more creative. One good rule of thumb is to try a more literal approach first. If the images transfer easily into the language of translation and can be understood and appreciated despite their foreignness, then they may, and perhaps should, be preserved. However, when certain lines make no sense whatsoever, when the wrong meaning is conveyed, or when the outcome is very far from what is considered poetic in the target language, translators are forced to take a more creative approach and use dynamic equivalents to get the message across.

If images must be adapted, there are some limitations. The essential content and function of the original text must be preserved. Furthermore, translators should be careful not to bring in images that are foreign to the biblical context. For example, translators should avoid referring to items that are modern or are out of place in a biblical context. We do not want to transform biblical poetry into today's image, but to render—with as much beauty as possible—what is in the original text.

Questions for review

1. Consider the following parallel lines from Psa 6.1-2. Decide if it would be helpful to reduce the pairs to one line each in your language, or if the two lines should be maintained. Give reasons for your decisions.

> O LORD, rebuke me not in thy anger,
>   nor chasten me in thy wrath.
> Be gracious to me, O LORD, for I am languishing;
>   O LORD, heal me, for my bones are troubled.

2. Study the following passage from Song of Songs 3.7-8:

> About it are sixty mighty men
>   of the mighty men of Israel,
> all girt with swords
>   and expert in war,
> each with his sword at his thigh,
>   against alarms by night.

How many swords does each soldier have? How will you handle the repetition in your language?

3. Evaluate the following translation of Song of Songs 5.14. What is wrong with this translation? Can you suggest something better?

> His hands are gold rings
>   where they placed a stone called "chrysolite."
> His body is the polished tooth of an elephant,
>   where they placed a stone called "safire."

4. Consider each of the following passages where there is a shift in person. What does the shift in person indicate in each context? What is the best translation solution in your language: harmonizing or keeping the original person shift? If you choose to harmonize, can the function of the shift be expressed in another way? If so, tell how.

1. Psalm 50.13-15
2. Psalm 18.26-30
3. Psalm 13
4. Psalm 23

5. Consider the following translation of Psalm 1 (Peterson). How have the original images and poetic devices been handled? What are some of the strong points of the translation? What are the weaknesses or drawbacks? Should your translation adapt or update the psalms like this? Explain your answer.

> How well God must like you—
>   you don't hang out at Sin Saloon,
>   you don't slink along Dead-End Road,
>   you don't go to Smart-Mouth College.
>
> Instead you thrill to Yahweh's Word,
>   you chew on Scripture day and night.
> You're a tree replanted in Eden,
>   bearing fresh fruit every month,
> Never dropping a leaf,
>   always in blossom.
>
> You're not at all like the wicked,
>   who are mere windblown dust—
> Without defense in court,
>   unfit company for innocent people.
>
> Yahweh charts the road you take.
> The road *they* take is Skid Row.

6. Consider the various problems that have been discussed in this chapter. Which one seems to give the most difficulty in your language, and why is this the case?

7. Have you encountered any other problems in the translation of biblical poetry that have not been dealt with in this chapter? If so, briefly explain what the problem is, and give an example from your language.

Chapter 6:

The Importance of Format:
Lining Up the Poetic Text on the Printed Page

6.1 Introduction

In chapter 1 we saw that there is a basic distinction between poetry and prose. Though in the original text Hebrew poetry was not placed in lines, most poems are made up of parallel or measured lines that balance and correspond to each other in various ways (section 3.2.1). In much the same way that sentences in a prose text are grouped together into paragraphs, poetic lines are grouped together into strophes or stanzas. This means that poems have a different format or arrangement than prose texts.

In chapter 1 we also learned that in poetry, form and meaning are connected in a much closer way than in prose texts. How words are used and how they are arranged contribute a great deal to what the text means. That is why it is important for readers to be able to recognize poetry even before they begin to read a text. In this chapter we will discuss the importance of formatting poetic text and will give some suggestions for lining up texts on the printed page in an effective way.

6.2 The shape of the translated text

What happens to a translated poetic text when we transform it into print? What happens to the natural format of the original poetry? This depends first of all on how the source text has been translated. If a poetic text such as a psalm has been translated as prose, then much of the original Hebrew structure will be lost. The form of the poem may be sacrificed in order to preserve the meaning, or to maintain a natural, clear style in the language of the translation. Similarly, if a poem has been adapted or made to conform to a certain genre in the target language, much of the ordering and arrangement of the original will be lost. On the other hand, if a more literal translation is done, then it is possible to preserve, at least to some extent, the parallel lines and stanza forms of the Hebrew. Of course, as we noted in the preceding chapter, such conservative renderings can also be made to sound natural or dynamic, depending on the skill of the translators and how well they can apply their talents to the various poetic features of the text.

6.3 Displaying a poetic text on the printed page

One of the most important factors involved in the recognition and appreciation of a text as poetry is how the text is displayed on the printed page (Louw and

Wendland, 1993). Readers have a certain expectation as to how poetry should look in print. This affects their perception and even their interpretation of the text. Consider the following example:

> Happy are those who reject the advice of evil people, who do not follow the example of sinners or join those who have no use for God. Instead, they find joy in obeying the Law of the LORD, and they study it day and night. They are like trees that grow beside a stream, that bear fruit at the right time, and whose leaves do not dry up. They succeed in everything they do. But evil people are not like this at all; they are like straw that the wind blows away. Sinners will be condemned by God and kept apart from God's own people. The righteous are guided and protected by the LORD, but the evil are on the way to their doom.

If we were to ask where this passage comes from, some might guess it is taken from a New Testament epistle such as James or Jude. In fact it is Psalm 1 presented in a prose format. Even though there are poetic images, we do not recognize this text as a poem. Though there are parallel lines, we cannot immediately identify them. We would need to study the text carefully and write out the text in poetic lines to see the real structure of the text. Presenting a poem in prose format is not helpful to readers because it does not highlight any of the poetic features in the text. Nevertheless, this is the way many common language versions render some important poetic passages.

Another method of formatting is to set off every verse as its own separate unit. The text is spread out on the page to line up with the left and right margins. These are called "justified" margins. King James and some modern versions such as Living Bible use this type of formatting. Consider Psalm 1 again, this time in the King James Version:

> 1 Blessed is the man that walketh not in the counsel of the ungodly, nor standeth in the way of sinners, nor sitteth in the seat of the scornful.
>
> 2 But his delight is in the law of the LORD; and in his law doth he meditate day and night.
>
> 3 And he shall be like a tree planted by the rivers of water, that bringeth forth his fruit in his season; his leaf also shall not wither; and whatsoever he doeth shall prosper.
>
> 4 The ungodly are not so: but are like the chaff which the wind driveth away.
>
> 5 Therefore the ungodly shall not stand in the judgment, nor sinners in the congregation of the righteous.

> 6 For the LORD knoweth the way of
> the righteous: but the way of the un-
> godly shall perish.

Note, however, that in this type of formatting as well, readers cannot readily see that they are dealing with a poem. We cannot see any parallel lines, and there are no stanza divisions. This text is also difficult to read because there are hyphenated words. Again, this manner of displaying the text does not really help readers to interpret the passage as a poem.

Fortunately some modern translations in English and other major languages pay much more attention to the poetic format of the text on the printed page. Such versions try to indicate poetic lines in the text and often mark off distinct stanza divisions. In the Zondervan edition of the New Revised Standard Version reproduced below, we note that the text looks much more like a poem. There is a clear break marking a new stanza at verse 4:

> [1] Happy are those
> who do not follow the
> advice of the wicked,
> or take the path that sinners
> tread,
> or sit in the seat of
> scoffers;
> [2] but their delight is in the law
> of the LORD,
> and on his law they
> meditate day and night.
> [3] They are like trees
> planted by streams of
> water,
> which yield their fruit in its
> season,
> and their leaves do not
> wither.
> In all that they do, they
> prosper.
>
> [4] The wicked are not so,
> but are like chaff that the
> wind drives away.
> [5] Therefore the wicked will not
> stand in the judgment,
> nor sinners in the
> congregation of the
> righteous;
> [6] for the LORD watches over the
> way of the righteous,

> but the way of the wicked
> will perish.

While this formatting is much improved over the two types seen above, it still has some serious weaknesses. This publication has followed the standard procedure of printing the Bible in a two-column format, which means that there is often not enough space for the poetic lines to be printed as a single line without running past the right-hand margin onto the next line. When there is a new line in a verse, it is indented one space. When any line runs over, the remainder of the line is indented yet another space.

The most serious consequence of this type of formatting procedure is that poetic lines are ended or divided in very awkward places. The result is a series of broken utterances. For example, in verse 1, one line reads "who do not follow the." In verse 6 we find "for the LORD watches over the." Many noun phrases are split up: "seat of scoffers" (verse 1), "law of the LORD" (verse 2), "streams of water" (verse 3), and others. Verb phrases are also divided: "do not wither" (verse 3).

But there are other problems as well. It is not at all clear which words should be indented one space or several spaces. For example, in verse 3, three parallel descriptions of the tree follow the first line, and the concluding remark "In all they do, they prosper" has been put in line with the three descriptive phrases. But this sentence is in fact an independent statement and seems to need a distinguishing format.

Indenting new lines by one space does not allow the reader to see that two lines may be exactly parallel, as they would appear if they were put side by side. For example, it may be more helpful for the reader to see that lines match in a systematic way, as in verse 2:

> but their delight is in the law of the LORD,
> and on his law they meditate day and night.

This artificial system of formatting has other negative consequences. A single poetic line such as "nor sinners in the congregation of the righteous" (verse 5) may be spread over three formatted lines. There are many isolated words and obvious spaces, so the page does not appear neatly ordered. This mechanical procedure of typesetting greatly hinders the readability of the text. Since natural groupings of words are not preserved, when readers read out loud or silently, they will have trouble knowing how to group words and when to pause. This in turn also affects how the text is understood, because the meaningful parallels and correspondences or contrasts between the paired lines and larger units are not immediately evident.

One recent version that tries to take poetic format into account is the new CEV. Compared to the formatting of the NRSV seen above, the page formatting of CEV looks much more ordered. Though this version also follows the standard procedure of two columns, an attempt is made to break only where there are natural divisions in the translated text. Most major groupings of words (noun phrases, relative clauses, and verb phrases) appear on the same line. Strophe divisions are clearly marked. Because of this type of formatting, the text is much easier to read, and some poetic features of the original are highlighted. In verses 1 and 5, for example, the original parallelism can be seen, and the verses retain some of the rhythm of the Hebrew:

[1] God blesses those people
   who refuse evil advice
   and won't follow sinners
   or join in sneering at God.
[2] Instead, the Law of the LORD
   makes them happy,
   and they think about it
   day and night.

[3] They are like trees
   growing beside a stream,
   trees that produce
   fruit in season
   and always have leaves.
   Those people succeed
   in everything they do.

[4] That isn't true of those
   who are evil,
   because they are like straw
   blown by the wind.
[5] Sinners won't have an excuse
   on the day of judgment,
   and they won't have a place
   with the people of God.
[6] The LORD protects everyone
   who follows him,
   but the wicked follow a road
   that leads to ruin.

Of course, to format a text like this forces translators to make a number of decisions. Where are the strophe breaks? Which lines are parallel? Thus, in verse 3 in the above example, we may question whether bringing "fruit in season" out to the main line of indentation is justified. We can also ask what motivated the strophe divisions. Should verse 3 begin a new strophe, when it continues the description of the righteous person begun in verse 1? Why is verse 6 attached to verses 4-5, when there is a change of subject (the LORD), and it seems that this is a separate unit marking the end of the poem? Questions of formatting bring us back to the original text, to think about how a poem is structured in Hebrew and what the intent of the author was.

Another version that seems to take text formatting seriously is *God's Word*. It uses only a single column of print, thereby allowing most poetic lines to stand on their own without running over to the next line. Furthermore, the indentation of lines is used to highlight important parallels that occur in the original. The following is how Psalm 1 looks in this version (slightly modified in verse 5 due to the length of the lines). Notice that this formatting also highlights the structure of the poem. There are three strophes that become progressively shorter: verses 1-3 describe the righteous person, verses 4 and 5 describe the wicked person, and verse 6 gives the conclusion:

[1] Blessed is the person who does not
    follow the advice of wicked people,
      take the path of sinners,
        or join the company of mockers.
[2] Rather, he delights in the teachings of the LORD
    and reflects on his teachings day and night.
[3] He is like a tree planted beside streams—
    a tree that produces fruit in season
    and whose leaves do not wither.
He succeeds in everything he does.

[4] Wicked people are not like that.
    Instead, they are like husks that the wind blows away.
[5]   That is why wicked people will not be able to stand in the judgment
      and sinners will not be able to stand where righteous people gather.

[6] The LORD knows the way of righteous people,
    but the way of wicked people will end.

This version comes a long way in helping the reader to identify the text as a poem right from the start, to discern its overall structure (in terms of the strophes), and to appreciate parallel lines.

6.4 Special problems in formatting
Each book in the Old Testament is unique. Therefore special consideration should be given to different formatting styles for each book. Below, however, we consider some general issues that may affect many Old Testament books.

6.4.1 Mixed genres
We have noted that there is not always a neat division between poetry and prose. While no one would dispute that the Song of Songs is poetry, things are not so clear-cut in other books. Parts of Isaiah, for example, appear to be written in prose, while other parts are clearly poetry.

When confronted with such a situation, some versions have simply picked a single genre and formatted the entire book in the same way. This is the case in some common language versions. But a more helpful approach is to recognize that books may contain various genres. Therefore it is necessary to translate and to format each section of the book in a way fitting each particular passage. This does not mean that every section of poetry in the Hebrew Bible will be rendered as poetry in the translation. It does mean, however, that literary units must be examined on their own, and decisions must be made about each one in keeping with its particular style and function.

For example, the book of Ecclesiastes contains a mixture of genres. There are passages that are clearly narrative, as when Qoheleth (the teacher or speaker) describes his building activities (2.4-6). There are passages that are clearly poems: 1.4-11; 3.1-8. There are also sets of proverbs throughout the book: 7.1-8; 10.8, 9, 11 (to name only a few). There are also other passages that involve debate. Some scholars see these sections as proverbs or poems, while others think they are poetic prose (for example, 12.1-8).

With the exception of the time poem (3.1-8), some versions flatten out all these genres and translate the entire book in prose (TEV, REB, FRCL). At times this makes it hard for the reader to see the style and the logical intent of the writer. Qoheleth often quotes various bits of wisdom literature to make a point. For example, in 4.1 Qoheleth begins a section on oppression. He leads off with a prose statement and then cites a poem. If we compare the two versions below, however, we see that in one (REB) we cannot tell that a poem is being quoted, while in the other (NIV) this is very clear:

REB:
> Again, I considered all the acts of oppression perpetrated under the sun; I saw the tears of the oppressed, and there was no one to comfort them. Power was on the side of their oppressors, and there was no one to afford comfort.

NIV (Single column version):
> Again I looked and saw all the oppression that was taking place under the sun:
>
> > I saw the tears of the oppressed—
> > > and they have no comforter;
> > power was on the side of their oppressors—
> > > and they have no comforter.

In NIV the poem is indented and separated from the prose text by a blank line. Parallel lines become very clear, and in fact two items stand out, as was certainly the intent of the author: "oppress" and "no comforter." Hebrew speakers certainly were able to recognize that a poem was being recited at this point. Proper formatting will help modern readers to realize the same thing. It will also assist public readers to articulate the text more clearly, thus benefiting hearers as well.

However, formatting mixed genres is no easy task. Scholars often differ as to where various genres begin and end. For example, in the case of chapter 5 of Ecclesiastes, NAB interprets the opening verses as containing a prose statement followed by a proverb:

Be not hasty in your utterance and let not your heart be quick to make a promise in God's presence. God is in heaven and you are on earth; therefore let your words be few.

2 For nightmares come with many cares,
      and a fool's utterance with many words.

3 When you make a vow to God, delay not its fulfillment. For God has no pleasure in fools; fulfill what you have vowed.

NIV, on the other hand, considers even the first lines, "Be not hasty . . . ," to be a proverb or poem, and puts the lines in a poetic format. Faced with such difficult decisions, translators can consult commentaries, translation manuals, and many different versions to see how various passages are analyzed and laid out on the printed page. If it can be determined that there are mixed genres in the text, then proper formatting will help the reader to see this at a glance.

Translators should not be afraid of mixing format types. Poems and proverbs are mixed into narrative texts, beginning with Genesis (2.23; 3.14-19; 4.23, 24) and continuing throughout the Old Testament (Exodus 15; Judges 5; Ruth 1.16-17, to name only a few). Setting these portions out in a poetic format will help rather than hinder the reader. And it must be stressed that, if one reads a text properly, those who are listening will be helped as well.

6.4.2 Formatting envelope structures

We have seen that envelope structures are a typical feature of Hebrew literature (section 3.2.4). Especially when there is a refrain-type phrase, poems can be laid out in such a way that readers can easily see the envelope or inclusio pattern. For example, in Psalm 8 translators can leave an empty line between the envelope and the rest of the poem, or even boldface the enveloped verses, thus highlighting the special structure of this psalm:

O LORD, our Lord,
   how majestic is thy name in all the earth!

Thou whose glory above the heavens is chanted
   by the mouths of babes and infants,
thou hast founded a bulwark because of thy foes,
   to still the enemy and the avenger.

When I look at thy heavens, the work of thy fingers,
   the moon and the stars which thou hast established;
what is man that thou art mindful of him,
   and the son of man that thou dost care for him?

Yet thou hast made him a little less than God,
   and dost crown him with glory and honor.

Thou hast given him dominion over the works of thy hands;
　　thou hast put all things under his feet,
all sheep and oxen,
　　and also the beasts of the field,
the birds of the air, and the fish of the sea,
　　whatever passes along the paths of the sea.

O LORD, our Lord,
　　how majestic is thy name in all the earth!

In the book of Ecclesiastes an envelope structure surrounds the whole book. The phrase "Vanity of vanities, says the Teacher, all is vanity" appears as the book opens (1.2) and as it closes (12.8). In fact this envelope seems to be very significant. Some scholars believe that the material both before and after these lines was added by a later editor. Whether this is the case or not, proper formatting will help readers to see this stylistic feature of the book. That is, these two verses should be separated from the rest of the text, possibly with blank space around them (or perhaps even in a special kind of print such as italics), allowing the reader to clearly see this poetic device. A note may be added to the introduction to explain the significance of this format.

6.4.3 Formatting for understanding

We know that many features of Bibles today were not present in the original. For example, verse numbers and chapter divisions were added at a much later date. According to modern studies, not all these divisions are correct. For example, in Ecclesiastes the division between chapters 6 and 7 seems artificial. At the end of chapter 6, Qoheleth asks "For who knows what is good (*tov*) for man while he lives the few days of his vain life, which he passes like a shadow? For who can tell man what will be after him under the sun?" The Hebrew word *tov* or its root occurs repeatedly in the beginning of chapter 7. In fact we can say that here Qoheleth is answering the question he asked in 6.12:

[1]　A good (*tov*) name is better (*tov*) than precious ointment;
　　　and the day of death, than the day of birth.

[2]　It is better (*tov*) to go to the house of mourning
　　　　than to go to the house of feasting;
　　　for this is the end of all men,
　　　　and the living will lay it to heart.

[3]　Sorrow is better (*tov*) than laughter,
　　　　for by sorrow of countenance the heart is made glad (*t-v*).

Most versions follow the traditional division and leave several lines of space between chapters 6 and 7. But this hinders the reader from seeing that there is a close connection in the original text. NJB, however, does a very good job of showing that chapter 7 is an answer to the end of chapter 6 through its formatting procedures. Verses 6.11-12 are grouped with chapter 7, with only one intervening line, so that it is clear that 7.1 and the following verses answer the question in 6.12:

> 11 The more we say, the more futile it is: what good can we derive from it? 12 And who knows what is best for someone during life, during the days of futile life which are spent like a shadow? Who can tell anyone what will happen after him under the sun?

>> 1 Better a good name than costly oil,
>> the day of death than the day of birth.
>> 2 Better go to the house of mourning
>> than to the house of feasting . . . .

This kind of formatting according to the original discourse structure helps the reader see the important logical connections and breaks in the text. We also note that this version makes a good attempt at distinguishing mixed genres, that is, by formatting prose as prose and proverbs as proverbs.

6.4.4 Formatting the Song of Songs

The Song of Songs is a particularly difficult text, because in the original there is no indication of how many characters there are and who is speaking. In the majority of cases, however, scholars agree on who is speaking, and in many versions poems are formatted to show when there is a change of speaker. Usually this is done by leaving an extra line between the different speeches. Many versions go even farther by identifying in the margin or in italics who they think the speaker is (TEV, CEV, FRCL, REB, NJB). They insert "young woman" and "young man," "he" and "she," "bride" and "bridegroom," or similar expressions to allow the reader to know who is speaking. CEV similarly adds indications of who is speaking in the book of Job and in Lamentations.

Without such helps these books would be extremely difficult to follow. So translators are encouraged to follow the majority of versions in providing this special format. In the Song of Songs there are a few passages where scholars cannot decide on who the speaker is. In this case the best approach is to pick one interpretation and use that in the text. If necessary a note may be added stating that some scholars believe that another person is speaking. A proper formatting of this book will go a long way in assisting readers to understand the meaning of the individual poems, and also to help them see how the book fits together as a whole.

6.5 The importance of punctuation

One way to help readers is to use punctuation that is clear and straightforward. Generally speaking, a **period** (.) marks the end of a sentence or a complete thought. A **comma** (,) marks a pause within a sentence. **Semicolons** (;) may be used to join independent clauses in a compound sentence. In most languages **questions** and **exclamations** are indicated by special markers at the end of the sentence: **?** and **!** (Spanish marks both the beginning and end of such sentences). In many languages a **colon** (:) is used after an independent clause to introduce a list of items, to expand on an idea, or to introduce a quote. If there is already a substantial literature in the language, translators should attempt to follow standard principles of punctuation in that language. Punctuation should be determined by what is natural in the language, not by what appears in any base text. Remember that the ancient Hebrew text had no punctuation!

In some versions, especially the more literal ones, we note a great number of semicolons (;), as seen in a sample below from KJV:

> [3] And he shall be like a tree planted
> by the rivers of water, that bringeth forth
> his fruit in his season; his leaf also shall
> not wither; and whatsoever he doeth shall
> prosper.

Sentences joined by semicolons are often confusing. The reader doesn't know whether there is to be a full stop or merely a pause. The relationship between the sentences is not clearly defined. Similarly, in some versions colons are used in a way that does not correspond to modern usage (KJV):

> [6] For the LORD knoweth the way of
> the righteous: but the way of the ungodly
> shall perish.

Contrary to the way colons are used in modern English, this colon introduces a contrasting thought.

This shows why translators should never blindly copy punctuation as they find it in a base text. In verse 3 above, the text would be easier to read and to understand if the passage were broken up into at least two independent sentences, even if a poetic format is not used:

> And he shall be like a tree planted by
> the rivers of water, that bringeth forth his
> fruit in his season. His leaf also shall not
> wither, and whatsoever he doeth shall
> prosper.

Simple periods and commas are sufficient to guide the reader here. In verse 6 a comma could easily replace the colon. While generally it is the case that long sentences should be avoided to promote easy reading, some languages do favor long series of clauses, each marked off by a short pause. If translators are dealing with such a language, they may wish to follow this style in the translation. If sentences are punctuated properly, with commas marking each breath group, readers should have no problem understanding the text. To test punctuation, texts should always be read out loud to make certain that the utterances flow naturally.

The point to remember is that punctuation is a key to reading and to understanding any text, but it is especially important in poetic passages, which are very likely to be read out loud.

6.6 Guidelines for formatting

Rules that have already been established for printing are very difficult to change or modify. However, there are a number of steps translators can take to improve the presentation of their translated texts. It is recommended that translators think about details for formatting before they begin translating biblical poetry. Decisions taken at this early stage may not be final, but keeping these issues in mind from the beginning can save a lot of time at the end of the project.

1. **Study various formats for poetry and decide which is best for your translation.** Due to various factors beyond their control, some translators will be obliged to follow the standard two-column format. However, some teams may be able to negotiate with the printer or publisher for a single-column format in the Psalms and in other poetic books.

2. **Be careful about how words are combined on a line**. If possible, natural word groups should not be broken up. For example, short noun phrases such as "the teachings of the LORD" should appear on only one line. If there are relative clauses or other short dependent clauses such as "whose leaves do not wither," these should not be broken up.

If at all possible, hyphenated words should be kept to a minimum. When dealing with typesetters, translators must be very specific about how words may be divided. Sometimes an unjustified right-hand margin may be used.

3. **Pay close attention to the strophe divisions in each poem**. Very often versions do not divide poems in the same way. Before beginning to translate a poem, translators should see how various versions divide it up. Considering the principles given in section 3.8, and considering their own analysis of the poem, they can decide where strophe divisions should be marked. Most often their decisions will agree with reliable models such as TEV, CEV, or NIV. But translators may propose a different division if they have well-founded reasons for doing so. Unless they are well trained in discourse principles and in Hebrew, however, it will be wise to check their proposals with a consultant.

Languages often differ as to the preferred length of strophes in the various types of poetic text. As with many issues in translation, translators will feel a tension between wanting to preserve what is basic to the original text and wanting to adapt to what is natural in their own language. Some languages do not tolerate very long strophes. If this is the case, it is possible to break poems up into groups of shorter strophes. But again, it will be wise to consult someone trained in discourse analysis and in Hebrew, to make sure that these divisions do not distort the meaning of the text.

Strophe divisions should be clearly marked in the text from the very first draft. Furthermore, it is necessary for translators to work hand-in-hand with manuscript examiners, typesetters, and printers, to let them know that sections of poetry in their text have been set out in a purposeful way.

4. If possible, **arrange poetic lines to highlight any parallelism**, as seen in the CEV example below:

> God blesses those people
> who refuse evil advice
> and won't follow sinners
> or join in sneering at God.

5. **Think about the role of punctuation**. Use standard punctuation for the language. Avoid blindly following the punctuation found in foreign versions used as base or model texts. Read the text aloud, and let the natural breaks in the translation guide the placement of punctuation. Punctuation marks should be chosen with the average reader in mind.

6. Type the poem on the page exactly as you want it printed. **Read the text out loud, to see if it flows smoothly as formatted and punctuated**. If possible, lines should match natural intonation patterns in the language. This will help to make certain that the translation is well received and understood.

6.7 A practical example

The following is an experimental version of Psalm 1 prepared in Chichewa, a language of South-Central Africa. It was finalized during a workshop on how to translate Scripture using poetic genres from target languages. A specific genre known as *ndakatulo* was chosen. This genre has many interesting poetic features: ideophones, figurative language, rhythmic diction, condensed expression, variations in word order, additional grammatical suffixes, concrete and graphic vocabulary, exclamations, intensifiers, as well as many types of sound effects. This translation is intended for an oral performance. What is interesting is that the poets have tried to make each line a single complete breath span and one natural intonation group. The English translation following the poem is a fairly literal rendering of the Chewa text that highlights word order parallels.

> *Kudalatu munthu woongoka—*
> *nzeru za oipa samverako,*
> *m'njira ya ochimwa sayendamo,*
> *onyoza Chauta sakhala nawo.*
> *Koma kukhosi mbee! akamva mau,*
> *ee, malamulo a Mulungu apo ndipo,*
> *usana ndi usiku mtima amaikapo,*
> *kusinkhasinkhatu salekezako.*
> *Ameneyu afanafana ndi mtengo—*
> *mtengo womera mwa mtsinje wosaphwa.*
> *Zipatso zili psa! pokhwima,*

onse masamba ali biliwiliwili!
Pakutero ndiko kukhoza iyeyo,
zonse zidzamuyendera bwinodi!

Nanga oipa nkutero kodi?
Ha! mpang'ono pomwedi!
Kunena iwo, angonga gaga—
mungu wouluka ndi mphepo,
angoti mwaa! basi, watha mwai!
Zimene adzaona nzothetsa nzeru.
Mulungu mwini mlandu adzawazenga,
chiweruzo chidzawagwera tsikulo.
Pampingo wa okhulupirika adzawachotsatu,
sadzakhala nawo pamsonkhano waodala.
Chonco, pali olungame ndi ochimwa:
ochita zabwino ali thi! m'manja mwa Chauta,
koma ochita zoipa Iye adzawataya psiti!
Motero anthu adziwe kui Mulungu alipodi!

How blessed is the straight person—
the wisdom of the wicked he pays no heed,
the way of sinners he does not walk in,
the despisers of Yahweh he has no part with.
But his neck is *MBEE!* clear, as he hears the Words,
yes, the laws of God, that's where he's at,
day and night his heart is placed there,
deep meditation he never gives up.
This sort of person resembles a tree—
a tree growing alongside a drought-proof stream.
Its fruit are *PSYU!* fully ripe at the right time,
all its leaves are *BILIWILIWILI!* bright green.
Herein lies the success of that one,
everything will go great for him!

Now does the same thing happen for the wicked, do you think?
Ha! no, it's not the least bit similar.
As for them, they are like husks—
like a piece of chaff carried off by the wind,
they go *MWAA!* straight up and away, that's it,
their fortune is finished!
What they are going to see is quite shocking,
judgment will befall them that day.
From the congregation of the righteous they will be removed,
they will not remain in the assembly of the blessed.
So there we have the righteous and sinners:
the faithful are *THI!* all together in the hands of Yahweh,

but those who do evil He will cast them *PSITI!* completely away.
Thus people ought to realize that there is indeed a God!

Looking at the psalm in Chichewa as it appears on the printed page, readers can readily identify it as a poem with two strophes. No word groups are broken up. There are no dangling words at the end of lines. Punctuation is particular to the language (note the exclamation point [!] after ideophones), but simple and straightforward. The last line, which was added as a kind of conclusion, may have to be modified in a written version. Nevertheless, both in translation and formatting, this rendering of Psalm 1 is clearly a success.

Translators should be encouraged to do their own experimenting while translating or re-creating a poem. They should pay special attention to intonation and tonal patterns, as well as to breath groups, so that hearers will easily understand what is being read. This kind of careful work will lead to overall clarity on the printed page as well. Certainly well-organized and well-formatted material will be easier to read, to understand, and to remember.

6.8 Conclusion

In chapter 1 we have stressed that form is part of the total meaning of a poem. If this is true, then how a poem is formatted or set out on the printed page contributes significantly to how it is read and interpreted. Formatting is an area that has been seriously neglected in the past. Yet we have seen how important the "packaging" of a message is. Every effort should be made to make poetry recognizable to readers. Translated poems should appear on a page in a way that highlights their patterned structure and poetic features. This will help make a somewhat difficult genre more accessible to readers.

Questions for Reflection

1. Consider the following rendering of Eccl 12.1-7 from NRSV. Rewrite this passage, formatting the verses and lines in a way that highlights the poetic features of this text. The punctuation may be modified.

Remember your creator in the days of your youth, before the days of trouble come, and the years draw near when you will say, "I have no pleasure in them"; 2 before the sun and the light and the moon and the stars are darkened and the clouds return with the rain; 3 in the day when the guards of the house tremble, and the strong men are bent, and the women who grind cease working because they are few, and those who look through the windows see dimly; 4 when the doors on the street are shut, and the sound of the grinding is low, and one rises up at the sound of a bird, and all the daughters of song are brought low; 5 when one is afraid of heights, and terrors are in the road; the almond tree blossoms, the grasshopper drags itself along and desire fails; because all must go to their eternal home, and the mourners will go about the streets; 6 before the silver cord is snapped, and the golden bowl is broken, and the pitcher is broken at the fountain, and the wheel broken at the cistern, 7 and the dust returns to the earth as it was, and the breath returns to God who gave it.

After you have completed this exercise on your own, check several modern versions to see how this passage has been formatted there. Where do the major differences occur and what are these? Which version do you find the easiest to read aloud? Which is the most difficult? Give reasons.

2. Study Isaiah 52.13–53.12 in TEV, CEV, NIV, and (N)RSV. What difference in text formatting do you notice? Which version do you think presents the text in the most effective way? Explain. What can you say about the chapter division at 53?

3. List some of the features of formatting discussed in this chapter that would help you to clarify the poetic structure of Job 28 in your language.

Chapter 7:

How Poetic Structures Can Help Determine Meaning

7.1 Introduction

We have already mentioned in chapter 1 that we do not have access to the original copies of any books of the Old Testament. Rather, we only have copies of copies, handed down through the centuries. Thus, in studying the Old Testament we are confronted with literally thousands of textual problems—places where it is very difficult to determine what the Hebrew text said. The vast majority of these are of minor importance, but they still need to be examined and evaluated. Some problems arise because vowels were not marked in the ancient text, leaving many words open to several possible interpretations. Other problems arise because word spaces were not present in the Hebrew text, so it was hard to know how to divide letter sequences to form words. In many Bibles, passages with problems of interpretation are marked by footnotes that say "Hebrew uncertain" or "Hebrew obscure." Certain biblical scholars specialize in textual problems, and they have various means of trying to determine what the Hebrew text said. For example, they have classified the most common errors that the scribes made, and are therefore able to explain many of the differences in variant texts. Thus they can make intelligent hypotheses about what the original text said. Another tool that can help in determining how a certain text should be read is a good working knowledge of the primary features of Hebrew poetry (Bascom). In this chapter we will examine a few cases of this last principle at work.

7.2 Poetic structure and variant meanings

When there are difficulties in a given text, there may be more than one way to understand it. Interpreters may offer many variant meanings. Understanding various stylistic features used in Hebrew poetry may help scholars and translators to choose the most likely of two or more interpretations. For example, in Pro 3.10 the RSV text reads:

> then your barns will be filled with plenty,
> and your vats will be bursting with wine.

NIV provides essentially the same translation:

> then your barns will be filled to overflowing,
> and your vats will brim over with new wine.

But many other versions have a slightly different reading at the end of the first line (TEV, REB, NAB, NJPSV):

> . . . your barns will be **filled with grain** . . .

Note that the difference revolves around the meaning of the Hebrew word, *sava'*, which RSV and NIV take to be a verbal participle, "overflowing," and the others take to be a noun meaning "grain." Which interpretation is correct? In searching for an answer we learn that some Greek manuscripts have "wheat" or "grain." Thus some versions may have chosen to follow the Greek text rather than the Hebrew one. In addition to this fact we may find other reasons for considering it a better choice. By studying the structure of the verse in detail, we may be able to find more convincing evidence. Taking the Hebrew word for word, there appears to be an envelope, or chiastic structure, at least at the edges of the verse:

so will be filled	a
your barns	b
********	
your vats	b'
will brim over	a'

This observation leads us to see that if we adopt the RSV/NIV interpretation ("to overflowing" or "with plenty"), the chiastic structure is incomplete:

so will be filled	a
your barns	b
to overflowing,	
with wine	
your vats	b'
will brim over	a'

But if we assume that the word is "grain," the verse has a perfect chiastic structure:

so will be filled	a
your barns	b
grain	c
(and) **new wine**	c'
your vats	b'
will brim over	a'

Analyzing texts from a poetic point of view may lead us to change our understanding of texts we have read and worked with for many years. F or example, we are all very familiar with the quote from Isaiah (Isa 40.3) cited by the writer of the Gospel of Mark (1.3). Christians see this verse as describing John the Baptist, crying out in the wilderness, calling people to prepare the way for the Messiah:

> the voice of one crying in the wilderness:
> Prepare the way of the Lord,
> make his paths straight—   (Mark 1.3)

However, if we study this passage in Hebrew in the book of Isaiah, we see that the original verse had a somewhat different structure and thus a slightly different meaning. RSV gives the following rendering of Isa 40.3:

> A voice cries:
> "In the wilderness prepare the way of the LORD,
> make straight in the desert a highway for our God. . . ."

We can be relatively sure that the interpretation of RSV is correct because of our knowledge of Hebrew poetry. There is a chiastic structure in the first part of the lines:

> in the wilderness   prepare
> make straight   in the desert

The last two expressions in the two lines, "the way of the LORD" and "a highway for our God," are parallel. Because this structure coincides perfectly with what we know about poetic patterns in Hebrew, it seems to be the correct structuring of the verse. Translators must be careful to translate the passage in Isaiah properly in order to preserve the true meaning.(See chapter 8 for a discussion of how this text should be handled in the New Testament).

7.3 Solving more difficult texts

Sometimes knowing how Hebrew poetry fits together can help us unravel very difficult texts (Bascom, 1994). One such passage is found in Song of Songs 3.9-11. In this passage we find the description of what appears to be King Solomon's royal litter, or palanquin (a sort of seat or enclosure hand-carried by several people):

> 9 King Solomon made himself a palanquin
>   from the wood of Lebanon.
> 10   He made its posts of silver,
>   its back of gold, its seat of purple;
>   it was lovingly wrought within*
>   by the daughters of Jerusalem.

it was lovingly wrought within*
    by the daughters of Jerusalem.
11 Go forth, O daughters of Zion,
    and behold King Solomon . . . .

*the meaning of the Hebrew is uncertain

The line marked by a footnote is the passage we want to study closely. The text seems to say literally "its-interior fitted out [with] love." There are many different renderings, but in many translations the noun "love" (*'ahavah*) is taken as an adverb of manner, explaining how the daughters of Jerusalem worked to make this carriage beautiful:

TEV	**lovingly** woven
NIV	its interior **lovingly** inlaid by the daughters
NJPSV	Within, it was decked **with love**
	By the maidens of Jerusalem
CEV	You women of Jerusalem
	have **taken great care**
	to furnish the inside.

There is something slightly odd about these translations, however, because never before, and never again in the Song, are the daughters involved in any overt actions. In all other passages they speak or are spoken to, but they do not carry out any actions or participate in any way.

Scholars have spent much time and energy trying to figure out the exact meaning of this passage. Some think "love" refers to love scenes painted on the inside of the carriage. Others think there is a mistake in the text, and claim that the word translated as "by" (a simple *m* affix) in "by the daughters of Jerusalem" is not "by" at all. They think that the sound *m* belongs rather to the word preceding it ("love"), which creates a new word altogether. Scholars have proposed various meanings for this word: "leather," "ebony," "ivory," or "precious stones." Looking back to the text, then, the meaning may be something like:

its interior was paved with precious stones

If we accept this interpretation, however, this leaves "daughters of Jerusalem" unattached to anything else in the context. They would not have been the ones to decorate this special carriage.

However, if we study the text more closely, we see that "daughters of Jerusalem" can fit nicely into the first line of the next verse. In fact, if it is placed just before the beginning of this verse, it forms a perfect chiastic structure with what follows:

daughters of Jerusalem ⟍ ⟋ (verse 11) Come out
    and behold [or, look] ⟋ ⟍ daughters of Zion

Note as well that the general "daughters of Jerusalem" would be seconded by a more specific "daughters of Zion" (Bascom, page 100), something we expect in Hebrew poetry.

This solution has several points in its favor. First, it eliminates a very awkward passage that has the daughters of Jerusalem acting out of character. Second, the poem's structure is rendered in a way that is much more in keeping with what we know about Hebrew poetry. We still do not know what the interior of the carriage was lined with: ivory? ebony? or something else? But we can be fairly confident that the carriage was not decorated by the daughters of Jerusalem. Rather, they are being called to admire the king, an event much more in keeping with their role in this book. At least some modern versions (NRSV and REB) adopt this restructuring in their own translations of the Song of Songs.

7.4 Signaling varying interpretations of a poetic text

How should we handle passages for which the meaning is not sure? There are several possibilities. First, translators can study the choices and simply pick what appears to them to be the best choice within the context, and incorporate this into the text. Taking the case of Pro 3.10, for example, we see that two well-respected versions (RSV and NIV) have one interpretation ("overflowing"), while other versions prefer another (TEV, REB, NAB, NJPSV "with grain"). Translators can pick the interpretation they feel is best, and translate that text without including a footnote.

Another possibility is to signal the problem of interpretation to the readers through footnotes. Translators can add footnotes stating "meaning in Hebrew unclear" or, better, give a slightly longer explanation such as CEV does: "One possible meaning for the difficult Hebrew text." A better procedure, when possible, is to give the most likely alternative reading. For example, in the case of Pro 3.10, translators may put "with grain" in the text and then add a footnote, "alternatively, this word may mean 'to overflowing.' " Or vice versa, they may put "to overflowing" in the text and put "or 'with grain' " in the footnote, and cite the Septuagint as a reference.

Translators will have to weigh each text that allows an alternative interpretation, or which contains a difficult reading, and judge whether it merits a footnote. Some of the alternative readings will be crucial to the understanding of the text, and some will not. In the Pro 3.10 example, there is a change in meaning if we choose "to overflowing" or "with grain," but the overall message of the verse is the same either way. We have seen that, in the case of Song of Songs 3.10, at least two versions have restructured the text on the basis of poetic principles and do not show this in a footnote.

We recommend that footnotes should be included in the translation of poetic material in the following cases:

(1) if the alternative reading makes a real difference in meaning, especially on an important theological point;
(2) if readers have access to many versions which note variant readings;
(3) if readers are especially aware of textual problems;

(4) if a minority view is taken of a text having two or more possible interpretations.

For example, if we have a situation where a group of readers rely heavily on one version in a trade language, and a new translation adopts an alternative reading, it will be wise to note this. In the example from the Song of Songs, we can set out the text in the following way:

> . . . inlaid with precious stones.
> O daughters of Jerusalem,* (11) come out!
> Look, O daughters of Zion!
>
> *The text in Hebrew is difficult to understand. Some think the text says "inlaid with love by the daughters of Jerusalem."

Note that the solution we have adopted leaves us with a verse number in the middle of a thought. This may bother the translator or the reader. However, we have already noted that chapter and verse divisions were inserted centuries after the original texts were first written down, and that they do not always occur in the correct place. Helping readers see the real structure of a book or a poem is more important than dividing texts at their commonly accepted breaking points.

Many people object by saying that readers do not really use footnotes. Others go so far as to imply that footnotes acknowledging textual problems can undermine the faith of believers. However, it seems virtually impossible to do an honest translation of the Old Testament without footnotes. Rather than undermining believers' faith, footnotes serve an important role. If they are simple and to the point, they help readers develop a healthy attitude toward the biblical text and make them aware of the difficult problems translators face. They also display the translator's determination to convey the intended meaning of the Scriptures as fully and accurately as possible.

To sum up, when there are two or more alternative translations, and all are acceptable, translators should make the best choice possible based on their study of the text, without introducing special footnotes. However, if a minority view is taken or if the chosen text or interpretation goes against the standard views of the versions already used in the community, it is best to acknowledge the alternative solutions in a footnote. It is recommended that teams ask their translation consultant for advice in these difficult matters.

7.5 Pushing the notion of poetic structures too far

While understanding poetic structures can help us understand the organization of a difficult passage, at times it can lead us astray. That is, translators must be careful not to go too far in trying to discover or create poetic structures or parallelisms where they do not exist. For example, in Psa 105.6 the Hebrew text is well reflected in the RSV translation:

> O offspring of Abraham, his servant,
> sons of Jacob, his chosen ones!

Despite the two expressions "offspring of Abraham" and "sons of Jacob," only one group of people is being referred to. As we noted earlier, if there is any ambiguity, translators should attempt to make the meaning clear. Some have accomplished this by inserting "you," as TEV does below, showing that the same person is being addressed:

> You descendants of Abraham, his servant;
> you descendants of Jacob, the man he chose . . . .

Note, however, in their zeal to make the structure of this parallelism clearer, TEV translators have apparently gone beyond the real meaning of the text. If we consider RSV (which here literally reflects the Hebrew), we see that "his servant" modifies "Abraham." But despite appearances and our own expectations, "his chosen ones" does not modify "Jacob" but rather modifies the entire phrase "sons of Jacob" (thus the people of Israel). TEV presents us with a clear and balanced parallelism but, unfortunately, one which does not reflect the true meaning of the text.

CEV corrects this error by putting "descendants of Jacob" and "his chosen ones" side by side:

> You belong to the family of Abraham, his servant;
> you are his chosen ones, the descendants of Jacob.

A few other changes also occur in this version. Note that the lines are rendered as statements, "you belong . . . you are." Also, the order of the elements in the line is reversed, creating a chiastic structure that is not present in the original:

This shifting of order is permitted, since it does not significantly affect the meaning. The CEV translation is really quite appealing. It avoids ambiguity by inserting "you," and at the same time maintains poetic balance and the correct meaning.

7.6 Conclusion

We have seen that a knowledge of poetic devices in Hebrew is important for understanding the meaning of difficult passages. When there are variant renderings in a text, our understanding of poetic structures can help point to the more likely of two solutions. Understanding such structures can also help us find new solutions to old textual problems.

Questions for reflection

(Note: in this chapter these are truly questions for reflection. There is no right or wrong answer.)

1. Consider the following translations of Song of Songs 1.5, concentrating on the last two lines:

RSV:

> I am very dark, but comely,
> O daughters of Jerusalem,
> **like the tents of Kedar,**
> **like the curtains of Solomon.**

NAB:

> I am as dark—but lovely,
> O daughters of Jerusalem—
> **As the tents of Kedar,**
> **as the curtains of Salma.**

REB:

> Daughters of Jerusalem, I am dark and lovely,
> **like the tents of Kedar**
> **or the tent curtains of Shalmah.**

"Kedar" is an area located in the northern Arabian peninsula. Why do you think there is a difference among versions in the last word of the verse (*Solomon-Salma-Shalmah*)? Why do you think some scholars think this word is a place name? What is your opinion? Can you think of any reason why the word "Solomon" could be the original meaning? Do you have any evidence in the rest of the poem?

2. For the Song of Songs 5.13, the Hebrew version we have today and the Greek translation (the Septuagint) do not match. The Hebrew text has something like:

> his cheeks are like a bed of spice,
> **towers of perfume**
> his lips, lilies dripping flowing myrrh

The Septuagint and many versions have interpreted the word "towers" in a different way. With a few minor changes in vowels, the phrase can be a verbal form meaning "yielding" or "producing":

RSV:

> His cheeks are like beds of spices,
> **yielding fragrance.**

His lips are lilies,
distilling liquid myrrh.

Can you see anything in the RSV translation above that will help you to decide in favor of one interpretation over the other? If you are translating, which interpretation will you choose? Do you think it is necessary to include a footnote?

3. There is a difficult text problem in Psa 22.26. The Hebrew Masoretic text has "like a lion" at the beginning of the second (B) line, but some Hebrew manuscripts, the Septuagint, and several other ancient versions have "they pierced." Consult several modern versions (especially their footnotes on the verse), study Bibles, and *A Handbook on the Psalms* to see what they advise concerning this issue. Then consider the problem in terms of poetic features and structures as we have in this chapter (for example, see Psa 22.20-21). Does this study lead you to favor one possible interpretation over the other? Explain.

Chapter 8:

Translating Old Testament Poetry
in a New Testament Context

8.1 Introduction

Almost without exception writers of the New Testament drew heavily on the ideas, images, and words of the Old Testament writings. They used wording from the Old Testament when giving examples or making important points. The writer of Matthew, for example, quoted the Old Testament prophets more than fourteen times, often with the statement "These things happened to fulfill what the Lord had spoken . . . ." This author was convinced that the major events of Christ's life had been foretold in the Old Testament writings. The apostle Paul and other New Testament authors also used Old Testament quotes throughout their writings to support their major theological points: the coming of the Messiah, the role of the Jews in salvation history, the "grafting in" of the Gentiles, and justification by faith. In many cases these quotes come from poetic contexts.

Normally translators of the New Testament should apply the same principles to their translation of quoted poetry as we have presented in the first seven chapters of this manual. But when such passages are quoted, rather than appearing in their original context, there are a number of issues that need to be addressed. First, the wording of the quotes in the New Testament may not be exactly the same as in the Old Testament. Secondly, the quotes appear in different sociological, political, and theological settings. Thirdly, translators may be tempted to "Christianize" Old Testament passages appearing in the New Testament. In this chapter we will discuss some of the special problems involved in translating Old Testament poetry in the context of the New Testament.

8.2 The nature of Old Testament quotes

New Testament translators dealing with quotes of poetic passages from the Old Testament are immediately confronted with a problem: the quotations in the New Testament are not always identical to the passages quoted from the Old Testament. Since the New Testament was written in Greek and not in Hebrew, passages could not simply be lifted out of the Hebrew text and inserted into the Greek text. During the period of time when the New Testament books were being written, many people used a Greek translation of the Old Testament instead of the original Hebrew text. Thus quotes from the Old Testament did not necessarily come directly from the Hebrew but from this Greek translation known as the Septuagint. Because there can never be a one-to-one correspondence between words in a translation, we find several discrepancies between passages occurring in Hebrew in the Old Testament and those quoted in Greek in the New Testament.

There are at least two ways in which the authors of the New Testament used passages from the Old Testament. We can categorize these two methods as **allusion** and **direct quotes**.

8.2.1 Scriptural allusions

It is evident that New Testament writers knew the Old Testament Scriptures well. The vocabulary, images, and concepts of the Old Testament (whether read in Hebrew or Greek) had penetrated their thought patterns and ways of expressing themselves. Thus, in writing down the New Testament records, authors made many allusions to the Old Testament. Sometimes they used expressions from the Old Testament without actually quoting specific passages. For example, in Revelation the text is full of allusions to geographical locations first mentioned in the Old Testament: the garden of Eden, Babylon, Jerusalem. The author also refers to many exotic spices and jewels that had first appeared in the Old Testament. In the gospel of Mark, even the words of God coming from heaven, "Thou art my beloved Son; with thee I am well pleased," echo the words of Psalm 2 and of the prophet Isaiah (42.1). Indeed, Jesus' own speech as recorded in the Gospels shows this kind of Old Testament pattern of thinking and manner of expression. Allusions to Jonah, Moses, Abraham, and other Old Testament personalities abound. Even the phrase Christ used to designate himself, the "Son of Man," seems to have its roots in the Old Testament.

8.2.2. Direct quotes from the Old Testament

The second type of Old Testament reference is a direct quote, and this is where we find many passages of Hebrew poetry. It is often the case that, when poetry from the Old Testament is cited, authors clearly mark their quotes in the text. The writer may identify the source of the quote by referring to either the person or the book:

> Then was fulfilled what was spoken by the prophet Jeremiah . . . (Matt 2.17)

> As it is written in Isaiah the prophet . . . (Mark 1.2)

> For David says concerning him . . . (Acts 2.25)

> As indeed he says in Hosea . . . (Rom 9.25)

If the book or author is not cited, there is often a reference to indicate that a quote is being made, either through a general statement, "it is written," or as a reference to "a prophet":

> All this took place to fulfill what the Lord had spoke by the prophet . . . (Matt 1.22)

As it is written . . . (Rom 3.10; 14.11; 15.9; Gal 4.27; and elsewhere)

It has been testified somewhere . . . (Heb 2.6)

Translators must be careful to preserve these introductory statements and, if possible, to format the material associated with them in a way that shows they are quotes—for example, by indentation. (For more on formatting, see chapter 6.)

8.3 Preserving key terms in quotes

New Testament authors used Old Testament quotes to make important points. This means there may be one or two words or longer expressions in the quote that link it to the surrounding text. Or one or two Old Testament words may introduce a concept that becomes a key term in the New Testament. Translators must be very careful in their translation of such expressions. This may mean adapting their approach to translation from a dynamic style to a more conservative or literal one in order to make sure that such key terms are preserved in the translation.

For example, in the second chapter of Acts, we find a lengthy quote from the prophet Joel concerning the pouring out of the Spirit of God. Near the end of the citation we read (2.19-20):

> And I will show wonders in the heaven above
> and signs on the earth beneath,
> blood, and fire, and vapor of smoke;
> the sun shall be turned into darkness
> and the moon into blood,
> before **the day of the Lord** comes,
> the great and manifest day. . . .

This passage contains a common feature of Hebrew poetry which we have seen in section 3.4.5: a shift from first person ("I" in the first line) to third person ("the day of the Lord"). Many translators who are used to applying the principles of dynamic translation will identify this person shift as a problem for the reader. They may automatically adapt a more natural style (section 5.5) and use the first person throughout the quote. For example, they may render "before the day of the Lord comes" as "before my day comes."

But the expression "the day of the LORD" is a key term in the Old Testament and was an especially important part of the message of the prophets. This expression becomes a key concept in the New Testament as well (1 Cor 5.5 "the day of the Lord Jesus"; 1 Thess 5.2 "the day of the Lord," Rev 16.14 "the great day of God the Almighty"). Therefore it seems better to translate this passage in a more conservative way than we would normally do. Giving a more literal translation (that is, keeping "the day of the Lord") allows the reader of Acts to study the text closely and see what the ties are to the surrounding text as well as to other books in both the New and Old Testaments. It is interesting to note that, despite its very modern language and approach to translation principles, CEV has chosen to maintain "the day of the Lord" in this context.

8.4 Preserving the link between the quote and the text

Translators need to determine what is the link, or connection, between the Old Testament quote and the text. This will direct them as to which part of the passage needs a more literal rendering. For example, in 1 Cor 1.19 Paul quotes from Isa 29.14:

> For it is written,
> "I will destroy the wisdom of the wise,
> and the cleverness of the clever I will thwart."

As we read on in the passage (verses 20-21), we note that it is the word "wisdom" or "wise" which is highlighted:

> Where is the **wise** man? Where is the scribe? Where is the debater of this age? Has not God made foolish the **wisdom** of the world? For since, in the **wisdom** of God, the world did not know God through **wisdom**
> . . . .

CEV has clearly recognized the importance of the key word in the quote. It gives a more literal translation of the first line of the quote from Isaiah, maintaining the word "wisdom," and goes on to give a more dynamic translation of the second line. To help the reader, it identifies the speaker (God) *outside* the quote, all the while maintaining the first person *within* the quote:

> As God says in the Scriptures,
>
> > "I will destroy the **wisdom**
> > of all who claim
> > to be **wise**.
> > I will confuse those
> > who think they know
> > so much."

> What happened to those **wise** people? . . . Didn't God show that the **wisdom** of this world is foolish? God was **wise** and decided not to let the people of this world use their **wisdom** to learn about him.

Translators must study the context of each quote very carefully in a more literal version such as RSV to determine exactly which words from the Old Testament text are repeated in the New Testament quote. If at all possible the rendering of these shared words should be the same, so as to maintain the literary and logical links in the passage.

8.5 Treating quotes as known information

Translators must also realize that, when authors quoted Old Testament passages, they usually assumed the audience was familiar with these texts and valued them highly. Thus the content of the quotes must be translated as **known information**. For example, when Matthew quoted Jeremiah (Matt 2.18), most of Matthew's readers (or listeners) knew where Ramah was, and they knew who Rachel was:

> A voice was heard in Ramah,
> wailing and loud lamentation,
> Rachel weeping for her children . . . .

Translators may be able to include in the line that Ramah is a town. They may even want to add a term of respect such as "Mother Rachel," as the Chewa translation has done. But it would not be right to put in explicit historical information about who Rachel was. Not only would this violate the poetic style (section 5.4.2), but it would present the material as if it were unknown to the audience. Most often, then, when Old Testament poetic passages are being quoted, it is because the author and the audience share a certain body of common knowledge. If the translation is a first New Testament, and people do not have an Old Testament background, it is appropriate to include explanatory footnotes for them. But it is not acceptable to modify the quotes themselves by adding implicit information to make them more understandable to today's readers.

While we can assume that the first readers (or hearers) of the New Testament knew that authors were quoting the Old Testament, many of today's readers will not. One way of helping readers understand that there is a quote present (other than including a cross reference) is to use proper formatting. In the passage quoted from 1 Cor 1.19 above, note how CEV indents the entire quote and puts quote marks around it. We can also let readers know that lines of poetry are being quoted by lining up parallel lines. For example, in the CEV example above, the quote would be clearer of the poetic lines were written out completely, with no overlapping material—provided the available space between margins is long enough:

> I will destroy the wisdom of all who claim to be wise.
> I will confuse those who think they know so much.

In many languages special quote formulas and particles exist which, when used properly, will signal to readers and hearers alike that a quote is being made.

To sum up, then, poetry from the Old Testament should be translated with great care in the New Testament. Often translators will need to take a more literal approach to maintain the verbal links between the quote and any parallel text, whether in the Old or in the New Testament. They should not introduce implicit information that would disrupt the text or make it sound artificial. If necessary such information can be added in a footnote.

8.6 Translating the text before us

We have noted that at times quotes of Old Testament poetry in the New Testament are not exactly the same as those found in the Hebrew. We said that a major reason for this is that New Testament writers often used the Greek Septuagint translation of the Hebrew Bible. Most translators consider this a serious dilemma. Should we translate the text as it is written in the New Testament, or should we go back to the source text and give a translation closer to that text?

In chapter 7 we mentioned one very important example from the Gospel of Mark, where an Old Testament passage appears to be misquoted. In Mark 1.2-3 we noted that in the Greek text the phrase "in the wilderness" is connected to "a voice":

> "Behold, I send my messenger before thy face,
> who shall prepare thy way;
> **the voice of one crying in the wilderness:**
> Prepare the way of the Lord,
> make his paths straight—"

But as we have already seen, in the Hebrew text the phrase occurs in the following line:

> A voice cries:
> **"In the wilderness prepare the way of the LORD,**
> make straight in the desert a highway for our God. . . ."

There is no doubt that this difference is due to the fact that the writer of Mark used the Septuagint as his base and not the Hebrew text. (Note that there is another adaptation: "the highway of our God" has become "his paths.")

From today's perspective we may be inclined to say that the writer of Mark quoted a translation that was not completely faithful to the original or that the Septuagint was too free in its translation of this verse. Alternatively, the Septuagint may have translated a Hebrew text that was slightly different from the Masoretic text that we have today. What should translators do? Should we accept the Greek text as it stands and translate that text, or do we correct it based on our knowledge of the Masoretic Hebrew text? Virtually all scholars agree that we must respect the integrity of the New Testament document and translate the Greek as we find it, without attempting to make it conform to the Hebrew. This follows a basic translation principle that we are to faithfully render the meaning of the text as the writer intended it.

We see the importance of following this principle in numerous cases throughout the New Testament, but probably one of the most famous and the most discussed example is that of Matt 1.22-23:

> All this took place to fulfill what the Lord had spoken by the prophet:
> "Behold, a virgin shall conceive and bear a son,
> and his name shall be called Emmanuel" . . . .

Many scholars suggest that the word translated here as "virgin" does not have such a narrow meaning in Hebrew. They say that in its original context (Isa 7.14) the Hebrew word 'almah meant simply "young woman" (with no indication as to whether this person had had previous sexual relations). Be that as it may, in translating from Hebrew the translators of the Septuagint used a more specific Greek word, "virgin." And it is clear from the context (Matt 1.20: "for that which is conceived in her is of the Holy Spirit") that Matthew intended the word to mean "virgin," not simply young woman.

We may ask: given the findings of modern scholarship, should translators change the word "virgin" to "young woman"? Though some versions include a brief footnote to explain the difference between the Hebrew and Greek texts (for example, the Harper-Collins Study Bible), virtually all translations use the word "virgin" in the New Testament text as the intended meaning of the author, and that is what is recommended here. We must render Matthew's intended meaning and not the meaning of the text he quoted from.

A slightly more complicated problem is found in Matt 21.5. Here there is some dispute as to what the author actually meant when he quoted the text. In referring to the triumphal entry of Jesus into Jerusalem, the author of Matthew cites the prophet Zechariah (9.9):

> Tell the daughter of Zion,
> Behold, your king is coming to you,
> humble, and mounted on an ass,
> **and** on a colt, the foal of an ass.

The major problem with this passage is that it seems to imply that there were two donkeys rather than one (see also Matt 21.7). Actually the rendering from the Septuagint is very close to the Hebrew. It has translated the text literally, replacing the Hebrew waw with the Greek conjunction kai. Most versions give a literal translation of the "and" in their translations of the Old Testament quote, as seen in the RSV above and the TEV below:

> He is humble and rides on a donkey
> **and** on a colt, the foal of a donkey.

However, when we examine the RSV, NIV, and TEV renderings of the text in the Old Testament, quite a different approach has been used. Since translating "and" literally here may give the impression that the person was somehow sitting on two donkeys instead of one, these versions do not translate waw literally. They recognize that waw is serving not as a true conjunction but rather as a linking device between two parallel lines (section 5.2.2.2). By removing "and" we see clearly that the last line is merely spelling out, or elaborating poetically on, the line preceding it:

RSV:

> Rejoice greatly, O daughter of Zion!
> Shout aloud, O daughter of Jerusalem!
> Lo, your king comes to you;
> triumphant and victorious is he,
> **humble and riding on an ass,**
> **on a colt the foal of an ass.**

NIV:

> gentle and riding on a donkey,
> **on a colt, the foal of a donkey.**

TEV:

> He comes triumphant and victorious,
> but humble and riding on a donkey—
> **on a colt, the foal of a donkey.**

So, while these versions have decided to translate dynamically in the Old Testament, they have followed the basic principle that in the New Testament we must not change the Old Testament passage as it has been quoted from the Greek translation.

Sometimes the New Testament author seems to have added to a Scriptural passage. In Matt 4.10 there is a quote from Deut 6.13. The Greek text has:

> You shall worship the Lord your God
> and him **only** shall you serve.

But when we look at this verse both in the Hebrew and in the Septuagint translation, we note that the word "only" does not appear:

> Yahweh your God you will fear
> and him you will serve
> and in his name you will swear.

However, when we examine this text in its context, we note that "only" is implied though not explicitly expressed. However, there is definitely a call to exclusiveness, as the rest of the passage in Deuteronomy makes clear (6.14-15): "You shall not go after other gods . . . for the LORD your God . . . is a jealous God." We conclude that the author of Matthew has himself given a dynamic equivalent of the text! In this case again, translators must follow the text of the Greek New Testament as it stands, incorporating the thought of the author. It would be wrong to remove "only" from the New Testament quote, to make it sound more like the original.

The quote appearing in Matt 4.10 reveals another area where it may be hard for a translator to come to terms with discrepancies between poetry in the Old and the New Testaments. This concerns how to treat the names of God. We know that in the Old Testament there are many names for God, the most common being *Yahweh* ("LORD" in RSV) and *'Elohim* ("God"). There is also the title *Adonai* ("Lord"). As Old Testament quotes have passed from Hebrew into Greek, the distinction between these names has been lost. In the Septuagint *Yahweh* ("LORD") becomes *kurios* ("Lord"), while the rendering of *'elohim* and *'adonai* remains unchanged. Thus, in the example just cited, *Yahweh* ("LORD") appears as "Lord." The name *Yahweh*, then, does not occur in the New Testament.

Translators who have worked on the Old Testament and who have put a lot of effort into finding acceptable equivalents for the many names of God in Hebrew may find it hard to give up their solutions when translating Old Testament quotes in the New. They will certainly be tempted to put their rendering for "Yahweh" back into the text. Nevertheless it is better to follow the text at hand (that is, the text of the Greek New Testament) rather than to introduce a distinction that was not made at the time this document was written. We know also that, even when reading the Hebrew text, Jews at the time of Jesus avoided pronouncing the name "Yahweh," replacing it with *'adonai* ("Lord"). People using the Greek translation of the Old Testament in New Testament times obviously used *kurios* ("Lord"). It would be wrong for a translator to reintroduce a distinction that was not functioning at the time when the text was being written. If necessary a note in the introduction to the New Testament can explain the rendering of Yahweh in Old Testament quotes. Such a not may also be needed to point out that the reference ins such passages is to Yahweh, not to Christ, which the vernacular term for "Lord" may suggest to many hearers.

8.7 Avoid "Christianizing" Old Testament quotes

Another temptation translators often face when translating Old Testament passages in the New Testament is trying to make the author's point too explicit. Christian writers purposely quoted the Old Testament to show that they saw important links between what the prophets said and what had happened or was currently happening in their own day. The events of Jesus' life and death, and their own Christian experiences, gave them a new understanding of the meaning of the Old Testament documents. The point of the quotations is to show this link. But if translators rewrite the quotes from the Old Testament, the point will be entirely missed. For example, while working on Rom 15.21:

> They shall see who have never been told of him,
> and they shall understand who have never heard of him.

one translation team had made explicit who "he" is in this text: "Those who have never been told of Christ, they will see him." Certainly the author, Paul, is thinking of the Messiah. The context preceding this passage makes this clear: "making it my ambition to preach the gospel, not where Christ has already been named, lest I build on another man's foundation." By quoting Isaiah, Paul is trying to show that he is taking this Old Testament reference to be a reference to Christ. But his goal is not to rewrite the Old Testament. He wants rather to show that the Old Testament Scriptures have new meaning in light of the events of his day. It will therefore be violating Paul's style and logic if translators try to "Christianize" this and other Old Testament passages.

Here we come back to the same basic principle that applies to translating Old Testament passages in the New Testament. Translators should render these passages as quotes by another author. They are not free to adjust these passages to make them conform to modern Christian understanding. That would entirely defeat their purpose.

Finally, we recommend that New Testament translators render poetic quotes directly from the Greek text, if possible, or from a literal version of this text, rather than looking back at their translations in the Old Testament. Once this rendering has been done, they can, of course, compare their translations. They may wish to harmonize certain vocabulary items or expressions that are the same in the Hebrew text and in the Greek. But they must be very careful to maintain those distinctions that have been introduced into the poetic passages— knowingly or unknowingly—by the writers who quoted them.

We may add that it is also a temptation for translators to Christianize Old Testament texts as they translate them for the first time. For example, in light of their understanding of Scripture as a whole, translators may wish to translate "virgin" in Isa 7.14, instead of rendering the original by its core meaning, "young woman." They may want to make very explicit certain references to the Messiah as they appear in Psalms or Isaiah. We strongly advise against such an approach. The Old Testament and the New Testament are separate documents and are themselves made up of individual books written by different authors over a large time span. We need to respect both the author and the time frame of each book, translating to the best of our ability, without imposing wider theological interpretations on the text.

Questions for reflection

1. Compare the quote in 1 Cor 2.16 with the original in Isa 40.13. Why does one passage have "LORD" and the other "Lord"? Explain your answer.

2. In the versions available to you, do you know any cases of translators "Christianizing" the text? How would you change these translations to make sure that the integrity of the original text is respected?

3. See if you can find an Old Testament quote in the book of Hebrews that differs in some respect from its original wording. Point out what this difference is and how it affects the meaning of the passage.

4. Study the Song of Zechariah (Luke 1.68-79) and identify the Old Testament references that you find. List two references where the New Testament texts are exactly the same, and two others where they differ. How should a translator render the latter two?

5. Compare Rev 15.3-4 with Psa 89.9-10; Isa 45.22-24; and Mal 1.11. Which concepts from the Old Testament did John incorporate into this passage? Why is the use of Old Testament poetry particularly appropriate in this context? How can you indicate this fact in your translation?

Appendix

Translating Poetry for Oral Presentation:
A Case Study

Edward R. Hope

The poetry of one culture differs considerably from that of other cultures, and may change drastically over a period of time. In some cultures poetry is recited; in others it is chanted or sung, while in some it is read silently, with as much interest in the calligraphy as in the words. In some cultures it is presented by one individual; in others it is expected that there will be audience participation or response. Thus when deciding to translate a biblical poem into another language hundreds of years after the original poem was written, an important conscious decision needs to be made:

> Will the translation attempt to retain the poetic structures of the original, or will it be recast in the poetic structures of the receptor language?

In the case which will now be described, a decision had been made to recast the poem in the structures of the audience, although using the medium of the English language. The project was an experiment, to test audience response, but also to investigate the translation issues involved in such an exercise.

The overall aim was to prepare a 60-minute cassette in English for a general African audience on poetic selections from the book of Isaiah. To do this, a list of features frequently used in Hebrew and African poetry was drawn up, as follows:

Hebrew Poetry	African Poetry
Parallelism	Rhythm and meter
Chiastic structures	Repetition
Rhythm and meter	Refrain for audience response
Repetitive consonants	Metaphors
Puns and wordplay	Juxtaposition of ideas
Repetition	Condensed style
Metaphors	
Juxtaposition of ideas	
Condensed style	

After making a comparison, it was decided that because juxtaposition of ideas was common in African poetry, Hebrew parallelisms could easily be retained and accommodated in the translation. The major effort would have to be in the areas of creating a poem with African rhythms and meters (which are usually

179

very complex, as can be seen in the sophisticated drumming that often accompanies oral presentations), and creating suitable refrains, without altering the emphasis of the original text.

The first step in the experiment was the choice of the Song of the Vineyard in Isaiah 5.1-7 as the first poem to be translated. Since styles of presentation of poetry differ considerably from region to region in Africa, it was decided to present the poem as a song.

Then a thorough exegetical study of the passage was done. This included looking at the Hebrew vocabulary and its meaning in various contexts. This enabled one to get a clearer idea of the range of meaning of the words in the context of the Isaiah passage. Since the central theme was wine farming, a study was done of the archeology of vineyards, wine presses etc.

From these studies it was noted that the verb used for digging in Hebrew was not the usual word for cultivating or hoeing a field, but for digging holes or ditches. Thus the reference seemed to be to digging an irrigation ditch. It was also discovered that the "wine vat" was probably a wine-press that was often dug from solid limestone. As the grapes were trodden in this wine press, the juice usually ran in a channel cut into the floor of the press and flowed from the press to a point where it was collected in jars.

The poem centers on the fact that after everything possible had been done to ensure a good crop, the resulting grapes were "wild," i.e., too small and too sour for making wine. Since African audiences are not usually familiar with grapes, and in the Bibles in their own languages the name of a wild fruit is often used, it was felt that the point would be lost if the term "wild grapes" was retained. "Grapes that were sour and small" seemed a better phrase, since it had rhythm as well as conveying the right emphasis.

An important feature of the Hebrew poem is the play on words at the climactic point of the poem: *mishpat* "justice" is expected but *mishpach* "violence, the wrong use of power" is the actual outcome; *tsedaqah* "righteous judgment" is looked for, but what is found is *tse'aqah* "a cry of pain." Try as one might, no way could be found to retain this play on words that still resulted in natural English. Every attempt seemed too artificial.

The next step was to translate the poem into English, using rhythmic phrases and a reasonably consistent meter. This latter feature was not as strict a restraint as it would have been if Western music had been envisioned. African music and singing styles allow a little more leeway in this.

The work proceeded on a trial-and-error basis. A stanza would be translated and then the rhythm and meter would be checked, and ways sought to make adjustments in wording. The first verse was the most difficult, and it took many adjustments to find something properly rhythmic. Other lines, such as

> He dug a water ditch,
> He gathered up the stones,
> He planted the choicest of vines,

seemed right from the first attempt. Some lines could only be made adequately rhythmic by repetition. However, care was taken not to allow the repetitions to give a line more emphasis than it had in the original Hebrew poem.

The final line, which carries tremendous emotional power in the Hebrew, was difficult to get right. It seemed unnatural to talk about finding a cry, so the verb "heard" was introduced. The draft line read:

> A cry of pain was what he heard.

When this was read with the previous few lines, however, the rhythm and meter were poor. A better result was obtained by rewording the line as:

> A scream was all he heard.

This was now better meter, but didn't seem to close the song properly. So it was decided to repeat the phrase "a scream" as a separate closing line.

Once the whole poem was in a near-final form, the refrains were worked on. It seemed exegetically and linguistically sound to take as a refrain a segment or two of the poem which were presupposed by other segments, and which were necessary for these other segments to be interpreted correctly. For instance, when the poem talks about the owner waiting for the harvest of grapes, it is against the background of all his efforts in preparing the vineyard. This background is also relevant when the question is asked "What more could I have done?" So the segment dealing with the preparation of the vineyard was chosen as suitable for the first refrain.

In the latter part of the poem, where judgment is pronounced on Israel, it is the destruction of the vineyard which is the relevant background against which many of the lines have to be interpreted, and this destruction segment was therefore chosen as the second refrain.

The next step, which was the final stage in the drafting of the poem, was to add notes for the musicians about the emotional tone of the various parts of the text. At this point, the text of the poem was as follows, with the refrains in italics (it had already been decided that the body of the poem would be sung by a single voice, and the refrains by a group):

[The song begins with a simple neutral mood]

> 1. Let me sing for you, my friend,
> Let me sing you my love-song
> About my friend and his vineyard,
> On a fertile hill.
> He dug a water ditch,
> He gathered up the stones,
> He planted the choicest of vines.

Refrain: *He dug a water ditch,*
He gathered up the stones,
He planted the choicest of vines.

2. In the center he built a look-out tower,
   And he chiseled out a pit for wine.

[At this point the mood becomes plaintive, even sad]

Then he waited . . . he waited . . .
He waited for it to produce
But the grapes were sour and small,
the grapes were sour and small.

Refrain, twice: *He dug a water ditch,*
He gathered up the stones,
He planted the choicest of vines,
But the grapes were sour and small.

[Tempo and rhythm change—the poet is now addressing Israel]

3. Now you citizens of Jerusalem,
   All you people of the land of Judah,
   Judge between me and this vineyard of mine,
   Judge between me and this vineyard of mine.

4. What more could I have done for my vineyard, I ask you,
   What more could I have done?
   Why, when I waited for it to produce,
   were the grapes so sour and small?

Refrain, slower: *He dug a water ditch,*
He gathered up the stones,
He planted the choicest of vines,
But the grapes were sour and small,
The grapes were sour and small.

[There is a great deal of pain in what follows]

Let me tell you what I will do now—
What I will do to my vineyard:

5. I will remove its hedge,
   And I will let it go to waste,
   And I will break down its protecting
wall.
   I will abandon it,

To be trodden underfoot,
And I ***will leave it in ruins.***

Refrain: *He will remove its hedge,*
            And he will let it go to waste,
            And he will break down its protecting wall.
            He will remove its hedge,
            And he will let it go to waste,
            And he will break down its protecting wall.
            He will abandon it, he will abandon it.

6. It shall not be pruned,
    And it shall not be hoed,
    And the thorns and weeds will flourish.
        I will forbid the clouds
        To provide it rain.
        I will forbid the clouds
        To provide it rain.

Refrain, sadly: *He will remove its hedge,*
            And let it go to waste
            He will break down its protecting wall.
            He will abandon it,
            He will abandon it.

7. Now the vineyard of the LORD of Hosts is Israel,
    And Judah is the plant in which he took delight.

Refrain: *He planted the choicest of vines,*
            But the grapes were sour and small,
            The grapes were sour and small.

[Slower, this is the climax]

    Where he looked for justice,
    Violence was what he found,
    And instead of a righteous verdict,
    A scream was all he heard.

[Faster, but slow on last line]

Refrain, twice: *Where he looked for justice,*
            Violence was what he found,
            And instead of a righteous verdict,
            A scream was all he heard,

[Try to put the pain of all the world's injustice into the last two words]

A *scream.*

Once the text had reached this stage it was shared with colleagues for exegetical assessment, and there was total agreement that the exegesis was sound, and that the repetitions did not warp the emphasis of the original.

The next stage was setting the song to music. For this my colleague Dr. Mae Alice Reggy, a very talented singer, was co-opted. She was in contact with an equally talented young Kenyan named Jack Odongo, himself a musician, singer and the director of his own recording studio. The three of us discussed the script together and decided on roughly the type of music and instruments that would be suitable (African xylophone, drums and rattles), and Mr. Odongo was then commissioned to create the music and the arrangements, with Dr. Reggy's advice. He prepared a demonstration tape and the three of us discussed it and made numerous suggestions for change. The final master tape was then recorded, and test copies made.

The tape was played to various small groups of Africans in Kenya, Zimbabwe and Ghana. The reaction was very enthusiastic, without exception. Particularly gratifying was the fact that very often the listening group would join in the refrains spontaneously. In cases where the test group heard the cassette repeatedly, most members of the group could sing the whole song after three or four playings. It is now hoped that the remaining songs for the project can be prepared in the same way.

Translating Psalm 23 in Traditional Afar Poetry

Loren F. Bliese

The Afar are a nomadic ethnic group living in the desert areas along the R ed Sea in Eritrea, east-central Ethiopia and northern Djibouti.

Afar poetry is expressed in songs sung at events such as weddings and in the evening when people are together in villages. Themes of herding, clan loyalty, companionship, love, and war are common in A far poetry. Recognized singers with special ability in memorizing and creating the poetic lines lead the songs. Others, especially the young people, join the singing by repeating the choruses. The rhythm of the song is maintained by a drum, or by hand-clapping and in some cases dancing in time to the music.

Features of Afar poetry

The Afar have a number of specific forms of songs (Bliese, 1982-83). The types vary in theme and structure. F or example, a war song called *horra* is sung by men boasting about their prowess. It has the structure of six syllables per line—usually only two or three words which make a short sentence. Another form is the *kassow*, which is used to challenge someone or to taunt opposing groups militarily or politically. It has twelve syllables per line. Another type with twelve syllables is the *saxxaq*, which is a dance song sung alternatively by young men and women in lines facing each other, moving back and forth in rhythm, clapping their hands and stamping their feet. This type was used in the translated version of the Song of Songs.

The type which has been chosen for translating some of the P salms is the praise song called *saare*. These traditional praise songs are subdivided as to whether they speak to camels, horses, or lovers. An attempt to sing P salm 23 using a camel praise song melody was found sacrilegious, since the A far immediately think of camels rather than of God. A new melody was composed to make it acceptable. Praise songs have lines of ten syllables, and a chorus of seven syllables, all matched with the same number of musical notes.

Afar songs are also characterized by thematic groupings or stanzas of two to four lines, sometimes extended to seven lines. The stanzas are marked by repetition of words in adjacent lines through the stanza—a feature of A far poetry in general (Bliese, 1991). The following two lines from a horse praise song illustrate this repetition:

matre	*wayti way*	*ku*	*cami-kkala*
arriving not	when	your	slander-but
tabse	*wayti way*	*yi*	*cami-kkala*
cross not	when	my	slander-but

> If we don't arrive, you'll be slandered.
> If we don't cross over, I'll be slandered.

Note that three of the five words in the first line are repeated in the second line, giving cohesion to the unit. Also take note of the ten syllables in each line, which can be found by counting the vowels. Afar also has long vowels which are written with two vowels together. However, in singing, no distinction is made, so long and short are counted the same. Also, if a word ends in a vowel and the next word begins with any vowel, they assimilate (become one vowel sound) and are counted only as one syllable. This feature requires special attention in translation, where one works with written material. However, in traditional singing the poet gets the rhythm in his or her head and forms the lines with the correct number of syllables automatically.

In preparation for doing a poetic translation, each culture's poetic pattern must be analyzed on its own.

Features of Hebrew poetry

The source language for a translation of the Psalms is Hebrew, so we should also look at some of the features of Hebrew poetry. The most obvious feature of Hebrew poetry is the use of a divided line in which the second half carries the thought of the first half forward. This is called parallelism or seconding, and traditionally has been noted to have several types, such as repetition (synonymous), contrast (antithetic), and progression (synthetic). Scholars have noted that the second part is usually more specific or emphatic.

Metrically the traditional analysis of Hebrew poetry counts accents, usually one accent in each word. In the examples that follow, one Hebrew word is indicated by a single English word or a group of hyphenated words. Hyphens appearing in the original Masoretic text (MT) are indicated by =. In my analysis I have found that Hebrew poems with the same number of accents per line generally lead to a climax at the end of the poem. For example, in the poem in Hosea 1.9, the basic line has four accents, and a three-accent climax comes at the end:

Call his-name <u>not my-people</u>	4
For you-are <u>not my-people</u>	4
And-I AM=<u>not</u> for-you	3

This climax will often be marked by a terrace pattern of words building up to the end, such as "not my people" (underlined above) or some special pattern of words or sound repetition in the climactic final line. Note the divine name "I AM" in the peak.

Another type of Hebrew poem has a different number of accents per line throughout the poem. They are structured on the common Hebrew literary principle of chiasm. This means that the first and the last lines have the same number of accents, and the second line and second line from the end have the same number. This pattern is repeated until one comes to the center. The central line (or lines if the poem has an even number) is often the high point, which can be identified as the peak of the poem. Besides the metrical structure which points to the center in these poems, there are often other markers such as word repetition within chiastic structures occurring centrally in the peak. In poems with final line peaks, there are also word or sound repetitions within the peak. In many Biblical poems, the peak or climax is the place where the names and actions of God are most explicit.

For example, in Hosea 3.1 there is a chiasm based on the number of accents per line: 7 4 7. The climax of the poem is in the middle. Note that the word love surrounds the peak passage (marked in bold) and is repeated within it. Also note the divine name LORD in the central peak:

> Again, go love(=)a-woman loved-of a-friend, an-adulteress;   6/7
> **As-the-LORD loves the-children-of Israel.**   4
> But-they turn to=other gods, and-love cakes-of raisins   7

Not all scholars agree on how various lines of poetry should be analyzed. They may differ in their analyses as to how words should be divided or how many accents occur in each line. The hyphen in the Masoretic text of the first line is not followed in this analysis and is marked by parentheses.

An analysis of Psalm 23

In Hebrew poetry the term cola ("colon" for singular) is used to identify the two or three parts of a line. In verse one of Psalm 23 below, indentation of the second line shows where the second colon ("I-shall-not want") begins. If the line has an odd number of accented units, the larger portion normally comes first. This can be seen below in verse 5, with the three-unit colon first and the two-unit colon indented. Sometimes a line of six or more accents divides into three units instead of two. This is shown by the second half of verse 4, which divides into three cola of two accentual units each. This line is the center of the poem. As indicated above, in a poem with varying accents per line, the central line often has special features which give it emphasis. Breaking into three instead of the normal two cola helps to give emphasis to this line. This peak line is set off in bold type below. The number of accents in each line of Psalm 23 below is noted at the end of each line. Departures from Masoretic text (MT) hyphenation are shown with the MT number of units first, followed by a slash and then the number in this analysis. A (+) in the text shows where separate MT words are proposed to be hyphenated, or read with only one accent. This analysis gives a metrical chiasm with lines of four units on each end, followed by lines of six units, and on each side of the central line, two lines of five units. This may be shown as the numerical inversion 4655 6 5564.

1 The-**LORD** is-my-shepherd,
    I-shall-not want.   4
2 He-makes-me-lie-down in-green pastures;
    he-leads-me beside=still waters.   6
3 He-restores my-soul;
    he-leads-me in-paths-of=righteousness for-his-name's (+) sake.
                                                              [2+3]6/5
*
4 Even (+) though-I=walk through-the-valley-of darkness,
    I-don't=fear evil   6/5
  For=YOU are-with-me
     your-rod and-your-staff,
     they comfort-me.   [2+2+2]6

**
5 You-prepare a-table before-me
    in-the-presence-of my-enemies;   5
  you-anoint my-head with-oil,
    my-cup overflows;   5
6 Surely goodness and-mercy
    will-follow-me all=the-days-of my-life;   6
  And-I-will-dwell in-the-house-of=the-**LORD**
    for-a-length-of days.   4

The central peak 4b has an exceptional structure of a three-cola rather than a normal two-cola line. It is marked by a chiastic inversion of suffixes with "me-your; you-me" ("with ME, YOUR rod and YOUR staff comfort ME"). Such inversions are a common way to mark important lines in Hebrew poetry. There is also a major grammatical change in that the word "you" of the central line marks a shift from third to second person for the LORD. Bazak (334) points out the importance of "you" in that "the pronoun designating God is in the centre of the central expression" *for you are with me,* which has 26 words before it and 26 after it. He further points out (335) that the "numerical value of the Tetragrammaton is 26," and that "it is quite possible that the central phrase . . . was so calculated in order to refer to the name of God." ("Tetragrammaton" means the name of YHWH or "Yahweh," which when read as numbers rather than letters totals 26 (Y =10, H = 5, W =6, and H =5.) It should also be noted that the number of accent units before and after the six-accent peak line total 20, which fills out to 26 by adding the peak from either end. The central metaphors, "your rod and your staff" (see Ahroni 1982:26-9), together with the biblically important words "with-me" and "comfort," also give emphasis to this line. Pardee notes the importance of the royal imagery suggested by "rod" (275, 279-80) in understanding the poem, and the significant change to human rather than sheep imagery with the word "comfort" (275).

Concentric word patterns in the whole poem also point to the central peak. The first word "LORD" is repeated only in the last line, forming an inclusio. As noted above, the third person is used for the LORD in the lines before the peak, and again in the last line, with the central section speaking directly to him. The emphatic "YOU" at the beginning of the central peak is the only occurrence, and makes a pivot for the inclusio of "LORD," especially considering the 26 words before and after the phrase. The object suffix -ni- "me" has a similar pattern, coming in the second line from each end, and at the end of the peak line. (It occurs twice in the second line, and once more in the third line.) The similarity of "waters" (Hebrew *mey*) in the second line to "days" (*yemey*) in the second line from the end also gives symmetry.

Parallelism is not obvious semantically except in verse two. Pardee points out that this line is the cue to the hearer to expect poetry, and in a thorough study shows how the lack of "semantic parallelism" is "made up for by other types of parallelism in other distributions . . ." (262-71, esp. 269). For example, he notes the similar structure of the three prepositional phrases: "in green pastures," "in paths of righteousness" and "in the valley of darkness" in verses 2-4a.

Thematically two stanzas can be noted (see C. O'Connor for a historical survey of structural studies of Psalm 23). The first stanza has the subject "The LORD my shepherd" in 3-4. (The stanza juncture is marked by ** above.) As is often the case in Hebrew poetry with two major divisions, the central peakline is the end of the first stanza. Hebrew poems normally group lines thematically in strophes of two lines or sometimes three lines. The juncture after the first strophe occurs after verse 3 (marked by * above). Thematically this is the end of the first picture of quiet, peaceful existence in the fold of the LORD. Verse 4 brings in new elements of danger, "the valley of darkness" and "evil."

The second stanza, 5-6, has the picture of being hosted by the LORD. Danger in the form of "enemies" comes in the first line after the center, chiastically matching that of the "valley of darkness" and "evil" just before the peak. The same confidence in the protection of the LORD is shown here. The last lines, with dwelling in the "house of the LORD" in "goodness and mercy," are chiastically parallel to the picture of "lying down in green pastures beside still waters" with "the LORD my shepherd."

An Afar translation of Psalm 23

Mr. Muusa Mohammed has a talent for composing Afar songs. In the past we have worked together in composing Psalm 8 as an Afar Praise Song published in the New Readers Series. He has also composed and recorded summary songs for the 28 chapters of Matthew for audio-cassette, and is now working on poetic translation of various other portions of the Old Testament. Muusa had already translated the Psalm in a basically prose style, keeping some of the obvious parallelism of the Hebrew poetic lines, and putting it in a poetry format following the Hebrew lines. No Afar poetic structure was chosen as the model for this initial translation. For example, the lines varied from four to fifteen syllables, in spite of the Afar poetic constraint to have the same number throughout the poem. This restricts the Psalm to only reading, when the original function of the Psalms was singing. The feature of repetition of words to give cohesion within each stanza was also not followed. The format suggests poetry, but the expectations for Afar poetry are not met.

189

The value of the prose translation was that it put the message into the Afar language. This gave an intermediary step before trying to write Afar poetry with the same message. Before poets can begin, they must have the ideas in their head that they want to express. By putting these first in Afar prose, we were able to begin manipulating the lines into the form which would be recognized as poetry. This is what happened with the present translation. We counted syllables to see what combinations would fit into a ten-syllable line, and we noted places where repetitions could be included from line to line to give stanza cohesion. The Psalm went through several versions trying to achieve faithfulness and naturalness, as well as fulfilling the constraints of Afar poetry. The result was as follows:

YALLI YI LOYNAYTU
GOD IS MY SHEPHERD

1   Yalli yi loyna 'kkal tuh waam mayyu.
      God is my shepherd, so I won't lack anything.
    Yoo miraacisah ikkal waam mayyu.
      He leads me, so I won't lack anything.

2   Meqe mano geya'gid yoo beyah;
      He takes me in order that I get a good living.
    Salalteeh meqe leeh fan yoo beya;
      He takes me to clear, good water.
3   Luk suge mano yok yuqusbuuseeh;
      He renewed the living I have;
    luk suge rooci yok yuqusbuuse;
      He renewed the spirit I have.
*

Isih le nabnal xagna yoh culeh;
      He enters an appointment with me for his own glory;
cakkik yan gital yoo miraacisa.
      he leads me on a road of uprightness.
*

4   Rabah daqar fan yoo beyaanamah,
      If they take me to the valley of death,
dite le boodoh fanah culaamah,
      if I enter a hole of darkness,

Yallaw, koo liyooh, hinigga maxca!
      God, I have you, I won't startle!
Yallaw, koo liyooh, tuk mameysita!
      God, I have you, I won't be afraid of anything!
*

Ku caxxat yoo cattah yoo dacrissah,
      You help me with a stick, you guard me,

yoh wakli takkeeh, yoo cattam digga.
you become a companion for me, you are active to help me.
**

5   Naqboytit abalih yoo-arcibissah;
      You host me when enemies watch;
maaqo yoh taceeh, caddi yoh abta.
      you give me food, you make honor for me.
Cayyam fan an wayya haam yoh abta.
      You do for me what I lack until I am satisfied.
*

6   Ku maqaane yo 'lih tan anim fan;
      As long as I live your goodness is with me.
an' anim fan ku kacni yo 'lih yan;
      As long as I live your love is with me.
buxah liyom anim fan ku buxa.
      As long as I live your house is my house.

A comparison of this version with the earlier prose version shows the
consistent pattern of ten syllables per line. This constraint forces many changes
which lengthen or shorten the lines of the prose translation. The important
feature of repetition of words within stanzas helps to fill short lines. One word
or phrase becomes the standard for the stanza, and the variable ideas from the
original are fitted around it. For example, the first line ends with "so I won't
lack anything," and the next line repeats the same phrase although the original
has this line only once. In verse 2 the opposite happens, where two Hebrew
words are both translated with the same Afar word. "Leads me" in the original
is translated with "takes me," which becomes the standard for the verse. Instead
of "makes lie down" as in the original, "takes me" is used again, giving
repetition. 3a gets its repetition by adding the phrase "renew my living" to the
original "renews my spirit." Since "living" is the same word as in verse 2, it gives
further cohesion between verses 2 and 3 within this stanza.

Verse 3b forms a stanza of its own in this translation. This change from the
original brings the number of verses closer to the length of normal Afar stanzas,
with two or three lines. The change to the spiritual themes of God 's "name" and
"uprightness" makes this appropriate. The repeated word in this unit is *yoo*
"me." The grammatical pattern of "me" coming before the final verb in both
clauses, and both of the lines starting with relative clauses, also gives cohesion
to this stanza.

In the first two lines of verse 4 the repetition of *-amah-* "if" in each line gives
strong cohesion. In this unit the original "valley" has been expanded to "valley"
and "hole." The Hebrew word for "darkness" is expanded to "death" and
"darkness" as in those translations which divide the Hebrew word into two
words, "shadow-of death". Pardee finds both meanings likely, calling this
"punning" (1990: 275).

The second two lines of verse 4 are the beginning of the peak in the Hebrew
poem. It is given emphasis by translating "You are with me" with the repetition
of the familiar phrase in Afar war songs *koo liyooh* "I have you," implying that

"you are all I need." The vocative "God" is added for clarity, emphasis and cohesion. This substitutes for the function of the 26 words or accent units referring to YHWH. The verb "fear" from the original 4a is repeated with two negative verbs, again giving emphasis and cohesion. Afar is a verb-final language, so the verb "fear" of the main clause in the original must come here at the end of the sentence. The peak lines beginning with "God, I have you" were later reduced to a chorus and repeated after every line.

In the last two lines of verse 4, "your rod and your staff, they comfort me" is restructured into two lines with *yoo* "me" repeated twice in each line. "Rod and staff" have been reduced to "stick" for lack of different terms. "Comfort" has been translated twice, as "help" and "active to help," also giving cohesion. The phrase "you become my companion" is another important phrase in Afar songs and here expands the key phrase "You are with me."

The triplet in verse 5 again has cohesion with "me" at least once in each line, including the final *yoh abta* "do for me" in the last two lines. Since the nomadic Afar don't have tables, "host" and "give me food" are the functional equivalents. "My cup overflows" doesn't fit the culture, so it is restructured as "you do for me what I need until I am satisfied." The last stanza (verse 6) is a triplet with cohesion, in that each line begins with *ku* "Your" and also has *anim fan* "as long as I live." The first two lines also have the repetition of *yo'lih -ani* "is with me" at the ends, and the last line has repetition of *buxa* "house," giving a strong poetic climax in the stanza. The repetition is achieved by restructuring the original "follow/pursue" twice as "is with me," and by changing from "live in the house of the LORD for a length of days" to "as long as I live, your house is my house." The change back to third person for LORD in the last line of Hebrew is not followed, since a Praise Song prefers direct address spoken to the one being praised. Such restructuring helps to make Psalm 23 as dynamic in Afar as it is in Hebrew.

The goal to have real poetry in Bible translation is a continuing concern for those seeking to make the best translation possible. Two of the three points in the definition of poetry which Stine (66) discusses on the basis of Easthope are "repetition" and organization into "lines." These are very well illustrated in the difference between the prose and the poetic versions of Psalm 23. The third point is that "information or communication is backgrounded" in the sense that poetry foregrounds the word or form of the words. Since Bible translation is closely tied to accurate transfer of information, this is a more difficult goal. The use of syllable counts and repetition within stanzas is an effort to achieve poetic effect. The repetition from well-known poetry forms, such as the "I have you" in the peak above, may be a means by which the hearer will identify this as poetry. By following such constraints the translator has put the use of poetic form forward, and perhaps from the standpoint of accuracy has backgrounded information in the original. Since the original would have had to do the same thing to be poetry in its own framework, such a transfer should be encouraged as necessary in translation of Biblical poetry.

In a basically illiterate culture such as the Afar, the importance of the use of an oral medium also needs to be emphasized. Written scripture has a very limited audience, but cassette players and radio programs can reach many more.

Klem (173-8) has shown that an oral community can assimilate scripture texts much more efficiently when put to music. The use of traditional forms of poetry and music in Bible translation is therefore motivated from two concerns: first, the concern for functional translation which tries to produce an equivalent form as well as the equivalent meaning in any language and culture (de Waard & Nida, 1986), and secondly, the special concern to reach those in an oral culture with an effective presentation of God's word.

REFERENCES

Ahroni, Reuben. 1982. "The Unity of Psalm 23." *Hebrew Annual Review* 6: 21-34.

Bazak, Jacob. 1988. "Numerical Devices in Biblical Poetry." *Vetus Testamentum* 38, 3: 333-337.

Bliese, Loren F. 1982-3. "Afar Songs", *Northeast African Studies* 4: 3, 51-76.

———. 1988a. "Chiastic Structures, Peaks and Cohesion in Nehemiah 9:6-37. *The Bible Translator,* 39.2: 208-215".

———. 1988b. "Metrical Sequences and Climax in the Poetry of Joel" *Occasional Papers in Translation and Textinguistics* 2.4: 52-84.

———. 1990. "Structurally Marked Peak in Psalms 1-24" *Occasional Papers in Translation and Textlinguistics* 4.4: 265-321.

———. 1994. "The Afar Drum Song Karambo." *Proceedings of the Eleventh International Conference of Ethiopian Studies*. Vol. 1. Bahru Zewde, Richard Pankhurst, and Taddese Beyene, editors. Addis Ababa: Addis Ababa University. 583-594.

———. 1994, "Symmetry and Prominence in Hebrew Poetry with Examples from Hosea," *Translating Biblical Poetry*. UBS Monograph, Ernst Wendland, ed.

de Waard, Jan, and Eugene Nida. 1986. *From One Language to Another: Functional Equivalence in Bible Translating*. New York: Nelson.

Easthope, Anthony. 1983. *Poetry as Discourse*. New York: Methuen.

Klem, Herbert V. 1982. *Oral Communication of the Scripture: Insights from African Oral Art*. Pasadena: William Carey.

The NIV Study Bible. 1985. Zondervan: Grand Rapids, 807-8.

O'Connor, Charles. 1985. "The Structure of Psalm 23." *Louvain Studies* 10:206-30.

Pardee, Dennis. 1990. "Structure and Meaning in Hebrew Poetry: The Example of Psalm 23." *MAARAV* 5-6: 239-280.

Stine, Philip C. 1987. "Biblical Poetry and Translation" *Meta* 32, 1: 64-75.

Philippine Poetry and Bible Translation

Louis Dorn

(Condensed from "Philippine Poetry and Translation : A General Survey," 1994, *TBT* 45: 301-315)

When the Tagalog Good News Bible (*Magandang Balita Biblia*) was published in 1980, one of the initial reactions was that of general pleasure at the use of normal forms of Philippine poetry where such forms were called for. Principles of dynamic equivalence provided enough freedom of word choice and of structure so that poetry could have appropriate equivalence of meaning and impact. It may be useful to reexamine the material, to determine both strengths and weaknesses in the translated poetic material.

This study touches upon a wide range of poetic features. We will first look at some features of Philippine poetry before reviewing samples from the Tagalog *Magandang Balita Biblia*.

Tagalog Poetry Forms

Formal Structure of Classical Poetry

A simple introduction into the formal nature of Philippine poetry can be accomplished by showing some details of the first stanza of the classical Tagalog poem, *Plorante at Laura* [Plorante and Laura], by Francisco Baltasar, who is also known by his pen name, "Balagtas." A good number of languages in the Philippines have lengthy poems passed on orally from one generation to the next, and these have been referred to as "epics." The opening stanza is as follows:

> Sa isáng madilím / gúbat na mapangláw,
> dáwag na matiník / ay waláng pagítan,
> hálos naghíhirap / ang kay Pébong sílang
> dumálaw sa loób / na lubháng masúkal.

In a dark / forest that is gloomy
the vines, thorny / have no space [for squeezing] between,
[so that] it is almost difficult / [even] for rising Phoebus [the sun god]
to visit the interior / that is so very cluttered.

This stanza has twelve syllables per line, with the line regularly divided in the middle. Other poems that follow classical form regularly have an even number of syllables per line, and the lines can be rather long with eighteen or more syllables. The divisions do not necessarily divide the line in half as they do here, but they regularly occur at the same point in the line, with an even number of syllables in each half. (Note that these observations on counting syllables apply only to that poetry which attempts to imitate the classical form, especially that of Balagtas.)

Rhyming follows a strict pattern in the Balagtas epic. Each stanza has its own set of mutually rhyming syllables at the end of every line (not at the middle point), and no two adjacent stanzas use the same set of rhyming syllables. Rhyming rules in all Philippine languages we have examined are as follows:

Syllables that rhyme with each other must have identical vowels.

The syllables that rhyme with each other must be vowel-final or all consonant-final.

Vowel-final syllables must all either
  (i) end in a glottal stop (normally not written, although significant; for example, *wikà* 'language', *basâ* 'wet', and *paksâ* 'topic') or
  (ii) end without a glottal stop (for example, *halina* 'come' and *bumása* 'read').

Consonant-final syllables must all be either
  (i) voiced continuants (for example, the endings *-an, -al, -aw, -ay*) or
  (ii) stops, or the voiceless *s*; (for example, the endings *-ad, -at, -as, -ap*).

There are, therefore, four possible rhyming sets multiplied by the number of vowels in a given language. It has been surprising to find local poets who never realized that this was the rhyming pattern of their language, yet they adhered to it perfectly.

Stressed syllables are here indicated by accent marks, and in this poem they occur at the rate of two per half line, but within each half line they can occur in any position. This feature of stress is important to remember when poems are sung to rhythmic music. Tagalog is spoken with a fairly level pitch maintained during a given clause, and stress is a matter of loudness that does not change the pitch. Somehow this has meant that rhythmic stresses in sung music do not need to match spoken stresses. The only warning is that ambiguities may occur occasionally, in which the sung stress may signal a similar word form with a different meaning; e.g., *bumása* 'to read' and *bumasâ* 'to become wet'. The first two lines of the popular folk song "Bahay Kubo" demonstrate how spoken stress need not coincide with sung stress; here the sung stresses are underlined while the spoken stresses are accented:

Báhay kúbo, káhit muntî,	Nipa hut, although tiny,
Ang haláman doón ay sári-sári.	The plants there are various.

In terms of language structure, the above stanza of classical poetry uses a word order and sentence structure that is normal for standard prose, and this feature is common in Tagalog poetry. However, certain words serving as grammatical markers can be dropped, but only at the beginning of a line or of a half line. For example, in the Balagtas poem the connector/relator word *na* is implied at the beginning of the second half line, and the case marker *ang* is implied at the beginning of line 2. Again, it cannot be stated that this pattern is adhered to by all modern poets.

In terms of content, the poem has devices commonly used in the poetry of other cultures. It establishes a gloomy setting, almost chaotic, from the beginning. Other stanzas will reveal figurative language and similar devices anticipated in poetry. One can see already in the first stanza that Balagtas has borrowed a classical Greek image that was filtered through his Spanish education as he refers to the sun god in the third line. The rays of the sun that cannot penetrate the forest are spoken of figuratively as the visit of Phoebus, which meets with obstacles.

This borrowed feature from the western culture is important to note, for it signals the readiness of the Tagalog culture to adopt foreign features and adapt them so that they fit into the local culture.

Tagalog poetry in general appears to follow a system of poetic rules more closely than do certain other Philippine languages with regard to their respective traditions of poetry. For example, the life and death of Jesus Christ has been set to poetic form in several of the major languages, and these lengthy poems are sung or chanted in homes and in communities during the week between Palm Sunday and Easter. The Tagalog *Kasaysayan ng Pasiong Mahal ni Hesukristong Panginoon Natin,* "Narrative of the Precious Passion of Jesus Christ our Lord," is composed of five-line stanzas throughout, the lines of each stanza consisting of eight syllables, with all lines rhyming with each other on their final syllables, and no adjacent stanza employing the identical set of rhyming syllables. In the Cebuano version the form is less restricted, as one stanza may have a rhyming pattern of A-A-B-B-B, A-B-A-B-A, A-B-A-C-A, and so forth, or all lines may rhyme with each other. Not only may the various patterns exist within one poem, but adjacent stanzas may share the same rhyming set of syllables or the same rhyming pattern. This feature gives Cebuano hymn writers, for example, greater freedom within which to work.

As to the number of syllables per line, Cebuano poetry appears to be quite regular, as is true of Tagalog. However, the poetry and songs of certain language groups in the mountains of northern Luzon demonstrate freedom in this regard. If the regular beat of a song calls for eleven syllables per line, in some songs relatively few lines will adhere to this requirement. Shorter lines will have some syllables carried over two musical notes or beats, while longer lines will be adjusted by having two syllables sung where only one is normal. And the practice appears to be quite acceptable. All of these variations cause one to question whether the language groups more influenced by western culture have correspondingly regularized their indigenous poetic patterns, or whether such strict regularization preceded the arrival of westerners. This would be an area for further research.

An Example of Modern Poetry

In contrast with the classical style, modern, popular poetry is far more flexible. The following poem by Ronnie M. Halos appeared in the weekly magazine *Liwayway* (October 28,1985, page 32):

197

LOUIS DORN

| MGA ANAY SA HALIGI | TERMITES IN THE SUPPORT-POSTS |
| Line | rhyme | syllables |

		rhyme	syll	
1	*Nabaghan si Tata Gustin*	A	8	Daddy Gustin was surprised
2	*isang umaga nang kanyang*			
	mapansin	A	11	one morning when he noticed
3	*na may mga anay na namahay*	B	10	there were termites residing
4	*sa haligi ng kanyang bahay*	B	9	in the support-posts of his house.

5	*Mapuputi at manilaw-nilaw*	B′	10	Somewhat white and yellow
6	*ang mga anay na iyon*	C	8	were those termites
7	*na ang mga ngipin*	A′	6	whose teeth
8	*ay kumikinang*	B′	5	were sparkling.

9	*Si Tata Gustin ay nag-isip*	D	9	Daddy Gustin pondered
10	*at biglang nagulumihanan*	B″	9	and suddenly was perplexed
11	*ngayong nasinop na niya*	E	8	now that he had fixed up
12	*ang kanyang bahay*	B″	5	his house
13	*ay saka naman may*			
	tatampalasan	B″	11	there was, in turn, a destroyer.

14	*Si Tata Gustin bagamat may*			
	poot	F	11	Daddy Gustin, although angry,
15	*ay di makasigaw*	B″	6	could not shout
16	*bagkus ay napaiyak,*	G	7	but only cried
17	*ang sugat sa kanyang didib*	D	8	the wound in his breast
18	*ay nagdurugo at nagnanaknak...*	G	10	was bleeding and infected...

19	*Alam ni Tata Gustin*	A″	7	Daddy Gustin knew
20	*bukas ay darami pa ang mga anay,*	B‴	12	tomorrow the termites will multiply further,
21	*bukas din ay hindi niya alam*	B‴	10	and also tomorrow he will not know
22	*ang kanyang kinabukasan.*	B‴	8	his tomorrow [his future].

In the center column, after each line, the rhyming pattern is shown. Prime markers (B′, B″, B‴) show the same rhyming set of syllables used in later stanzas in separate, subsequent patterns. Upon first inspection there seems to be no real pattern except that several lines seem to rhyme with each other haphazardly. Horizontal lines have been added above to mark off the sentences from one another and to identify possible patterns. This seems to break the poem into five stanzas. The first four lines follow a common pattern seen in

198

poetry (AABB). The second stanza, lines 5-8, rhymes on its first and last lines (BCAB). The third stanza, 9-13, rhymes on its second, fourth, and fifth lines. The fourth stanza, 14-18, rhymes on its third and fifth lines. The last stanza rhymes on all but its first line. The first and last stanzas share the same rhyming types (A and B), forming a kind of inclusio around the poem. In the final stanza the word *bukas*, "tomorrow," is used in a skillful play on words in the last three rhyming lines.

The poem does not seem to have been prepared for singing, or at least not for use with a melody with even lines; the number of syllables varies considerably from line to line. However, Ruel F. Pepa (coordinator of the Tagalog Old Testament revision) reminds me that "free-verse poems like this are the favorite of modern Tagalog rock-and-roll ('soft' rock to be specific) musicians/singers." In any case, one wonders if the poet used shorter lines, possibly spoken more slowly, to give dramatic emphasis, especially toward the end of the poem.

In the following examples the number of accented syllables per line does not seem significant." This was certainly an important feature in the classical style of Balagtas. Some today continue to believe that this is an important feature. However, it seems that this feature was among the first to be abandoned by many writers as poetry moved into other forms such as those in use today.

What is the general meaning of the poem? When an assembled group of translation reviewers from several language areas was asked whether this poem is about termites, they responded with a resounding "No!" The poem appeared during the last months of the Marcos dictatorship, and so it could be thought of as a reflection on the political situation. However, this poem could be resurrected under different circumstances and applied in a completely different manner—also without reference to termites.

Other poetic forms

Proverbs and riddles also occur as a tradition in poetic form. Some believe that these forms were close to the life of the people and that they developed earlier, so that the forms of longer poems have their roots in these shorter forms. These forms need to be studied so that they can serve as models for translation.

Riddles

The Tagalog riddle is regularly composed of two rhyming lines, equal in length. Two images are presented to the hearer, usually contrasting images or even conflicting ones. For example:

> *Munting dagat-dagatan*
> *Binabakor ng danglay.*
> A tiny little lake
> fenced with bamboo strips.

Fish traps formed of bamboo strips are normally inside a lake, not surrounding it. The answer to the riddle is the human eye, with its eyelashes that surround it. Another example:

> *Bumbong kung liwanag*
> *Kung gabi ay dagat.*
> A bamboo tube by daylight
> at night a sea.

The mat for sleeping is rolled up by day so that it looks like a large bamboo tube, but at night it is wide and flat like the surface of the sea.

It will be noted that both riddles have their own rhyme. The first consists of two seven-syllable lines, while the second consists of two six-syllable lines. Comparison with riddle patterns from other language groups indicates that such a pattern is in common use in many areas of the Philippines. It seems that the challenge of the riddle is enhanced when fewer words are used, so that the number of hints toward a solution are kept to a minimum.

Proverbs

The form of the Tagalog proverb follows the same pattern as the riddle:

> *Nuti ang gumamela*
> *nula ang sampaguita*
> The hibiscus turns white;
> the jasmine turns red.

Since the normal color of these two flowers is the reverse, this proverb speaks of a completely unexpected reversal. Another example:

> *Ubos, ubos biyaya*
> *Bukas nama'y tunganga*
> Use up, use up what is granted
> Tomorrow, then, the mouth hangs open.

This proverb reminds those who have material blessings today not to squander them, lest they be left tomorrow with nothing. A third example shows how certain proverbial themes are repeated across the globe:

> *Ipinakataas-taas;*
> *dumagundung nang lumagpak*
> It was raised to a great height;
> it made a resounding noise when it fell.

These proverbs follow the same formal structure as the riddles, namely, that the two lines are equal in number of syllables, and each pair rhymes on the final syllable. The first two have seven syllables per line, while the last has eight. An economy of words is used, as in the riddle, and perhaps this feature helps people remember the proverb. The terseness also seems to emphasize the simplicity and clarity of principles that hold true for proper living.

Balagtasan

One more form of Tagalog poetry must be mentioned, namely, the *Balagtasan*, a spontaneous debate in which two contestants must argue their points strictly within the accepted forms of Tagalog poetry. A third poet is involved, a kind of middleman, who serves as referee and judge, and who, also in poetic style, introduces the topic and the contestants. In the end he usually does not state who won the debate (that would be impolite), but he suggests that each party had valid things to say, and we should all go home and think it over. Some features of this form have counterparts in the book of Job, where Job debates with his three friends (thus involving more than the two protagonists of the Balagtasan), and where Elihu appears out of nowhere and says nothing, really, beyond recapitulating what has been said.

The *Balagtasan* may eventually die out if people do not grow up in an environment where they are stimulated by this intellectual pastime. However, it is apparent that the form continues to be appreciated. One missionary told how he had just arrived by public transport at the public square of a large rural town where some Christian evangelists had arranged for an expert in spontaneous Tagalog poetry to address the public in that medium. The driver's attention was captured immediately by what he heard, and he didn't even pay attention to the payment the missionary was counting out into his hand. The Christian message apparently was heard more intently in this genre than would have been the case otherwise.

"Doggerel"

The Random House dictionary speaks of "doggerel" as "(verse) comic or burlesque, and usually loose or irregular in measure." Ogden Nash has proven that the English-reading public enjoys doggerel when it is used for comic purposes. Something similar is happening in the Philippines today, as demonstrated by newspaper clippings, in which verse is used for humorous purposes. Here is an excerpt from a contribution by a reader to *Sports Flash* (June 4-10, 1990), in which he discusses certain basketball players:

> *Kung* point guard *ang pag-uusapan*
> *Walang panama si Calma* or *Jaworski diyan*
> *Maging sa* assist or steal *ay talagang maaasahan*
> *Pati sa* rebound *kay Gray lumalaban*

Even without a technical description or translation, one can see how English and Tagalog are mixed, and that is all part of the humor of this one verse taken from a longer poem. The point is that translators should be aware of what makes for doggerel, chiefly so that such features do not by accident creep into what is supposed to be serious biblical text. Sometimes there may be a contraction that is normal elsewhere but should not be found in the best poetry, or there may be the misuse of a figure of speech, or the forced twisting of sentence structure to fit a required format.

There is much more to Tagalog poetry and to Philippine poetry in general than has been presented in these few lines. However, the above information may serve as sufficient background to demonstrate that forms are available for use in the Tagalog Bible translation. It is especially important to note that rules exist, but that these rules are bent frequently. It is also important to note that certain nonindigenous forms and concepts can be borrowed effectively. Philippine poetry resembles Hebrew poetry in that there is a great variety of forms and devices available to the poet, and one never knows from poem to poem what to expect next.

Although features such as parallelism and chiasmus may occur in Philippine poetry, they do not function in the same ways as in Hebrew poetry; they are not of central importance. For example, the Kugel/Alter concept of the second line serving as a further development of the first line has not been noted as a regular feature nor as significant in Tagalog. Similarly chiasmus, if it occurs, carries no significance other than structural beauty, and indeed it is difficult to find examples. As is true of English speakers, the reader or hearer may not recognize them, nor will they have any special significance, unless the reader is trained to watch for them.

Poetry in the Tagalog Bible

Riddles and proverbs

Samson's riddle, in Judges 14.14, makes an interesting study in Hebrew, to say nothing of its rendering into Tagalog. As with Tagalog riddles, this Hebrew riddle involves an unexpected clash or contrast in the images presented. The translators treated it as follows:

> *Mula sa mangangain / ay lumabas ang pagkain;*   7+8 A, A
> *at mula sa malakas, / matamis ay lumabas*   7+7 B, B
> From the eater came out the food;
> and from the strong, sweet came out

This rendering seems well done. Following classical style the translators could have deleted the particle *ay* in line 1, leaving equal half lines all around. Perhaps there are more hints available than in indigenous riddles, since this one is almost like a double riddle in length and style; each half has the form of a single Tagalog riddle, and each half has its distinct set of rhyming syllables. Regalada A. Herrera (a teacher and staff member of the Translation Department of the Lutheran Church) reports that "this may resemble the *talinhaga*, an extended form of the riddle."

To complete the picture, it seems appropriate to look at verse 18. The answer to the riddle:

> *May tatamis pa ba sa pulutpukyutan*   12 A
> *at may lalakas pa ba sa leong matapang?*   13 A
> Is there something more sweet than bee-honey
> and is there anything that will be stronger than a fierce lion?

And Samson's response:

Kundi pa ninyo sinapakat ang aking maybahay   15 A
hindi ninyo malalaman kung ano'ng kasagutan   15 A
If you had not conspired with my house-owner [wife]
you could not know what was the answer.

The chief purpose for rendering this part of the conversation in poetic form seems to have been to reflect the Hebrew word-game being played out at Samson's wedding feast—and the Tagalog reader will have no problem recognizing this fact. There seems to be a genre for such brief poetic statement-with-response in the final words of a typical *Balagtasan*, and Pepa agrees with this possibility. The contestants may become rather heated and shout brief sets of lines at each other. The translators have simply rendered each quotation as a pair of rhyming lines of equal length. (In order to keep the same number of syllables in the two lines of the answer, the translators could have left *at* implicit, second line, ending the first line with a semicolon.) The Hebrew of Samson's response uses the figure of plowing with Samson's heifer. That figure has been abandoned in the translation. As Pepa states, "The figure of plowing with Samson's heifer has been abandoned in the Tagalog translation . . . simply because a direct translation of it in Tagalog would not mean what the figure wants to say. There is no such idiom in Tagalog to mean 'conspiring with the wife.' The more functional alternative is to directly state the meaning, as has been done in the translation." There are other features of the Hebrew form of this repartee that cannot be duplicated in Tagalog, but this is typical of the loss of form in translating poetry.

The model of the proverb was perhaps the first form which the Tagalog Bible translators used after they decided to translate according to normal Tagalog poetic structures. They came to 2 Peter 2.22b: "The dog turns back to his own vomit and the sow is washed only to wallow in the mire" (RSV). After they rendered the two proverbs in standard prose form, they realized that the translation was accurate, but it simply would not function as a pair of proverbs. They therefore revised the translation and came up with the following final form:

Ang aso ay hayop, likas ang damdamin   12 A
Na sa isinuka ay nagbabalik din.   12 A
Ito namang baboy, paliguan mo man,   12 B
Babalik na muli sa dating lubluban.   12 B

The dog is an animal, natural its instinct
That to what it vomited it also returns.
As for this pig, even if you bathe it,
It will return again to its former wallowing-place.

It is evident, of course, that the translators made the saying somewhat wordy by making explicit some implicit information. Perhaps this was necessary in order to have the traditional two-line proverb. However, Pepa agrees that it would have been better to make them more brief and concise. Since the two proverbs are twins, so to speak, and since the second is related to the first by *naman,* "as for," it may have been better to consider the pair as a single quotation. However, note that each of the line pairs rhymes separately from the other. Each line consists of twelve syllables, and a break occurs in the middle of each line. Such line divisions don't seem to occur in proverbs, and the lines themselves are more verbose than any local proverbs we have encountered. It is clear that the normal, terse form for Tagalog proverbs has not been followed strictly. Proverbs and riddles that grow spontaneously from images and sounds available within a language group's culture can often be kept terse quite easily. Translators normally have difficulty matching such terseness when they are forced to use the same images and explicit referents.

Naturally the translators decided to use as much as they could of the Tagalog poetic form when they translated the book of Proverbs. Whether this was successful is difficult to determine. For example, 1.1-6 is translated as a prose introduction, since it does not resemble Tagalog proverbs in form and function (although Pepa feels that it could have been rendered as poetry anyway). Verse 7 is a proverb, is translated as such. It lacks the figurative speech normally seen in a Tagalog proverb, yet it is a wise saying expressed in a rhyme:

> *Ang pagkatakot kay Yahweh ay panimula ng karunungan,*
> *Ngunit walang halaga sa mga mangmang ang aral at mga saway.*
> Fear of Yahweh is the beginning of wisdom
> But of no value to fools is the teaching and corrections.

The ends of the two lines rhyme; the first line consists of eighteen syllables, the second, twenty. This does not pass a rigid test of poetic form, and the lines are much longer than normal for a proverb. Whether this fact is important must be determined by native speakers. Pepa, for example, feels that "the two lines of Prov 1.7 can be taken as two distinct proverbs, and they should be made to appear as such. Each line should therefore be revised to create rhyming syllables. Other similar cases in the book of Proverbs should be treated the same."

Verses 8-19 then continue with what in Hebrew is a poetic form of admonition and therefore in some languages should be rendered as a formal speech, not as poetry. However, the translators continue to use rhyming syllables at the end of each pair of lines. The lines themselves do not match at all in terms of syllable count, although no pair differs by more than two or four syllables. If there is a good reason to translate these verses into poetic form, it is not that these are proverbs, and Pepa agrees. However, Herrera informs me that this kind of admonition may well be stated in Tagalog poetic form. It would be useful to deal with this kind of problem at a translation workshop.

Proverbs 10 begins a series of statements that are considered proverbs in the Hebrew sense. The translators turned every one of them into a pair of lines rhyming at the end, but only in rare cases does the syllable count match. Furthermore, although the habit of pairing lines in Tagalog is a convenient match for parallelism in Hebrew, the resulting translation becomes somewhat lengthy. The shorter lines in the translation contain sixteen syllables, some over twenty, while the samples we reviewed of native Tagalog proverbs have at the most only eight syllables per line. One must, say, therefore, that what we find may perhaps be a good adaptation in the direction of the normal Tagalog proverb form, but these proverbs do not yet appear dressed in native Tagalog costumes.

Standard poems

In many instances the Tagalog translation committee took the cues of RSV in determining what was done originally in poetic form, and in deciding to render such sections as poetry in Tagalog. This applies to many sections of prophecy, for example. At some time it will be necessary to review all instances and determine whether some principles can be found by which to determine whether poetry is the proper medium for such material. Pending such an evaluation we turn to some examples at hand.

In Gen 2.23, Adam's response upon seeing his wife is rendered as follows:

> *Sa wakas, narito ang isang tulad ko,*   A 12
> Finally, here is one like me,

> *Laman ng aking laman, buto ng aking buto*   A 14
> Flesh of my flesh, bone of my bone;

> *Babae ang siyang itatawag sa kaniya*   B 14
> Woman is what will be called to her

> *Sapagkat sa lalaki nagmula siya*   B 12
> Because from the man she came forth.

The position and number of accented syllables has no significance, nor is there a significant consistency in any central pause for each line. It is interesting that the rhyming pattern (A-A-B-B) and the pattern of number of syllables per line (12-14-14-12) do not coincide. The subject matter may possibly be suitable for a *diona*, or wedding song, although the form may not be right; but this question must be left to an expert.

The Song of Lamech yields similar results (Gen 4.23-24):

> *Dinggin ninyo itong aking sasabihin,*   A 12
> Hear this that I will say,
> *Ada at Zilla, asawa kong giliw;*   A 11
> Ada and Zilla, my beloved wife;
> *May pinatay akong isang kabataan,*   B 12
> There is a young man I have killed,
> *Ako ay sinaktan kaya ko pinatay*   B 12
> I was wounded therefore [he] was killed by me

> *Kung saktan si Cain, ang parusang gawad*   C 12
> If Cain is hurt, the punishment paid

Sa gagawa nito'y pitong patong agad;   C 12
    To the one who will do this is seven times immediately;
Nguni't kapag ako ang siyang sinaktan,   B' 12
    But if I am the one he wounded,
Pitumpu't pitong patong ang kaparusahan.   B' 13
    Seventy-seven times is the punishment.

Here the rhyming pattern is very regular. The last two lines are not regarded as rhyming with lines 3 and 4, but only with each other. One of the eight lines lacks a syllable for perfect syllable count, while the last line has one syllable too many. Further research may determine whether this song resembles the *kumintang*, the war or battle song.

Psalms

Although the following study will demonstrate problems with the psalms in their present form, Herrera reports that they have been gladly received and used at worship in the church which she attends. This includes singing the Psalms and other portions of Scripture, using the medium of chant.

Psalm 1

b. *Mapalad ang taong naaakit niyong masasama,*   18 A
    Upang sundan niya ang kanilang payo't maling halimbawa   18 A
    Hindi sumasama sa sinumang taong ang laging adhika'y   18 B
    Pagtawanan lamang at hamakhamakin ang Diyos na dakila.   18 A
c. *Nagagalak siyang laging magsaliksik ng banal na aral,*   18 B
    Ang utos ni Yahweh siyang binubulay sa gabi at araw;   18 B
d. *Ang katulad niya'y isang punongkahoy sa tabing batisan*   18 B
    Sariwa ang daho't laging namumunga sa kapanahunan   18 B
    At anumang gawin ay nakatitiyak na magtatagumpay.   18 B

e. *Ngunit ibang-iba ang masamang tao; ipa ang kawangis,*   18 C
    Siya'y natatangay at naipapadpad kung hangi'y umihip;   18 C
f. *Ang masamang tao ay parurusahan, hindi magmimintis,*   18 C
    Iwawalay siya sa pagkakatipon ng mga matuwid,   18 C
g. *Sa taong matuwid ay itong si Yahweh ang s'yang ma-iingat,*   18 D
    Ngunit kailanman ang mga masama ay mapapahamak.   18 D

1. Blessed the person who is not drawn toward those evils
    So their advice and wrong example are followed by him;
    He doesn't join any person whose constant ambition is
    To laugh at and to ridicule the great God.
2. He always is happy to search the holy teaching,
    The command of Yahweh is what he meditates upon night and day;
3. What he is like is a tree by side of a spring-brook,
    Fresh in the leaf and it always bears fruit at the (proper) time,
    And whatever he does is certain that he will succeed.

4. But really different is the evil person; chaff is his resemblance,
   He is carried off and shipwrecked (stranded) if the wind should blow;
5. The evil person will be punished, he won't succeed,
   He will be separated from the gathering of the upright.
6. For an upright person this Yahweh will be the one who will protect [him],
   But for always the evil ones will be disgraced.

This psalm has perfectly matching syllable counts in all lines. The rhyming pattern varies slightly from verse to verse, apparently dictated by the number of lines needed to reflect the Hebrew message. The only possible flaw in the form of lines is the addition of the particle 'y (for ay) at the end of the third line. If that were dropped, the rhyming would be perfect. Pepa regards this as "inelegant." He also feels the sentences are not clear and not easy to understand.

Psalm 23

1. *Si Yahweh ang aking Pastol, hindi ako magkukulang*	16 A
2. *Ako'y pinahihimlay sa mainam na pastulan,*	15 A
At inaakay niya ako sa tahimik na batisan,	17 A
3. *Binibigyan nya ako niyong bagong kalakasan.*	16 A
At sang-ayon sa pangako na kaniyang binitiwan	16 A
Sa matuwid na landasi'y doon ako inaakay.	16 A
4. *Kahit na ang daang iyo'y tumatahak sa karimlan,*	16 A
Hindi ako matatakot pagkat ikaw'y kaagapay;	16 A
Ang tungkod mo at pamalo ang gabay ko at sanggalang.	16 A
5. *Sa harapon ng lingkod mo, ikaw ay may handang dulang,*	16 A
Ito'y iyong ginagawang nakikita ng kaaway;	16 A
Nalulugod ka sa akin na ulo ko ay langisan	16 A
At pati na ang saro ko ay iyong pinaaapaw.	16 A
6. *Tunay na ang pag-ibig mo at ang iyong kabutihan,*	16 A
Sasaaki't tataglayin habang ako'y nabubuhay;	16 A
Doon ako sa templo mo lalagi at mananahan.	16 A

1. Yahweh is my Shepherd, I will not lack.
2. I am made to lie down in a pleasant pasture,
   And I am led by him to a quiet spring-brook,
3. By him I am given that new strength.
   And according to the promise that he has rendered (released)
   In a straight path there I will be guided.
4. Even though that path makes its way in darkness,
   I will not fear because you are alongside;
   Your walking stick and [spanking/beating] paddle are my [hand-]guide
      and protection.

207

5. In front of your servant, you have a prepared dining-table,
   This is what you are doing that is seen by [the] enemy;
   You are pleased with me who my head is oiled
   And even my chalice is made to overflow by you.
6. Truly your love and your goodness/generosity
   Will be with me and carried/possessed as long as I am living;
   There in your temple I will remain and dwell.

In this psalm only the second and third lines have a syllable count which differs slightly from that of the other lines; the sentence structure is such that this could have been adjusted quite easily.

Tentative Conclusions

It is clear that there is great potential in the Philippines for translating certain portions of the Bible in poetic form, following common poetic style in the country.

Before such translation is undertaken, it is important to get a clear understanding of the norms of good indigenous poetry. The study should include:

    a. Overt forms such as meter, line length, rhyming patterns.

    b. Varieties of poetic genre, such as epic, song, riddle/proverb, free verse.

    c. Style of expression, including differences from prose, discourse markings that signal poetic form, kinds of imagery, etc.

Principles must be established as to what genres of biblical text lend themselves to poetic form, and what genres should not be rendered poetically.

After reviewing the above points, translators should find it possible to study the nature of biblical poetry of both Testaments. It is important to evaluate features of biblical poetry and determine whether counterparts exist in the poetry of the receptor language. If counterparts exist, there should be no problem in using them. If counterparts do not exist, it must be determined whether the biblical features can be utilized effectively in the receptor language. If they can not, and if there is no substitute, they must be abandoned or ignored. Chiasmus, for example, as mentioned above, may have no significance whatever for the reader or hearer unless trained to notice and interpret that poetic device. And so, for example, if the intended meaning of a chiasmus will escape notice by a reader untrained in recognition of that device, some other means must be utilized to make the intended meaning clear for a Tagalog reader.

Bibliography

Dorn, Louis. "Philippine hymns and songs: guidelines for translation." Shareletter, February 1971: pages 48-58. Manila: Department of Parish Education, Lutheran Church in the Philippines.

Halos, Ronnie M. 1985. "Mga anay sa Haligi." *Liwayway* (October 28): page 32.

Herrera, Regalada A. "A brief history of Philippine poetry and music." Shareletter, February 1971: pages 26-47. Manila: Department of Parish Education, Lutheran Church in the Philippines.

Kasaysayan ng Pasiong Mahal ni Hesukristong Panginoon Natin. 1964. Manila: Aklatang Lunas.

Magandang Balita para sa Ating Panahon. 1980. Manila: Philippine Bible Society. (Cover title: *Magandang Balita Biblia*.)

Panganiban, Jose Villa. 1972. *Diksyunaryo-Tesauro Pilipino-Ingles*. Quezon City, Philippines: Manlapaz Publishing Co.

Random House Unabridged Dictionary. Second edition, 1993. New York: Random House.

Guidelines for Translating Poetry in Kinyarwanda

Giles Williams
Coordinator, Kinyarwanda Translation Project

1. Introduction

Kinyarwanda is a Bantu language spoken by over 10 million people in Rwanda and neighboring countries in central Africa. There is a rich oral tradition of proverbs, songs, and poetry, and the latter includes two major types: *imivugo*, which are rhythmic, lyrical poetry and songs, whose meaning is generally accessible, and *ibisigo*, which follow similar rhythms to *imivugo*, but tend to use obscure and esoteric vocabulary and expressions, only accessible to the initiated. *Ibisigo* were highly prized at the former royal court.

When translating the poetry of the Old Testament, the Kinyarwanda translation team took into account various principles of translation but also tried to develop a sensitivity as to what sounded "right." We took care to read poetic passages aloud to one another and asked our reviewers to do the same.

The "guidelines" which follow are a synthesis of the translation principles and the intuition mentioned above. We have called them "guidelines" rather than "rules" because we have not applied them mechanically and systematically and do not feel it would be right to do so. But they do represent our general approach to translating poetry, and they will, we hope, ensure a certain amount of consistency in the poetic style of our translation. It is inevitable that the intuitive aspects of our approach to poetry will not suit everyone's stylistic sensibilities, but response to our "poetry" generally seems to be favorable.

Having made our observations on what helps to make Kinyarwanda poetry sound "poetic," we produced a document primarily for reference for the translation team, although we have given copies to certain reviewers and others. This article is based on the "guidelines" document.

2. Poetry within the wider context of functional equivalence translation

Our project has a set of Basic Principles which we abide by, and the following quotations have a bearing on the translation of poetry:

- The translation is to be in contemporary Kinyarwanda, as spoken today by people aged between 25 and 35. We therefore avoid archaic and obscure language on the one hand, and slang and "unstable" language on the other.
- Meaning always takes priority over the form of the Hebrew/Aramaic original.

211

● Metaphors, images and figurative language will only be translated literally in as much as they convey the same meaning in Kinyarwanda as in the original. Otherwise they will be translated by non-figurative language or else by a Kinyarwanda figure of speech which conveys the same meaning/effect (*e.g.,* "white as snow" could be translated by the corresponding expression, *kwera nk'inyange,* "white as a certain sort of bird.") Similarly it is legitimate to introduce a Kinyarwanda metaphor or idiom to translate a non-figurative expression in the original, provided that it is contextually appropriate and does not introduce extraneous elements.

The two existing Bibles in the language, *Bibliya Yera* and *Bibiliya Ntagatifu,* have not generally followed such principles, preferring a formal, literal correspondence to the original. The existence of these two translations in some ways makes our job simpler; if ours were the only Bible in the language, perhaps we should have agonized further over the degree of formal equivalence we felt necessary to retain in poetry. Normally these Bibles have communicated the figures of speech of Hebrew poetry, sometimes at the expense of comprehensibility. The distinctive approach of our translation is to communicate the meaning of the original, sometimes at the expense of its figures of speech. For example, Psalm 5.10b (N.B.: our translation follows the Hebrew verse numbering, the convention normally used in francophone countries):

| literal translation: | "Their throat is an open grave" |
| our translation: | "They are plotting to commit murder" |

3. Considerations of style

Our Basic Principles also force us to resist the temptation to embellish the translated text:

● Meaning also has priority over a perceived beauty of style.

But our Basic Principles also state that:

● Nevertheless, the translation attempts as far as possible to represent the different literary styles of the Bible by their Kinyarwanda equivalents.

The following points detail certain procedures which we have adopted to represent Biblical poetry by something that will be recognizably "poetic" in translation in Kinyarwanda.

3.1 Rhythm

We attempt to be sensitive to rhythm in the translated text, taking our inspiration from Rwandan poetic traditions. If the rhythm is awkward, we attempt to express the same meaning using a different form: changes in word order, use of synonyms with different numbers of syllables, vowel-length, etc.

We invited a well-known Rwandan poet and literary expert to one of our training workshops, to advise us in these matters.

3.2 Parallelism

In Hebrew poetic parallelism, a single idea is often repeated, with certain modifications in the following line(s). We attempt to reproduce this style as much as possible. For example, Psalm 12.2:

> The godly have disappeared,
> the faithful are no longer to be found.

We could have expressed the same meaning as "The godly and the faithful are no longer to be found," but this would obviously be simple prose.

Nevertheless, care needs to be taken in translating synonymous parallelism, as it is easy to convey the idea that two (or more) events are taking place, or two persons are involved, when in reality there is only one; e.g., Psalm 147.7:

> Sing to the LORD with thanksgiving,
> Make melody to our God upon the lyre! (RSV)

Someone hearing this text without any Judeo-Christian background might imagine that two distinct orders were being given, to worship two deities in different ways! We make the assumption that our readers realize that God and the LORD are the same, but in other cases we attempt to show the identity of elements in the two lines. For example, Psalm 14.7b:

literal translation: "Jacob shall rejoice, Israel shall be glad."
our translation: "Then Israel, the descendants of Jacob, will be glad."

This translation is less evocative but avoids various potential misunderstandings.

3.3 What is a line of poetry?

Simply setting our prose in short lines does not make it poetry. We attempted to analyze what constitutes a "line" in Kinyarwanda poetry, and we offer the following conclusions with some confidence, although we are aware that there are many exceptions. A "line" tends to be a simple independent sense-unit, avoiding complex structures and subordinate clauses. As a result we have generally followed the following guidelines.

3.3.1 Each line should have a main verb

For example, Psalm 92.2-4 in the RSV translation:

> It is good to give thanks to the LORD,
> to sing praises to thy name, O Most High;
> to declare thy steadfast love in the morning,
> and thy faithfulness by night,

> to the music of the lute and the harp,
> to the melody of the lyre.

Here there is only one main verb in six lines, and a literal translation would sound very unnatural in Kinyarwanda. We translated:

> LORD, it is good to praise you,
> God Most High, it is good to sing to you:
> It is good to proclaim your kindness each morning
> It is good to proclaim your faithfulness every night.
> Let us sing to you whilst playing a ten-stringed instrument
>   and a "bow-shaped stringed instrument";
> Let the "rectangular stringed instrument" also be played.

3.3.2 Verb tenses should be in their basic mode

In Kinyarwanda prose narrative, the first verb tends to set the time frame with the appropriate tense; subsequent verbs are in simplified form (e.g., the simple present is used in past narrative, the consecutive particle -ka- or -ga- is used to replace "and" in successive verbs, etc.). However, in poetry each line functions independently, and so this prose pattern is no longer appropriate.

It is not easy to show this phenomenon in an English back-translation, but the following examples may show how we have translated past and future consecutive verbs.

> Bibliya Yera: It is he who struck many nations,
>   he kills mighty kings. (Psalm 135.10)

The grammatical present tense of the verb "kills" in the second line accurately conveys a "past" meaning, but sounds like prose).

> Our version: He ravaged many nations,
>   he killed mighty kings.

> Bibiliya Ntagatifu: He will vindicate the masses
>   save the destitute,
>   and trample on their oppressor. (Psalm 72.4)
> Our version: The king will vindicate the masses,
>   he will save the poor,
>   he will destroy those who oppress them.

3.3.3 Logical subordination

Since each line of poetry should normally be an independent sense-unit, we have avoided beginning lines with subordinate conjunctions such as "because." There are various ways of showing the logical subordination of the second line without making it grammatically subordinate; for example, repeating the verb in the following line with "because," etc., after this verb.

Bibiliya Ntagatifu:	Expel them because of their many sins,
	because they rebel against you! (Psalm 5.11)
Our version:	Expel them because of their many sins,
	expel them because they have rebelled against you.

The second or subsequent line can be introduced with a formula which shows the logical subordination, such as "therefore," "in this "way," "that is why," etc., while still retaining its grammatical independence. For example, Psalm 91.9-10:

Bibliya Yera:	Because you are my refuge, LORD,
	you have made the Most High your dwelling,
	then no evil will get to you
Our version:	You have made the LORD your refuge,
	The Most High, you have him as your hiding place.
	Therefore no evil will get to you . . . .

Or Psalm 122.9:

Bibiliya Ntagatifu:	Because of the temple of the LORD our God,
	I wish you well-being and prosperity.
Our version:	The temple of the LORD our God is built within you:
	for this reason I (continually) wish you well-being and
	prosperity.

The preposition *kî* in Hebrew can equally be translated by "because" or "indeed," and the latter possibility has often suited our stylistic needs. For example, Psalm 1.6:

| Bibliya Yera: | For the LORD knows the path of the righteous |
| Our version: | Indeed, the LORD protects the righteous . . . . |

In many cases the logical relationship between two propositions can remain implicit without any loss of communication.

3.3.4. The use of conjunctions
Similarly we sense that the use of certain conjunctions and connective particles, which would be natural in prose, are inappropriate at the beginning of a line of poetry. It is usually possible to put them in median position, or to convey the same meaning differently. We have avoided words like "and" or "then" at the start of a line.
For example, Psalm 2.2:

Bibliya Yera:	The kings on the earth have prepared to make war,
	and its chiefs have made a plot . . .
Our version:	Its kings are ready for action,
	its rulers have gathered together as well . . .

215

Or Psalm 18.7:

Bibiliya Ntagatifu: Then, in my woes, I called out to the LORD
Our version: Being in danger, I called out to the LORD

3.3.5 Line-length

The fact that each line of poetry is a single sense-unit tends naturally to restrict the number of words per line and the length of the line on paper. However, translation often requires us to attempt things that would not be stylistically normal in the receptor language, and if a line appears to be excessively long (even with only one main verb), we have often tried to find a way of dividing it into two shorter lines. See the example of Psalm 92 above.

Another obvious example would be in invocations of God using many different names. For example, in Psalm 84.4 we have set out the text as follows, despite the lack of a verb in the first line:

> O LORD of Hosts, my King, my God,
> the sparrows have found a shelter in your temple. . . .

(The invocation in the first line takes up considerably more space in Kinyarwanda than in English).

3.3.6 Lay-out

We start each line with lower-case (except for new sentences and proper nouns, of course). Normally each new line begins on the left margin, except for special cases such as Psalm 136, where we have indented the "refrain." For "Selah" lines we use a greater level of indentation.

4. Testing

We read all our texts aloud, prose or poetry, but as mentioned at the beginning, we take special care to read poetic passages aloud, to hear the rhythms and sounds of the text. In many cases this leads to a change in word order, or substituting one word by a synonym that fits the sounds and rhythms better. When sending the Psalms to our reviewers, we specifically asked them to read them aloud, to hear them as well as to study them. One religious sister undertook to sing them for us, and she reported that they "sang well." Generally people's reactions to the Psalms have been positive.

5. Conclusions

I repeat that these "guidelines" are not rigid rules to be followed at all costs, and we freely admit the subjective, intuitive nature of some of them. Not everyone agrees with all of our observations. But these guidelines have been useful to the team for three reasons:

1. They assure a certain consistency in the poetic style of our translation.
2. Our team has seen a number of changes in personnel, and the guidelines have served to initiate new translators into the rationale behind our poetic style.

3. They have also served to explain this style to others, notably some of our reviewers, who have asked about our approach to translating poetry.

Many—or most—of the stylistic techniques and considerations mentioned above would not apply in other languages, but we would be delighted if what we have done stimulated other translation teams to identify certain "tricks of the trade" which give a more authentic poetic "feel" to the poetic passages of their translations.

Bibliography

Alter, Robert. 1985. *The Art of Biblical Poetry*. New York: Basic Books.

――. 1987. "The Characteristics of Ancient Hebrew Poetry." In *The Literary Guide to the Bible,* edited by Robert Alter and Frank Kermode, 611-623. Cambridge, Mass.: Harvard University Press.

Alonso Schökel, Luis. 1988. *A Manual of Hebrew Poetics*. Rome: Editrice Pontificio Istituto Biblico.

Bascom, Robert. 1994. "Hebrew Poetry and the Text of the Song of Songs." In *Discourse Perspectives on Hebrew Poetry in the Scriptures,* edited by Ernst R. Wendland, 95-110. UBS Monograph Series 7. New York: United Bible Societies.

Berlin, Adele. 1985. *The Dynamics of Biblical Parallelism*. Bloomington: Indiana University Press.

Bliese, Loren. 1988. "Chiastic Structures, Peaks, and Cohesion in Nehemiah 9:6-37," *The BibleTranslator* 39 (April): 208-215.

――. 1994. "Symmetry and prominence in Hebrew poetry." In *Discourse Perspectives on Hebrew Poetry in the Scriptures,* edited by Ernst R. Wendland, 67-94. UBS Monograph Series 7. New York: United Bible Societies.

――. "The Poetics of Habakkuk." Unpublished manuscript.

Bratcher, Robert G., and William D. Reyburn. 1991. *A Handbook on the Book of Psalms*. New York: United Bible Societies.

Dorn, Louis O. 1994. "Philippine poetry and translation: A general survey," *The Bible Translator* 45 (July): 301-315.

Fox, Michael V. 1985. *The Song of Songs and the Ancient Egyptian Love Songs*. Madison, Wisconsin: University of Wisconsin Press.

Gottwald, Norman K. 1984. "Poetry, Hebrew." In *The Interpreter's Dictionary of the Bible,* 829-838. Nashville: Abingdon Press.

BIBLIOGRAPHY

Krabill, James. 1995. *The Hymnody of the Harris Church among the Dida of South-Central Ivory Coast (1913-1949)*. Frankfurt: Peter Lang.

Kugel, James. 1981. *The Idea of Biblical Poetry: Parallelism and Its History*. New York: Yale University Press.

Loader, J[amer] A. 1986. *Ecclesiastes: A Practical Commentary* (Text and Interpretation). Translated by John Vriend. Grand Rapids: Eerdmans.

Louw, Johannes P., and Ernst R. Wendland. 1993. *Graphic Design and Bible Reading*. Cape Town: Bible Society of South Africa.

Martin, Ralph P. 1986. "Poetry, Hebrew." In *The International Standard Bible Encyclopedia*, Vol. 3: 891-899. Grand Rapids: Eerdmans.

Moomo, David O. 1993. "Hebrew and Ebira Poetry," *Notes on Translation* 7:4, 9-25.

Newman, Barclay M. 1993. "Biblical Poetry and English Style," *The Bible Translator* 44 (October): 405-410.

———, and Philip C. Stine. 1988. *A Handbook on the Gospel of Matthew*. New York: United Bible Societies.

Noss, Philip A. 1976. "The Psalms and Gbaya Literary Style," *The Bible Translator* 27 (January): 110-118.

Ogden, Graham S. 1994. "Poetry, Prose, and Their Relationship: Some Reflections Based on Judges 4 and 5." In *Discourse Perspectives on Hebrew Poetry in the Scriptures*. Edited by Ernst R. Wendland, 111-130. UBS Monograph Series 7. New York: United Bible Societies.

———, and Lynell Zogbo. 1998. *A Handbook on Ecclesiastes*. New York: United Bible Societies.

———, and Lynell Zogbo. 1998. *A Handbook on the Song of Songs*. New York: United Bible Societies.

Reaske, Christopher Russell. 1966. *How to Analyze Poetry*. New York: Simon and Schuster.

Reyburn, William D. 1992. *A Handbook on Lamentations*. New York: United Bible Societies.

———. 1992. *A Handbook on the Book of Job*. New York: United Bible Societies.

———. 1994. "Anatomy of a Poem: Lamentations 1." In *Discourse Perspectives on Hebrew Poetry in the Scriptures,* edited by Ernst R. Wendland, 147-169. UBS Monograph Series 7. New York: United Bible Societies.

Sherzer, Joel. 1983. *Kuna Ways of Speaking.* Austin, Texas: University of Texas Press.

Schneider. Théo R. 1986. "From wisdom sayings to wisdom texts, Part I," *The Bible Translator* 37 (January): 128-135.

———. 1987. "From wisdom sayings to wisdom texts, Part II" *The Bible Translator* 38 (January): 101-117.

Sterk, Jan. 1989. "Bible Poetry in Translation," *Occasional Papers in Translation and Textlinguistics* 3, No. 1: 36-48.

———. 1994. "Translation as re-creation," *The Bible Translator* 45 (January): 29-139.

Watts. 1985. *Isaiah* (Word Biblical Commentary). Waco, Texas: Word Books.

Webster's New Collegiate Dictionary. 1981. Springfield, Massachusetts: G. and C. Merriam Company.

Wendland, Ernst R. 1993. *Comparative Discourse Analysis and the Translation of Psalm 22 in Chichewa, a Bantu language of South-Central Africa.* Lewiston, New York: Edwin Mellen.

——— 1998. *Discourse Analysis and the Psalms: An Introduction with Exercises for Exegetes and Bible Translators.* Dallas: Summer Institute of Linguistics.

Yilbuudo, Jean T. 1971. *Elaboration d'une tradition orale.* Memoire du Seminaire de Koumi. Haute Volta. [Thesis. Seminary of Koumi. Upper Volta.]

Zogbo, Lynell. "Issues in Poetic Transfer." Paper presented at the UBS Triennial Translation Workshop, Victoria Falls, Zimbabwe, 1991.

———. "Enallage, the Shifting of Persons in Hebrew Poetry." Paper presented at the UBS Triennial Translation Workshop, Chiang-Mai, Thailand, 1994.

Poems cited

Aldan, D. 1969. *Poems from India.* New York: Thomas Y. Crowell.

Chaves, Jonathan, editor. 1986. *The Colombia Book of Later Chinese Poetry.* New York: Columbia University Press.

Finnegan, Ruth. 1970. *Oral Literature in Africa.* Nairobi: Oxford University Press.

Hughes, Langston, editor. 1968. *Poems from Black Africa.* Bloomington: Indiana University Press.

Lewis, Richard, editor. 1965. *In a Spring Garden.* New York: Dial Press.

Olaleye, Isaac. 1995. *The Distant Talking Drum: Poems from Nigeria.* Honesdale, PA: Boyds Mills Press.

Sharpe, J. Edward, editor. 1985. *American Indian Prayers and Poetry.* Cherokee, North Carolina: Cherokee Publications.

Sneve, Virginia H., editor. 1989. *Dancing Teepees: Poems of American Indian Youth.* New York: Holiday House.

Untermeyer, Louis. 1966. *A Concise Treasury of Great Poems: English and American.* 1966. New York: Pocket Books.

Bible Texts and Versions Cited

La Bible en français courant avec les Livres Deutérocanoniques. 1991. Paris: Alliance Biblique Universelle. (Cited as FRCL French common language version.)

Good News Bible: The Bible in Today's English Version. 1976; second edition, 1992. New York: American Bible Society. (Cited as TEV.)

The Holy Bible (Authorized, or King James Version). 1611. (Cited as KJV.)

The Holy Bible: Contemporary English Version. 1995. New York: American Bible Society. (Cited as CEV.)

The Holy Bible: New International Version. 1973, 1978, 1987. New York: New York International Bible Society. (Cited as NIV.)

The Holy Bible: New Revised Standard Version. 1989. New York: Division of Christian Education of the National Council of the Churches of Christ in the United States of America. (Cited as NRSV.)

The Holy Bible: Revised Standard Version. 1952. New York: Division of Christian Education of the National Council of the Churches of Christ in the United States of America. (Cited as RSV.)

The Message: New Testament with Psalms and Proverbs in Contemporary Language. 1994. Translated by Eugene Peterson. Colorado Springs, CO: NavPress.

The New American Bible. 1983. New York: Thomas Nelson Publications. (Cited as NAB.)

The New Jerusalem Bible. 1985. Garden City, NY: Doubleday. (Cited as NJB.)

The Revised English Bible. 1989. London: Oxford University Press; and Cambridge: Cambridge University Press. (Cited as REB.)

TANAKH: A New Translation of the Holy Scriptures According to the Traditional Hebrew Text. 1985. Philadelphia: The Jewish Publication Society. (Cited as NJPSV, New Jewish Publication Society version.)

Traduction œcuménique de la Bible. Nouvelle édition revue. 1988. Paris: Éditions du Cerf et Alliance Biblique Universelle.

Glossary

ACROSTIC refers to poems whose lines or stanzas follow the order of the letters of an alphabet. In the Hebrew Bible this type of poem occurs in many psalms (34, 37, 119) and in the book of Lamentations. The first stanza begins with the first letter of the Hebrew alphabet "aleph," and the last stanza begins with the last letter "taw."

ADJECTIVE is a word that limits, describes, or qualifies a noun. In English, "red," "tall," "beautiful," and "important" are adjectives.

ADVERB is a word that limits, describes, or qualifies a verb, an adjective, or another adverb. In English, "quickly," "soon," "primarily," and "very" are adverbs.

AFFIX is an added part of a word and cannot stand alone. It is attached to a word, root, or stem. In English "im-" is an **AFFIX** on the word "impossible." In many languages of the world, **AFFIXES** on verb and noun stems indicate **PLURAL** or **SINGULAR**, **PERSON**, **MASCULINE** or **FEMININE**, as well as tense, mode, or aspect.

AGENT is one who does the action in a sentence or clause, regardless of whether the grammatical construction is active or passive. In "John hit Bill" (active) and "Bill was hit by John" (passive), the agent in both cases is "John."

ALLITERATION is the repetition of consonant sounds, either at the beginning of a sequence of words or throughout an utterance, in order to create a special literary effect. "Peter Piper picked a peck of pickled peppers" is an example of **ALLITERATION** in English.

ALLUSION is an indirect or general reference to a text which is already well known. For example, when the Preacher in Ecclesiastes says "and the dust returns to the earth" (12.7), this appears to be an **ALLUSION** to a passage in Genesis (3.19).

AMBIGUITY refers to words or sentences that have more than one possible meaning in a given context. For example, in the sentence "Mike said that if Joe comes, he will speak to the president," "he" could refer to Mike or to Joe. Thus this sentence is **AMBIGUOUS**. Often what is ambiguous in written form is not ambiguous when actually spoken, since intonation and other features of speech help to make the meaning clear. In written discourse, context also helps to indicate which meaning is intended by the author.

ANALYSIS is the process of determining how an oral or written text is composed, in terms of distinct units and connective relationships.

ANTHROPOMORPHIC means attributing human characteristics to a non-human entity. For example, when biblical authors speak of "God's arm," they are using an **ANTHROPOMORPHISM**.

ANTITHETIC PARALLELISM refers to parallel poetic lines where one or more contrasts is being made. For example, in Prov 13.1 there is a contrast between a wise son and a scoffer:

> A wise son hears his father's instruction,
> but a scoffer does not listen to rebuke.

There are further contrasts between "hear" and "does not listen," and between the words "instruction" and "rebuke." Such a contrast is often marked by the conjunction "but" in English.

ARAMAIC is a Semitic language that was widely used in Palestine and in the surrounding regions during the time of Christ. After the Jews were taken into exile in Babylonia, **ARAMAIC** became the common language of many Jews instead of Hebrew.

ASSONANCE is the repetition of vowel sounds throughout an utterance in order to create a special literary effect. In Robert Frost's lines from "Stopping by Woods on a Snowy Evening," repetitive **o** sounds contrast with long **e** sounds:

> The **o**nly **o**ther s**o**und's the sw**ee**p
> Of **ea**sy wind and d**o**wny flake.

CHIASTIC STRUCTURE (CHIASMUS, CHIASM) refers to a reversal of the order of words in a parallel construction in order to create some special literary effect (such as focus or emphasis) or to serve as a discourse boundary marker. This device produces a cross-over (X) structure, as in the following example from Eccl 3.8:

> a time to love ⟍⟋ and a time to hate
> a time for war ⟋⟍ and a time for peace

However, more complex chiastic structures also appear, as in Psa 51.5:

A	I
B	was brought forth
C	in iniquity
C'	in sin
B'	did my mother conceive
A'	me.

CLAUSE is a grammatical construction, normally consisting of a subject and a predicate. An **INDEPENDENT CLAUSE** may stand alone as a complete sentence. A

DEPENDENT (or subordinate) **CLAUSE** is dependent on a main or independent clause, and it does not form a complete sentence.

CLIMAX refers to a place in a story, poem, or speech, which is the high point or turning point in the action or in the development of the message. One **CLIMACTIC** point in the story of Esther is when she enters the king's presence and he holds out his royal scepter. In the Song of Deborah (Judges 5), the climax comes at verse 27:

> He sank, he fell,
> he lay still at her feet;
> at her feet he sank, he fell;
> where he sank, there he fell dead.

The climax of a section is normally marked by the presence of one or more special stylistic features (such as many actors, much action, figurative language, or intensified speech).

COLON is a rhythmic line of poetry. Two **COLA** (or a **BICOLON**) make up a parallel pair of poetic lines. A **TRICOLON** consists of three parallel lines of poetry.

COMMON LANGUAGE TRANSLATION uses language that is widely understood and accepted by most speakers. In such a translation, substandard speech, dialect peculiarities, and highly literary or technical terms are avoided.

CONCESSIVE describes a clause that admits something is true, usually something of a contrary, opposing, or unexpected nature. **CONCESSIVE** clauses in English are often introduced by "though," "even though," or "although." For example, *"Though your sins are like scarlet,* they shall be as white as snow" (Isa 1.18).

CONDITION is that which shows the circumstance under which something may be true. In English a **CONDITIONAL** phrase or clause is usually introduced by "if." For example, *"If you dig a pit,* you may fall into it," or "The story, *if true,* will cause much joy."

CONJUNCTIONS are words that serve as connectors between words, phrases, clauses, and sentences. "And," "but," "if," "because," and "or" are typical conjunctions in English.

CONSEQUENCE is that which shows the result of a condition or event. In the sentence "If you dig a pit, you may fall into it," falling is the consequence of the first action, digging.

CONSONANTS are speech sounds that are produced by blocking or restricting the passage of air as it comes from the lungs through the mouth. The written letters representing those sounds are also called **CONSONANTS**; for example, "b," "c," "d," or "f" in English. **CONSONANTS** were originally the only spoken sounds written in the Hebrew alphabet. Marks for **VOWELS** were added later above or below the **CONSONANTS**. See also **VOWELS**.

CONSTRUCTION. See **STRUCTURE.**

CONTEXT refers in general to the situation in which something occurs. More specifically, the verbal **CONTEXT** is the material that precedes or follows any part of an oral or written discourse. The **CONTEXT** of a term often affects its meaning, so that a word may not mean exactly the same thin in one context as it does in another. The **CONTEXT** also helps us to determine meaning. In Job 28.23 the **CONTEXT** (Job 28.1-28) shows us that "it" refers to "wisdom."

CULTIC is an adjective formed from the noun "cult"; it is used to describe any custom or action that is required in the performance of religious practices. It is synonymous with the adjectives "ritual" and "ceremonial."

CULTURE (**CULTURAL**) is the combination of beliefs, values, social institutions, customs, and material objects (such as tools or ornaments) of any group of people. A culture is passed on from one generation to another but undergoes development or gradual change.

DEPENDENT CLAUSE is a grammatical construction consisting normally of a subject and predicate, which is dependent upon or embedded within some other construction. For example, "if he comes" is a dependent clause in the sentence "If he comes, we'll have to leave." See **CLAUSE.**

DIRECT SPEECH (or, **DIRECT DISCOURSE**) is the reproduction of the actual words of one person quoted and included in the discourse of another person. For example, "He declared *'I will have nothing to do with this person.'* " **INDIRECT SPEECH** is the reporting of the words of one person within the discourse of another person. Usually the form of indirect discourse is different from an exact quotation. For example, "He said *he would have nothing to do with that person.*"

DISCOURSE is the communication of thought or meaning through spoken or written words. One can study the **DISCOURSE STRUCTURE** of both oral and written texts to see how thoughts, words, sentences, and other units are arranged to communicate a message.

DYNAMIC EQUIVALENCE TRANSLATION refers to a translation that tries to give the intended meaning of the **SOURCE TEXT** in a natural and meaningful way so that it produces a response in today's reader that is essentially equivalent to that of the original reader. **LITERAL** translations pay more attention to reproducing the forms found in the **SOURCE** text. For example, RSV follows the Hebrew wording of Psa 104.29 and says: "they die and return to their dust." CEV tries to give a **DYNAMIC EQUIVALENT TRANSLATION**: "they die and rot."

ELLIPSIS refers to words or phrases intentionally omitted in a discourse when the sense is perfectly clear without them. **ELLIPSIS** occurs in the following example from Psa 103.7, where the words "He made known" have been omitted in the second line:

> He made known his ways to Moses,
> *************** his acts to the people of Israel.

What is elliptical in one language may need to be expressed in another. For example, some languages will need to repeat "He has made known" in the second line of the example.

EMOTIVE refers to human emotions such as anger, joy, fear, or gratitude. The **EMOTIVE** impact of a discourse is its effect on the emotions of the person(s) to whom it is addressed.

EMPHASIS (EMPHATIC) is the relative importance given to an element in a discourse. **EMPHASIS** is conveyed by many different devices, depending on the language; for example, positioning of words, emphatic particles, intensifiers, or ideophones. In "Oh, that you had heeded my commandments!" (Isa 48.18, NKJV), the particle "Oh" marks this statement as **EMPHATIC**.

ENVELOPE. See **INCLUSIO**.

EXAGGERATION is stating more than the speaker or writer knows to be true. **EXAGGERATION** may be used to express humor, **IRONY**, or **SARCASM**, or to make a particular point. For example, "Everyone is doing it" can mean "Many people are doing it" (implying "and I want to do it, too"). See also **HYPERBOLE**.

EXPLICIT refers to meaning that is expressed overtly in the words of a discourse. This is in contrast to **IMPLICIT** information.

FEMININE is a grammatical category usually referring to the female **GENDER**. In some languages nouns, pronouns, and affixes may be **MASCULINE** or **FEMININE**. However, sometimes words that seem unrelated to the female gender appear in this category. For example, in Hebrew the words for "stone" and "city" are feminine.

FIGURE, FIGURE OF SPEECH, or **FIGURATIVE LANGUAGE** involves the use of words in other than their literal or ordinary sense in order to bring out some aspect of meaning by comparison or association. For example, when the psalmist says "my cup overflows," he is not saying his cup is too full. He is rather using a **FIGURE OF SPEECH** to say that he is as content as someone who has been served a generous portion. **METAPHORS** and **SIMILES** are common figures of speech.

FINITE VERB is a verb form that distinguishes person, number, tense, mode, or aspect. It contrasts with an infinitive verb form, which does not indicate these features but only the action or state.

FIRST PERSON. See **PERSON**.

FOCUS is the center of attention in a discourse. It may be marked in a special way such as by word order, a special particle, or repetition.

FORMAL CORRESPONDENCE, or **FORMAL EQUIVALENCE**, is a type of translation in which many features of the source text, especially the form of the discourse, have been literally reproduced in the translation. This approach often results in an unnatural style in the receptor language, or sometimes in the lack of any meaning at all. See **LITERAL**.

FULL STOP is a punctuation mark indicating the end of a sentence; this mark is also called a "period."

FUNCTIONAL EQUIVALENCE is a type of translation that attempts to convey the same set of communicative functions as that of the original **SOURCE** text. Some important functions of communication are to convey information, to express or evoke emotions, to promote changes in thinking or behavior, or to maintain good interpersonal relations. See also **DYNAMIC EQUIVALENCE**, which has a similar meaning.

FUTURE TENSE. See **TENSE**.

GENDER refers to categories of nouns and pronouns based on distinctions between male and female. However, many languages assign certain terms to such categories without regard to whether a term is male, female, or neither. Not all languages have gender distinction, though English, Greek, and Hebrew do. See also **FEMININE** and **MASCULINE**.

GENERAL. See **GENERIC**.

GENERIC refers to a general class or kind of object. It contrasts with **SPECIFIC**. For example, the word "food" is a generic term, while "fruit" is more specific. However, the word "fruit" is a **GENERIC** term for the more specific word "orange."

GENRE refers to different types of literature that can be distinguished from each other by their communicative function (goal of speaking), content, and particular stylistic features. In the Old Testament, praise poetry is one **GENRE**, while proverbs is another.

GRAMMAR refers to the rules governing the formation and arrangement of elements of meaning, words, and larger constructions in a language. If a sentence is **GRAMMATICAL** it follows the rules of normal speech, and sounds correct to a speaker of that language.

GREEK is the language in which the New Testament was written. It belongs to the Indo-European family of languages and was the language spoken in Achaia, which is Greece in modern times. By the time of Christ Greek was used by many of the people living in the eastern part of the Roman empire. By that time the entire Hebrew Old Testament had been translated into Greek, a version referred to as the **SEPTUAGINT**.

HEBREW is the language in which the Old Testament was written. It belongs to the Semitic family of languages. By the time of Christ many Jewish people no longer used Hebrew as their common language, but spoke Aramaic (a language related to Hebrew) or Greek.

HONORIFIC is a form used to express respect or deference; for example, "my lord," "sir," or "I am your humble servant." In many languages such forms are obligatory in talking to or about royalty and persons of social distinction.

HYPERBOLE is a figure of speech that makes use of **EXAGGERATION**. A deliberate overstatement is made to create a special effect. "He cries night and day" is an example of **HYPERBOLE**. The statement does not mean that the person cries every moment of the day and night, but that he cries a great deal.

IDEOPHONE is a form of expressive language that can describe anything that a person's senses may feel or observe. It can express an emotion, a sound (onomatopoeia), a smell, quality, texture, or movement. Ideophones use sounds and combinations of sounds that make them stand out from other words in a language. They are especially common in African languages. For example, in one language *prrrr!* expresses whiteness or brightness. In another language *yaa* indicates complete emptiness.

IDIOM, or **IDIOMATIC EXPRESSION**, is a combination of terms whose meanings cannot be understood by adding up the meanings of the parts. "To hang one's head" is an English idiom. "A drop in the bucket" is an idiom coming from Hebrew (Isa 40.15). Idiomatic expressions almost always lose their meaning or convey a wrong meaning when translated literally from one language to another.

IMMEDIATE CONTEXT refers to the words which immediately precede or follow a discourse or segment of discourse, and which often help one to interpret the meaning of the whole section. For example, Psalm 1.2 is a passage in the immediate context of Psalm 1.1 and helps to interpret it. See also **CONTEXT**.

IMPERATIVE refers to forms of a verb that indicate commands or requests. In Psa 34.11 there are two imperative forms, "*Come*, you children, *listen* to me." Imperatives are often used together with **VOCATIVE** expressions ("you children"). In some languages imperatives occur only in the second person; but in others imperatives also occur in the first and third persons. These are usually expressed in English by the use of "must" or "let"; for example, "They *must work* harder!" or "*Let us go* to the house of the LORD."

IMPLICIT (IMPLIED) refers to information which is conveyed by a text, but which is not expressed in words. The speaker assumes that the hearer understands the meaning. Often the meaning is clear from the **CONTEXT**. For example, when Hannah says in 1 Sam 2.6 "He brings down to Sheol and *raises up*," the **IMPLIED** or **IMPLICIT** meaning is *"raises up to life."* See **EXPLICIT**.

INCLUSIO is the use of the same or similar words or phrases at the beginning and end of a literary unit. In Psalm 20, for example, the words "LORD" and "answer" occur in the first and last lines, forming a kind of **ENVELOPE** around the poem. **INCLUSIOS** help to show the unity of a few lines, several **STANZAS**, or even an entire book.

INDEPENDENT CLAUSE. See **CLAUSE**.

INDIRECT SPEECH. See **DIRECT DISCOURSE**.

IRONY occurs when a person says one thing but means another, often for the purpose of criticism, rebuke, or instruction. When Job says to his friend, "How you have helped him who has no power!" he is using **IRONY**. He means "You have not helped at all!"

LEADING QUESTIONS in a poem are those questions that are asked and then answered by the speaker or writer. This literary device often begins a new discourse unit. In Psa 24.3, for example, the psalmist asks "Who shall ascend the hill of the LORD?" and then answers the question: "He who has clean hands and a pure heart . . . ." See also **RHETORICAL QUESTION**.

LINGUISTIC refers to language, especially the formal structure of language.

LITERAL refers to the ordinary or primary meaning of a word, phrase, or clause. For example, the **LITERAL** meaning of "my cup overflows" is that liquid is streaming over the top of the speaker's cup. The **FIGURATIVE** meaning is that the person is happy or satisfied. A **LITERAL TRANSLATION** follows the **SOURCE** text very closely, trying to imitate the order of words or sentences, and translating expressions word-for-word. Such translations are frequently unnatural, meaningless, or even incorrect.

LITERARY DEVICE refers to a particular use of words or of language by an author to achieve special effects or to conform to a particular style. This includes, for example, figures of speech, repetition, wordplays, and rhetorical or leading questions. See also **STYLE**.

LITURGICAL refers to liturgy, or public worship, including songs, prayers, responses, and so forth. **LITURGICAL** language is often traditional or old-fashioned.

MANUSCRIPTS are books, documents, or letters written or copied by hand. A **SCRIBE** is one who copies a manuscript.

MARKERS (**MARKING**) are features of words or of a discourse that signal some special meaning or some particular structure. For example, words for speaking may mark the onset of direct discourse, a phrase such as "Once upon a time" may mark the beginning of a fairy story, and various types of parallelism are the dominant markers of biblical poetry.

MASCULINE is a grammatical category usually referring to the male **GENDER**. In some languages nouns, pronouns, and affixes may be **MASCULINE** or **FEMININE**. However, sometimes words that seem unrelated to the male gender appear in this category. For example, in Hebrew the word for "mountain" is masculine.

MASORETIC TEXT is the traditional written text of the Hebrew Old Testament established by Hebrew scholars during the eighth and ninth centuries A.D.

METAPHOR is likening one object, event, or state (the "topic") to another (the "image") to which it is not directly or closely related in meaning. For example, when a person says "I am a worm," he is describing his state as being lowly, miserable, or of no value. Biblical metaphors are often difficult to understand because the basis for the comparison is not always stated, as in the line "The LORD is my rock" (Psa 18.1). At other times either the image or the basis of comparison is unfamiliar or used differently in the receptor language. For example, when the psalmist says "He remembers that we are dust" (103.14), he is not referring to the dirt or dust on our bodies. Metaphors are the most commonly used figures of speech and are often so subtle that a speaker or writer is not conscious of the fact that he or she is using figurative language. See **SIMILE**.

METER refers to a special rhythm in a verse, usually determined by the number of stressed syllables or accented words in a given line. In Hebrew poetry the most common form is three accents per poetic line (**COLON.**).

MODIFY is to directly affect the meaning of another part of the sentence, as when an adjective modifies a noun or an adverb modifies a verb.

MOOD defines frame of mind or psychological background of an action or event, and involves such categories as possibility, necessity, and desire. Some languages (for example, Greek) use specific verb forms to express mood.

NOMINAL refers to nouns or noun-like words. See **NOUN**.

NONFIGURATIVE involves the use of words in their literal or ordinary sense. See **FIGURE, FIGURATIVE**.

NOUN is a word that names a person, place, thing, quality, action or idea.

ONOMATOPOEIA (ONOMATOPOEIC) is the use of words or series of words that cause one to think of the sounds that they refer to; for example, "swishing," "bang!" or "the buzzing of bees."

OVERLAPPING is the way in which part of the meanings of two words cover the same general area of meaning, although the remainder of the meanings covered by the two words is not the same. For example, "love" and "like" overlap in referring to human affection.

PARAGRAPH is a distinct unit of prose discourse that usually deals with a single topic or theme. A **PARAGRAPH** is made up of **SENTENCES**.

PARALLELISM refers to two or more poetic lines (**COLA**) that are alike in some way and need to be interpreted together. They may be related in sound, meaning, or grammatical structure (or all three). In the following lines from Eccl 3.4, the lines are **PARALLEL** in meaning and structure. In Hebrew, there are also similarities in sound:

> a time to weep and a time to laugh
> a time to mourn and a time to dance

PARTICIPLE is a verbal adjective, that is, a word that retains some of the characteristics of a verb while functioning as an adjective. In the phrase "land flowing with milk and honey," "flowing" is a participle. Participles are very common in Hebrew.

PARTICLE is a small word whose grammatical form does not change and which has a particular function. In English the most common particles are prepositions and conjunctions, such as "with," "into," or "and."

PERSON, as a grammatical term, refers to the speaker, the person spoken to, or the person or thing spoken about. **FIRST PERSON** is the person(s) speaking (such as "I," "me," "my," "mine," "we," "us," "our," or "ours"). **SECOND PERSON** is the person(s) or thing(s) spoken to (such as "thou," "thee," "thy," "thine," "ye," "you," "your," or "yours"). **THIRD PERSON** is the person(s) or thing(s) spoken about (such as "he," "she," "it," "his," "her," "them," or "their"). The examples given here are all pronouns, but in many languages the verb forms have affixes that mark first, second, or third person and also indicate whether they are **SINGULAR** or **PLURAL**.

PERSONIFICATION is a reference to an inanimate object or an abstract idea in terms that give it a personal or a human nature. This figure of speech often emphasizes or highlights an idea. In "Wisdom is calling out," "wisdom" is referred to as if it were a person.

PHRASE is a dependent grammatical construction of two or more words, but less than a complete clause or a sentence. A phrase is usually given a name according to its function in a sentence, such as that of a "noun phrase," "verb phrase," or "prepositional phrase." For example, "the boy in front" is a noun phrase, "in front of the house" is a prepositional phrase, and "carried a heavy load" is a verb phrase.

PLAY ON WORDS. See **WORDPLAY.**

PLURAL refers to the form of a word that indicates more than one. See **SINGULAR.**

POETRY (POETIC) refers to a literary genre that differs from everyday speech and from **PROSE** because of its rhythmic and heightened style. Poets use special language to create a mood or image to be shared with the hearer or reader. Each language has special stylistic devices such as figurative language, word order variation, wordplay, repetition or rhyming that are especially frequent in **POETRY** (compare Judges 4 and 5). The boundary between beautiful, artistic **PROSE** and **POETRY** is sometimes difficult to determine, but speakers of a language can usually distinguish poetry from ordinary speech. **POETRY** is usually written or spoken in measured or balanced lines, while prose is not. See **PROSE.**

POINT OF VIEW. See **VIEWPOINT.**

PREPOSITION is a word whose function is to indicate the relation of a noun or pronoun to another noun, pronoun, verb, or adjective within a clause. Some English prepositions are "for," "from," "in," "to," and "with."

PREPOSITIONAL refers to **PREPOSITIONS.** A prepositional phrase or expression is one governed by a preposition. "For his benefit" and "to a certain city" are prepositional phrases.

PRONOMINAL refers to **PRONOUNS.**

PRONOUNS are words that are used in place of nouns, such as "he," "him," "his," "she," "we," "them," "who," "which," "this," or "these."

PROSE is the ordinary form of spoken or written language, without a special style and structure such as elaborate imagery, meter, and rhythm that are often characteristic of **POETRY.** However, literary **PROSE** may share some of the features of poetry such as figures of speech, wordplay, repetition, or even parallelism.

READ, READING, refers to a particular interpretation of a written text. Sometimes differences in versions or the uncertainty of the writing system make the interpretation of a text uncertain. For example, in 1 Sam 1.24 the Hebrew text says "three bulls," but the Greek and Syriac versions say "a three-year-old bull." These are different **READINGS.** See also **TEXT, TEXTUAL.**

REFRAINS are repeated lines or sets of lines which occur regularly throughout a song or poem. They may occur every other line, at the end of a stanza, or at the end of another literary unit.

RELATIVE CLAUSE is a dependent clause that describes the person, place, or thing to which it refers. In "those who hate me without cause," the **RELATIVE CLAUSE** is "who hate me without cause."

RENDER means to translate or express in a language different from the original. **RENDERING** is the manner in which a specific passage is translated from one language to another.

RESTRUCTURE. See **STRUCTURE**.

RHETORICAL QUESTION is an assertion or exhortation that is put in the form of a question, but one which is not intended to ask for information. Rhetorical questions are usually employed for emphasis and often express the mood, emotion, or attitude of the person asking them. When the prophet says "Have you not known? Have you not heard?" (Isa 40.21), he really means "You surely know and you have been told!" See also **LEADING QUESTION**.

RHYME is a sound pattern in a poem, where the endings of two or more words match. In the following lines from Joyce Kilmore, the words "see" and "tree" **RHYME**:

> I think that I shall never **see**
> A poem lovely as a **tree**.

RHYME may occur at the end of lines or in the middle of lines. The latter is called **INTERNAL RHYME**. Deliberate rhyming is not as common in Hebrew poetry as it is in English poems.

RHYTHM is the regular pattern of accented syllables in an utterance, a sequence of utterances, or line of poetry. In some forms of poetry each line will have the same number of stressed syllables or accents. This creates a regular beat. In the English example under **RHYME**, each line has four beats.

ROOT refers to the smallest element of a word, from which other words may be derived. For example, "friend" is the root of "friendliness." In Hebrew most roots are made up of three consonants, and many words are formed on the basis of this root. For example, the root *b-r-k* is the basis for the noun "blessing," the adjective "blessed," and the verb "to bless."

SARCASM is a strong form of irony. **SARCASTIC** comments are always negative and intended to ridicule or reprove the person or subject to which they are directed. For example, "Some king you are!" really means "You are a worthless king!" **SARCASM**, like irony, is often marked by special intonation, but in written form **SARCASM** must be recognized from the context.

SCRIBE. See **MANUSCRIPT**.

SECOND PERSON. See **PERSON**.

SEMANTIC refers to meaning. **SEMANTICS** is the study of the meaning of any element of discourse, oral or written.

SENTENCE is a grammatical construction composed of one or more clauses and capable of standing alone. **SENTENCES** that have the same topic or theme combine to form a **PARAGRAPH**.

SEPTUAGINT is a Greek translation of the Hebrew Old Testament. This translation was completed about 200 years before the birth of Christ and was the Scripture used by many New Testament writers. It is often abbreviated as LXX.

SIMILE (pronounced SIM-i-lee) is a **FIGURE OF SPEECH** that describes one event or object (the "topic") by comparing it to another event or object (the "image"). **SIMILES** always use words of comparison such as "like" or "as." "Your lips [the topic] are like a scarlet thread [the image]" is a **SIMILE** from Song of Songs 4.3. Similes differ from metaphors in that metaphors do not mark the image with words that indicate comparison. See **METAPHOR**.

SINGULAR refers to the form of a word that indicates one thing or person, in contrast to **PLURAL**, which indicates more than one. See **PLURAL**.

SOURCE LANGUAGE is the language in which an original message is produced. For the Old Testament the **SOURCE TEXT** is in Hebrew, while for the New Testament it is in Greek.

SPECIFIC refers to the opposite of **GENERAL**, **GENERIC**. See **GENERIC**.

STAIRSTEP PARALLELISM is a type of parallel poetic structure where one part of the first line is repeated in the second line, while something new replaces another part of the first line. Thus the poem moves upward one step as it focuses on some significant added information. Psa 29.1 is a case of **STAIRSTEP PARALLELISM**:

> **Ascribe to the Lord**, O heavenly beings,
> **Ascribe to the Lord** *glory and strength.*

STANZAS are major divisions in a poem. In written poems an empty line is normally used to mark the division between **STANZAS**. A pause longer than usual performs a similar function in the case of oral poetry.

STROPHE refers to a set of poetic lines which are grouped together by some common theme or pattern. **STROPHES** may combine together to form larger poetic units, which are called **STANZAS**. **STROPHES** in poetry correspond to **PARAGRAPHS** in prose.

STRUCTURE is the systematic arrangement of the elements of language, including the ways in which words combine into phrases, phrases into clauses, clauses into sentences, and sentences into larger discourse units. To separate and rearrange the various components of a sentence or some other unit of discourse in the translation process is to **RESTRUCTURE** it.

STYLE is the form or manner in which the content of a discourse is expressed. Each language has its own set of **STYLISTIC** devices that make a text pleasing to the reader or hearer. For example, in Hebrew, repetition is much appreciated, while in English, repetition is often avoided by the use of synonyms. Authors or storytellers may also have their own individual **STYLE**.

SUBJECT is one of the two major divisions of a clause, the other being the predicate. In "The small boy walked to school," "The small boy" is the subject. Typically the subject is a noun phrase.

SYNONYMOUS means that two or more words, phrases, or clauses are similar in meaning. "Happy" and "content" are **SYNONYMS** in English. **SYNONYMOUS PARALLELISM** refers to two lines that mean nearly the same thing, as seen in the example from Psa 62.10a:

>Put no confidence in extortion,
>set no vain hopes on robbery

SYNTACTIC refers to syntax, which is the arrangement of and relationship between words, phrases, clauses, sentences, and larger units of discourse.

SYNTHETIC PARALLELISM refers to a set of parallel lines in which the second line completes or builds upon the meaning of the first one. Each line has a separate sense, but the two lines together form a unit of meaning, as seen in Psa 79.10:

>Why should the nations say,
>"Where is their God?"

This type of parallelism differs from both **SYNONYMOUS** and **ANTITHETIC PARALLELISM**.

TARGET (or **RECEPTOR**) **LANGUAGE** refers to the language into which the **SOURCE TEXT** is being translated. In the case of Today's English Version, the **TARGET LANGUAGE** is English. **TARGET CULTURE** refers to the cultural **CONTEXT** or life-setting of the people who speak the **TARGET LANGUAGE**.

TEXT, TEXTUAL, refers to the various Greek, Aramaic, and Hebrew manuscripts of the Scriptures. **TEXTUAL PROBLEMS** arise when it is difficult to reconcile or to account for conflicting forms of the same text in two or more manuscripts. See also **MANUSCRIPTS.**

THEME is the central idea or main point of a discourse. For example, we can say that "purification from sin" is the major **THEME** in Psalm 51.

THIRD PERSON. See **PERSON.**

TONE is the psychological attitude, character, or emotional effect of a passage or discourse.

TONE LANGUAGE refers to a language that distinguishes words by their pitch structure. In many languages words with the same consonants and vowels may have different meanings, depending on their pitch. For example, in one language the word *su* with a high **TONE** means "push," with a mid **TONE** means "tree," and with a low **TONE** means "to be hot."

TRANSLATION is the transfer of a message from a **SOURCE LANGUAGE** text into another language, the **RECEPTOR LANGUAGE.** A good translation aims at giving the closest natural equivalent in the **TARGET LANGUAGE** in terms of meaning (content and function) and, if possible, also form (style and structure).

TRANSLITERATE is to represent in the **TARGET LANGUAGE** the approximate sounds or letters of words occurring in the **SOURCE LANGUAGE. TRANSLITERATING** is different from **TRANSLATING.** For example, "Amen" in Hebrew may be **TRANSLITERATED** in one language as *"amin,"* or it may be **TRANSLATED** as "so be it."

VERBS are a grammatical class of words that express existence, action, state, or occurrence, such as "be," "run," "become," or "think." In some languages ideas expressed by adjectives in English may be better expressed by verbs; for example, "to be hot" or "to be angry."

VERBAL refers to words being used in oral or written communication. It may also describe a word that is like a **VERB.**

VERSIONS are different translations of the same **SOURCE LANGUAGE** document. Some ancient **VERSIONS** of the Bible include the Greek Septuagint, the Syriac, and the Ethiopic versions. Modern **VERSIONS** in English include the Revised Standard Version and Today's English Version.

VIEWPOINT (POINT OF VIEW) is the location or situation or circumstance from which a speaker or writer presents a message. If, for example, the **VIEWPOINT PLACE** is the top of a hill, movement in the area will be described differently from the way one would describe it from the bottom of a hill. If the **VIEWPOINT PERSON** is a priest, he will speak of the temple in a way that differs from that of a common person.

VOCATIVE describes a word or phrase used to address a person or group in direct speech. In "Save me, O God" (Psa 54.1), "O God" is a **VOCATIVE**. Some languages have a special grammatical form to show that a word is used in this way.

VOWELS are speech sounds of the vocal cords, produced by unobstructed air passing from the lungs though the mouth. The written letters representing those sounds are also called **VOWELS**; for example, "a," "i," or "u," which are the most common vowels found in the world's languages. In Hebrew **VOWELS** were originally not written, but they were added later as small marks written under or above the consonants. See also **CONSONANTS**.

WORDPLAYS, or **PLAYS ON WORDS**, are constructions that highlight the similarity in sound between two words. In the Bible they are used to draw attention to a certain point or to create a special effect. For example, in Hebrew the name "Isaac" sounds like the word "laughs." This **PLAY ON WORDS** reminds the reader that his mother Sarah laughed when she was told that she, an old woman, would have a son.

Bible References

PRINTED IN THE UNITED STATES OF AMERICA